Scoring High

Iowa Tests of Basic Skills®

A Test Prep Program for ITBS®

Columbus, OH

The McGraw-Hill Companies

SRAonline.com

Send all inquiries to:
SRA/McGraw-Hill
8787 Orion Place
Columbus, Ohio 43240-4027

Printed in the United States of America.

ISBN 0-07-604384-3

1 2 3 4 5 6 7 8 9 QPD 09 08 07 06

On Your Way to Scoring High

On the Iowa Tests of Basic Skills®

Book 5

Family Letter

Greetings!

This year, your child, like many students across the country, will be taking a standardized achievement test called the *Iowa Tests of Basic Skills® (ITBS)*. We will be administering this test for several reasons.

- It gives us a snapshot of what your child has learned (achieved). It is one of many ways we assess the skills and knowledge of students because no one test or assessment tool can give an accurate, ongoing picture of your child's development.

- We use ITBS to help us determine where to strengthen our curriculum to better meet the needs of the students. It also helps us see if we are meeting the learning goals we set previously.

In order to give students the best opportunity to show what they know on this standardized achievement test, we will be using SRA/McGraw-Hill's test preparation program, *Scoring High on the Iowa Tests of Basic Skills.* It is designed specifically for the *Iowa Tests of Basic Skills.* Why will we be spending time preparing for this test?

- What happens to your heartbeat when you hear the word *test*? When students hear that word, their anxiety level can rise. However, when they know what to expect, their confidence soars—they are less nervous.

- Test-taking skills can be learned. When preparing, we focus on such skills as reading and listening carefully to directions; budgeting time; answering the easy questions first so more time can be spent on the harder ones; eliminating answer choices that are obviously wrong, and more. These are life skills that students will take with them and use again and again.

- Preparing for the test assures that students won't be surprised by the format of the test. They won't be worried about the type of questions they will see, or how hard the questions will be. They'll know how to fill in answers appropriately. These, and other skills learned ahead of time, will free students to focus on the content of the test and thus give a much more accurate picture of what they know.

How can you help?

- Talk with your child about the purpose of the test. Be positive about the experience.
- Talk to us here at school if you have any questions. Remember, we are a team with the **same** goals in mind—the improvement of your child's educational experience.
- Assure your child that the results of the test are private and won't be used on his or her report card. Remind your child that the test does not measure how smart he or she is, nor does it predict how successful he or she will be in the future.
- Encourage reading at home, and spend time together talking about what you read.
- Be sure your child has plenty of rest on a regular basis, and eats nourishing foods. That's important every day—not just on the day of the test.

Additional information will be provided about the specific subject areas and dates of the tests. Until then, please feel free to contact me if you have any questions about your child's performance or about standardized testing.

Sincerely,

____

Your child's teacher

Scoring High on the Iowa Tests of Basic Skills
A program that teaches achievement test behaviors

Scoring High on the Iowa Tests of Basic Skills is designed to prepare students for these tests. The program provides instruction and practice in reading, spelling, language, mathematics, study, and science skills. *Scoring High* also familiarizes students with the kinds of test formats and directions that appear on the tests and teaches test-taking strategies that promote success.

Students who are used to a comfortable learning environment are often unaccustomed to the structured setting in which achievement tests are given. Even good students who are used to working independently may have difficulty maintaining a silent, sustained effort or following directions that are read to a large group. *Scoring High*, with its emphasis on group instruction, teaches these test-taking skills systematically.

Using *Scoring High* to help prepare students for the Iowa Tests of Basic Skills will increase the probability of your students doing their best. Students' self-confidence will be at a maximum, and their proficiency in the skills tested will be higher as a result of the newly learned test-taking strategies and increased familiarity with test formats.

Scoring High can be used effectively along with your regular reading, language, science, and mathematics curriculums. By applying subject-area skills in the context of the test-taking situation, students will not only strengthen their skills, but will accumulate a reserve of test-taking strategies.

Eight Student Books for Grades 1–8

To choose the most appropriate book for each student, match the level of the Iowa Tests of Basic Skills that the student will take to the corresponding Scoring High book.

Grade Levels	Test Levels
Book 1	Level 7
Book 2	Level 8
Book 3	Level 9
Book 4	Level 10
Book 5	Level 11
Book 6	Level 12
Book 7	Level 13
Book 8	Level 14

Sequential Skill Development

Each student book is organized into units reflecting the subject areas covered on the corresponding levels of the Iowa Tests of Basic Skills. This book covers reading, spelling, language arts, mathematics, study, and science skills. Each lesson within a unit focuses on one or two of the subject-area skills and the test-taking strategies that complement the skills. The last lesson in each unit is designed to give students experience in taking an achievement test in that subject area.

The Test Practice section at the end of each book also provides practice in taking achievement tests and will increase students' confidence in their test-taking skills.

Features of the Student Lessons

Each student lesson in subject-area skills contains:

- A Sample(s) section including directions and one or more teacher-directed sample questions
- A Tips section providing test-taking strategies
- A Practice section

Each Test Yourself lesson at the end of a unit is designed like an achievement test in the unit's subject area.

How the Teacher's Edition Works

Since a program that teaches test-taking skills as well as subject-area skills may be new to your students, the Teacher's Edition makes a special effort to provide detailed lesson plans. Each lesson lists subject-area and test-taking skills. In addition, teaching suggestions are provided for handling each part of the lesson—Sample(s), Tips, and Practice. The text for the subject-area and Test Yourself lessons is designed to help students become familiar with following oral directions and with the terminology used on the tests.

Before you begin Lesson 1, you should use the Orientation Lesson on pages xii–xv to acquaint students with the program organization and the procedure for using the student book.

Scope and Sequence: Test-taking Skills

	UNIT										
	1	2	3	4	5	6	7	8	9	10	11
Analyzing answer choices		✓		✓	✓						✓
Comparing or evaluating answer choices						✓	✓		✓	✓	✓
Computing carefully							✓	✓			✓
Considering every answer choice	✓										✓
Converting items to a workable format							✓	✓			✓
Eliminating answer choices						✓					✓
Finding the answer without computing						✓	✓				✓
Following printed directions	✓			✓	✓						✓
Identifying and using key words, numbers, and pictures		✓				✓	✓			✓	✓
Indicating that an item has no mistakes			✓	✓	✓						✓
Indicating that the correct answer is not given							✓	✓			✓
Managing time effectively	✓	✓	✓	✓	✓	✓	✓	✓	✓	✓	✓
Noting the lettering of answer choices	✓										✓
Performing the correct operation							✓	✓			✓
Reasoning from facts and evidence		✓									✓
Recalling error types			✓		✓						✓
Recalling special capitalization rules				✓							✓
Recalling word meanings	✓										✓
Referring to a graphic						✓					✓
Referring to a passage to answer questions		✓								✓	✓
Referring to a reference source									✓		✓
Rereading a question						✓	✓				✓
Reworking a problem								✓			✓
Skimming a passage		✓									✓
Skimming a reference source									✓		✓
Skimming questions or answer choices					✓					✓	✓
Skimming text					✓						✓
Skipping difficult items and returning to them later				✓						✓	✓
Substituting answer choices	✓										✓
Subvocalizing answer choices					✓						✓
Taking the best guess when unsure of the answer	✓		✓					✓	✓		✓
Transferring numbers accurately							✓	✓			✓
Understanding unusual item formats				✓	✓						✓
Using charts, diagrams, and graphs							✓				✓
Using context to find an answer					✓						✓
Working methodically	✓	✓	✓	✓	✓	✓	✓	✓	✓	✓	✓

Scope and Sequence: Reading

	UNIT										
	1	2	3	4	5	6	7	8	9	10	11
Identifying synonyms	✓										✓
Analyzing characters		✓									✓
Comparing and contrasting		✓									✓
Deriving word meanings		✓									✓
Drawing conclusions		✓									✓
Identifying feelings		✓									✓
Making inferences		✓									✓
Making predictions		✓									✓
Recognizing an author's technique		✓									✓
Recognizing details		✓									✓
Recognizing genre or test source		✓									✓
Understanding literary devices		✓									✓
Understanding reasons		✓									✓
Understanding the main idea		✓									✓

Scope and Sequence: Language Skills

	UNIT										
	1	2	3	4	5	6	7	8	9	10	11
Identifying spelling errors			✓								✓
Choosing the best paragraph for a given purpose					✓						✓
Choosing the best word to complete a sentence											✓
Identifying capitalization errors				✓							✓
Identifying correctly formed sentences					✓						✓
Identifying mistakes in usage					✓						✓
Identifying punctuation errors				✓							✓
Identifying the best closing sentence for a paragraph					✓						✓
Identifying the best location for a sentence in a paragraph					✓						✓
Identifying the best opening sentence for a paragraph					✓						✓
Identifying the sentence that does not fit in a paragraph					✓						✓

Scope and Sequence: Mathematics Skills

	UNIT										
	1	2	3	4	5	6	7	8	9	10	11
Adding, subtracting, multiplying, and dividing whole numbers, fractions, and decimals								✓			✓
Comparing metric and standard units						✓					✓
Comparing whole numbers and fractions						✓					
Estimating and rounding						✓					✓
Estimating measurement						✓					✓
Finding area						✓					✓
Finding perimeter						✓					
Finding volume						✓					
Identifying a line of symmetry						✓					✓
Identifying multiples						✓					
Identifying parts of a figure						✓					✓
Identifying problem solving strategies						✓					
Identifying the best measurement unit						✓					✓
Interpreting tables, diagrams, and graphs							✓				✓
Naming numerals						✓					✓
Recognizing fractional parts						✓					✓
Recognizing plane figures						✓					
Sequencing numbers						✓					✓
Solving word problems							✓				✓
Telling time						✓					
Transforming plane to solid figures						✓					
Understanding average (mean)						✓					
Understanding characteristics of related numbers						✓					
Understanding discounts						✓					
Understanding elapsed time						✓					
Understanding factors and remainders						✓					✓
Understanding multiplication						✓					
Understanding number sentences						✓					✓
Understanding permutations and combinations						✓					
Understanding place value						✓					
Understanding ratio and proportion						✓					
Understanding simple probability						✓					
Using a number line						✓					

Scope and Sequence: Study Skills

	UNIT										
	1	2	3	4	5	6	7	8	9	10	11
Alphabetizing words or names									✓		✓
Differentiating among reference sources									✓		✓
Understanding a diagram									✓		✓
Understanding a map									✓		✓
Using a chart									✓		✓
Using a dictionary									✓		✓
Using a table of contents									✓		✓
Using an encyclopedia									✓		✓
Using key words											✓

Scope and Sequence: Science Skills

	UNIT										
	1	2	3	4	5	6	7	8	9	10	11
Classifying things based on characteristics											✓
Differentiating living and nonliving things										✓	✓
Differentiating the source of natural and manufactured products										✓	
Identifying the best unit of measurement										✓	
Recalling characteristics of Earth and bodies in space										✓	✓
Recalling characteristics and functions of the human body										✓	✓
Recognizing characteristics of a habitat										✓	✓
Recognizing chemical changes										✓	✓
Recognizing forms, sources, and principles of energy										✓	✓
Recognizing states, properties, and composition of matter										✓	✓
Understanding fossilization										✓	✓
Understanding gravity, inertia, and friction										✓	✓
Understanding the history and language of science										✓	
Understanding life cycles and reproduction										✓	✓
Understanding plant and animal behaviors and characteristics										✓	✓
Understanding scientific instruments, measurement, and processes										✓	✓
Understanding sound										✓	
Understanding the water cycle											✓
Understanding weather, climate, and seasons										✓	✓
Using illustrations, charts, and graphs										✓	✓

Orientation Lesson

Focus
Understanding the purpose and structure of *Scoring High on the Iowa Tests of Basic Skills*

Note: Before you begin Lesson 1, use this introductory lesson to acquaint the students with the program orientation and procedures for using this book.

Say Taking a test is something that you do many times during each school year. What kind of tests have you taken? *(math tests, reading tests, spelling tests, daily quizzes, etc.)* **Have you ever taken an achievement test that covers many subjects? An achievement test shows how well you are doing in these subjects compared to other students in your grade. How are achievement tests different from the regular tests you take in class?** *(many students take them on the same day; special pencils, books, and answer sheets are used; etc.)* **Some students get nervous when they take achievement tests. Has this ever happened to you?**

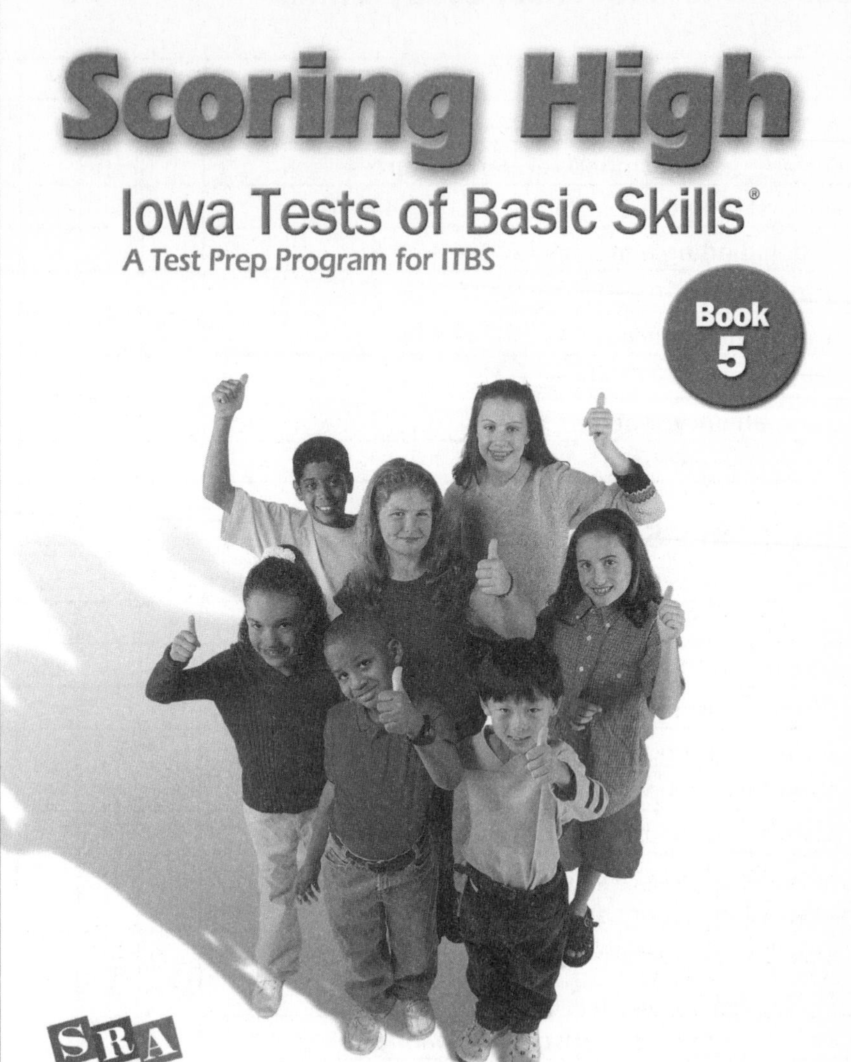

Encourage the students to discuss their feelings about test taking. Point out that almost everyone feels anxious or worried when facing a test-taking situation.

Display the cover of Scoring High on the Iowa Tests of Basic Skills.

Say Here is a new book that you'll be using for the next several weeks. The Book is called *Scoring High on the Iowa Tests of Basic Skills.*

Distribute the books to the students.

Say This book will help you improve your reading, language, mathematics, study, and science skills. It will also help you gain the confidence and skills you need to so well on achievement tests. What does the title say you will be doing when you finish this book? *(scoring high)* **Scoring high on achievement tests is what this program is all about. If you learn the skills taught in this book, you will be ready to do your best on the** *Iowa Tests of Basic Skills.*

Share this information with the students if you know when they will be taking the *Iowa Tests of Basic Skills.* Then make sure the students understand that the goal of their *Scoring High* books is to improve their test-taking skills.

Tell the students to turn to the table of contents of their books.

Say **This page is a progress chart. It shows the contents of the book. How many units are there?** *(11)* **Let's read the names of the units together. In these units you will learn reading, spelling, language, mathematics, study skills, science, and test-taking skills. The last lesson in each unit is called Test Yourself. It reviews what you have learned in the unit. In Unit 11, the Test Practice section, you will have a chance to use all the skills you have learned on tests that are somewhat like real achievement tests.This page will also help you keep track of the lessons you have completed. Do you see the box beside each lesson number? When you finish a lesson, you will write your score in the box to show your progress.**

Make sure the students understand the information presented on this page. Ask questions such as, "On what page does Lesson 10a start?" *(54)* "What is Lesson 2a called?" *(Reading Comprehension)* "What do you think Lesson 10a is about?" *(solving mathematics problems)*

On Your Way to Scoring High

On the **Iowa Tests of Basic Skills**®

Name ______________________________

Say Now let's look at two of the lessons. Turn to Lesson 1a on page 1. Where is the lesson number and title? *(at the top of the page, beside the unit number)* **What is the title of the lesson?** *(Vocabulary)*

Familiarize the students with the lesson layout and sequence of instruction. Have them locate the directions and sample items. Explain that you will work through the Samples section together. Then have the students find the STOP sign in the lower right-hand corner of the page. Explain that when they come to the STOP sign at the bottom of a page, they should turn to the next page and continue working.

Have the students locate the Tips sign below the Samples section.

Say What does the sign point out to you? *(the tips)* **Each lesson has tips that suggest new ways to work through the items. Tests can be tricky. The tips will tell you what to watch out for. They will help you find the best answer quickly.**

Have the students locate the Practice section below the tips. Explain that they will do the practice items by themselves. Tell the students they will have an opportunity to discuss any problems they had when they complete the Practice section.

Ask the students to turn to the Test Yourself lesson on page 3 of their books. Tell the students the Test Yourself lessons may seem like real tests, but they are not. The Test Yourself lessons are designed to give them opportunities to apply the skills and tips they have learned in timed, trial-run situations. Then have the students find the GO sign in the lower right-hand corner of the page. Explain that when they come to the GO sign at the bottom of a page, they should turn to the next page and continue working.

Explain that you will go over the answers together after the students complete each lesson. Then they will figure out their scores and record the number of correct answers in the boxes on the progress chart. Be sure to point out that the students' scores are only for them to see how well they are doing.

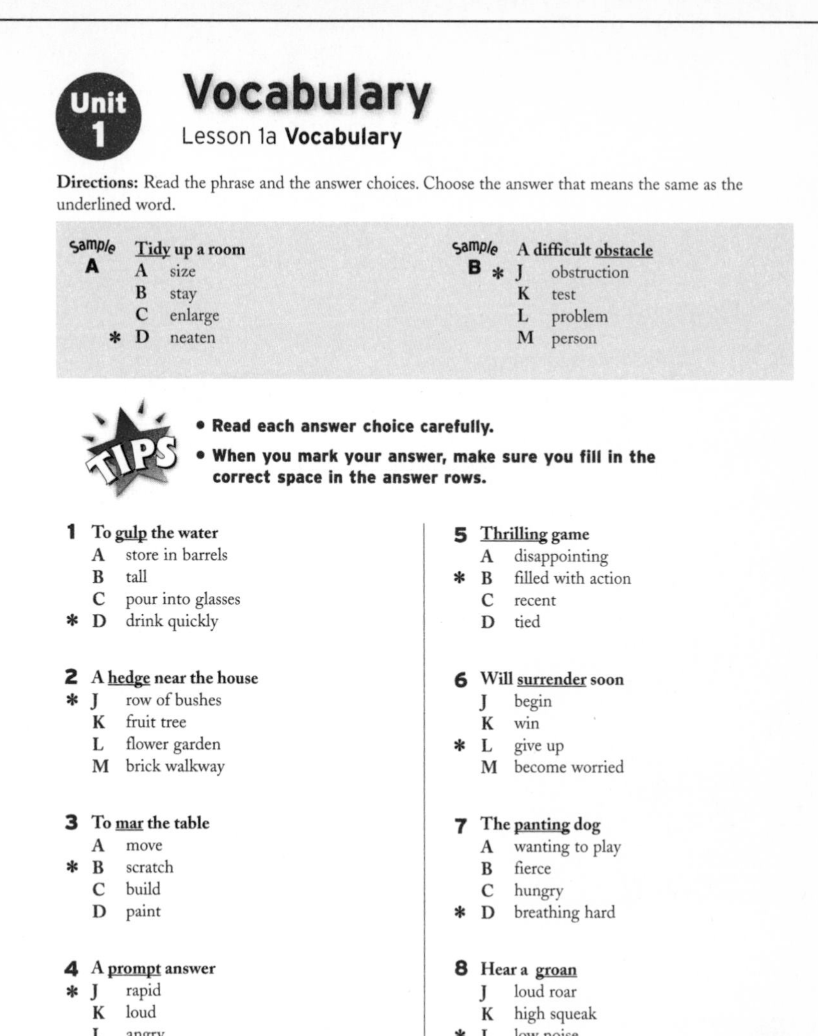

Unit 1 **Vocabulary**

Lesson 1a **Vocabulary**

Directions: Read the phrase and the answer choices. Choose the answer that means the same as the underlined word.

Sample A — Tidy up a room
- A size
- B stay
- C enlarge
- * D neaten

Sample B — A difficult obstacle
- * J obstruction
- K test
- L problem
- M person

TIPS
- Read each answer choice carefully.
- When you mark your answer, make sure you fill in the correct space in the answer rows.

1 To gulp the water
- A store in barrels
- B tall
- C pour into glasses
- * D drink quickly

2 A hedge near the house
- * J row of bushes
- K fruit tree
- L flower garden
- M brick walkway

3 To mar the table
- A move
- * B scratch
- C build
- D paint

4 A prompt answer
- * J rapid
- K loud
- L angry
- M kind

5 Thrilling game
- A disappointing
- * B filled with action
- C recent
- D tied

6 Will surrender soon
- J begin
- K win
- * L give up
- M become worried

7 The panting dog
- A wanting to play
- B fierce
- C hungry
- * D breathing hard

8 Hear a groan
- J loud roar
- K high squeak
- * L low noise
- M nice tune

STOP

Answer rows A ⒶⒷⒸ● 1 ⒶⒷⒸ● 3 Ⓐ●ⒸⒹ 5 Ⓐ●ⒸⒹ 7 ⒶⒷⒸ●
B ●ⓀⓁⓂ 2 ●ⓀⓁⓂ 4 ●ⓀⓁⓂ 6 ⒿⓀ●Ⓜ 8 ⒿⓀ●Ⓜ

1

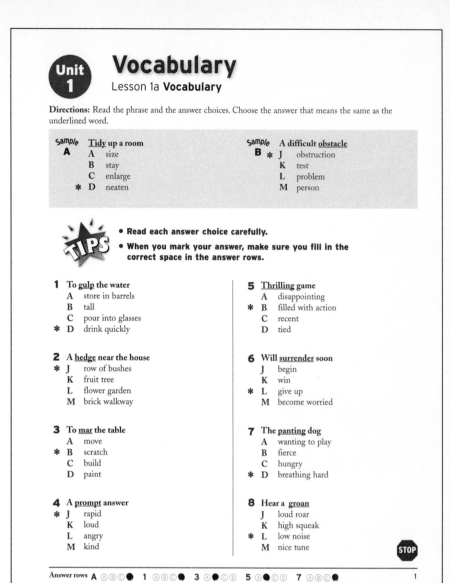

Say Each lesson will teach you new skills and tips. What will you have learned when you finish this book? *(vocabulary, reading, spelling, language, mathematics, study skills, science, and test-taking skills; how to do my best on an achievement test)* **When you know you can do your best, how do you think you will feel on test day? You may be a little nervous, but you should also feel confident that you are ready to do your best.**

Background

This unit contains three lessons that deal with vocabulary skills. Students are asked to identify words with similar meanings.

• **In Lesson 1a,** students identify words that have the same meaning as target words in phrases. Students are encouraged to follow printed directions. They note the lettering of answer choices, consider every answer choice, recall word meanings, and take their best guess when unsure of the answer.

• **In Lesson 1b,** students identify words that have the same meaning as target words in phrases. In addition to reviewing the test-taking skills introduced in Lesson 1a, students learn how to substitute answer choices.

• **In the Test Yourself lesson,** the vocabulary skills and test-taking skills introduced and used in Lessons 1a and 1b are reinforced and presented in a format that gives students the experience of taking an achievement test. Techniques for managing time effectively when taking a standardized test are reinforced.

Instructional Objectives

Lesson 1a	**Vocabulary**	Given a phrase with a target word, the student identifies which of four answer choices means the same as the target word.
Lesson 1b	**Vocabulary**	
	Test Yourself	Given questions similar to those in Lessons 1a and 1b, the student utilizes vocabulary skills and test-taking strategies on achievement test formats.

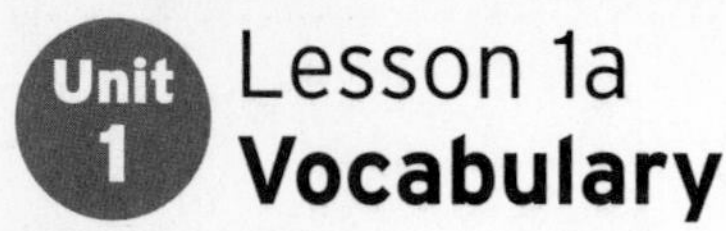

Lesson 1a Vocabulary

Focus

Reading Skill
- identifying synonyms

Test-taking Skills
- following printed directions
- noting lettering of answer choices
- considering every answer choice
- recalling word meanings
- taking the best guess when unsure of the answer

Vocabulary

Lesson 1a **Vocabulary**

Directions: Read the phrase and the answer choices. Choose the answer that means the same as the underlined word.

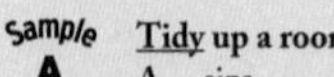

Sample A **Tidy up a room**
- A size
- B stay
- C enlarge
- * D neaten

Sample B **A difficult obstacle**
- * J obstruction
- K test
- L problem
- M person

- **Read each answer choice carefully.**
- **When you mark your answer, make sure you fill in the correct space in the answer rows.**

1 To gulp the water
- A store in barrels
- B tall
- C pour into glasses
- * D drink quickly

2 A hedge near the house
- * J row of bushes
- K fruit tree
- L flower garden
- M brick walkway

3 To mar the table
- A move
- * B scratch
- C build
- D paint

4 A prompt answer
- * J rapid
- K loud
- L angry
- M kind

5 Thrilling game
- A disappointing
- * B filled with action
- C recent
- D tied

6 Will surrender soon
- J begin
- K win
- * L give up
- M become worried

7 The panting dog
- A wanting to play
- B fierce
- C hungry
- * D breathing hard

8 Hear a groan
- J loud roar
- K high squeak
- * L low noise
- M nice tune

STOP

Answer rows A Ⓐ Ⓑ Ⓒ ● 1 Ⓐ Ⓑ Ⓒ ● 3 Ⓐ ● Ⓒ Ⓓ 5 Ⓐ ● Ⓒ Ⓓ 7 Ⓐ Ⓑ Ⓒ ●
B ● Ⓚ Ⓛ Ⓜ 2 ● Ⓚ Ⓛ Ⓜ 4 ● Ⓚ Ⓛ Ⓜ 6 Ⓙ Ⓚ ● Ⓜ 8 Ⓙ Ⓚ ● Ⓜ

1

Samples A and B

Say **Turn to Lesson 1a on page 1. The page number is at the bottom of the page on the right.**

Check to see that the students have found the right page.

Say **In this lesson you will find words that have the same or nearly the same meaning as another word used in a phrase. Read the directions at the top of the page to yourself while I read them aloud to you.**

Read the directions to the students.

Say **Let's do Sample A. Listen carefully. Read the phrase with the underlined word. Think about what the word means as it is used in the phrase. Now, look at the four answer choices below the phrase. Which of the four answers means about the same as the underlined word?** *(pause)* **The answer is D, *neaten*, because *tidy* and *neaten* mean about the same thing. Fill in the circle for answer D in the answer rows at the bottom of the page. Be sure your answer circle is completely filled in with a dark mark and that you have marked the correct answer circle.**

Check to see that the students have marked the correct circle.

Say **Now do Sample B by yourself. Read the phrase and fill in the circle for the word that means the same as the underlined word.** *(pause)* **Which answer choice is correct?** *(answer J)* **Yes, an *obstacle* is an *obstruction*. Make sure that circle J for Sample B is completely filled in. Press your pencil firmly so your mark comes out dark.**

Check to see that the students have marked the correct circle.

TIPS

Say **Now let's look at the tips.**

Read the tips aloud to the students.

Say **Think about where you might have heard or read the underlined word before. Pick the answer choice that means about the same thing. If you are not sure which answer choice is correct, take your best guess. It is better to guess than to leave an answer blank.**

Discuss with the students where they might have heard or read the words in the sample items. Mention places such as a book, television show, or movie. Encourage the students by telling them that they have probably heard or read all of the words in this lesson before.

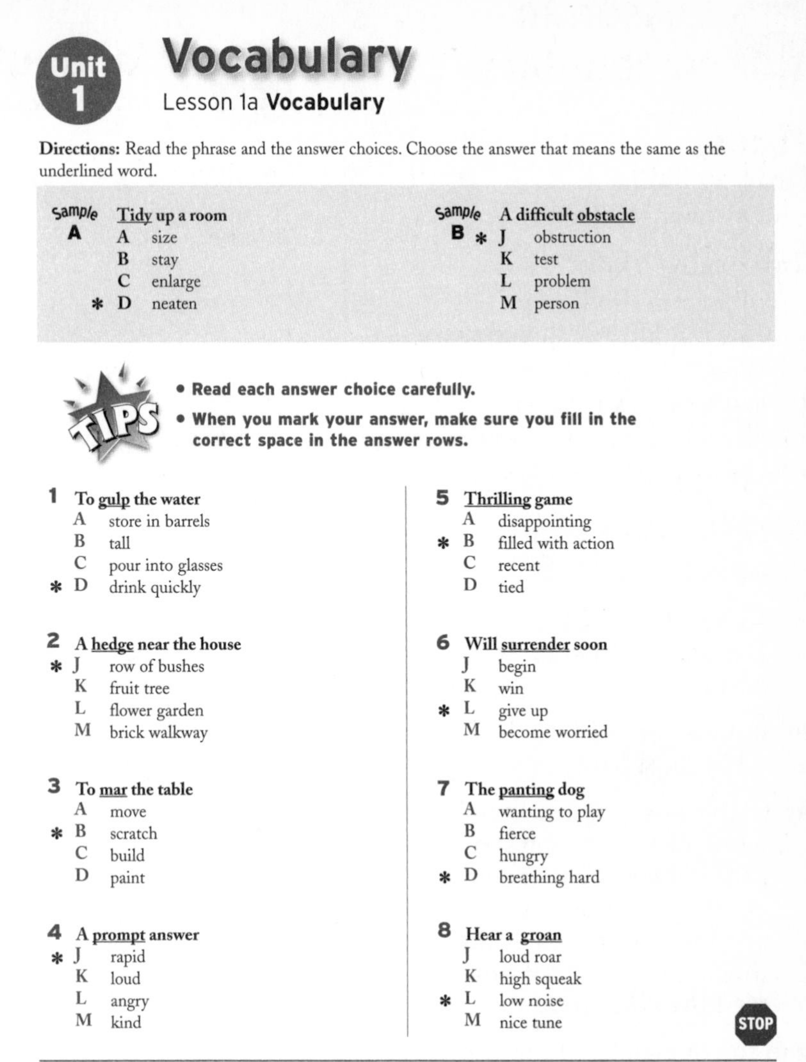

Unit 1 Vocabulary

Lesson 1a **Vocabulary**

Directions: Read the phrase and the answer choices. Choose the answer that means the same as the underlined word.

Sample A — Tidy up a room
A size
B stay
C enlarge
* D neaten

Sample B — A difficult obstacle
* J obstruction
K test
L problem
M person

TIPS
- Read each answer choice carefully.
- When you mark your answer, make sure you fill in the correct space in the answer rows.

1 To gulp the water
A store in barrels
B tall
C pour into glasses
* D drink quickly

2 A hedge near the house
* J row of bushes
K fruit tree
L flower garden
M brick walkway

3 To mar the table
A move
* B scratch
C build
D paint

4 A prompt answer
* J rapid
K loud
L angry
M kind

5 Thrilling game
A disappointing
* B filled with action
C recent
D tied

6 Will surrender soon
J begin
K win
* L give up
M become worried

7 The panting dog
A wanting to play
B fierce
C hungry
* D breathing hard

8 Hear a groan
J loud roar
K high squeak
* L low noise
M nice tune

STOP

Answer rows A ⒶⒷⒸ● 1 ⒶⒷⒸ● 3 Ⓐ●ⒸⒹ 5 Ⓐ●ⒸⒹ 7 ⒶⒷⒸ●
B ●ⓀⓁⓂ 2 ●ⓀⓁⓂ 4 ●ⓀⓁⓂ 6 ⒿⓀ●Ⓜ 8 ⒿⓀ●Ⓜ

1

Practice

Say **We are ready for the Practice items. Remember, the letters for the answer choices change from question to question. For odd-numbered questions, they are A-B-C-D. For even-numbered questions, they are J-K-L-M. You must pay careful attention to the letters for the answer choices and the circles in the answer rows at the bottom of the page. It's a good idea to double-check to be sure that you have filled in the circle for the answer choice you think is correct. Check both the item number and the answer letter. If you make a mistake when you fill in the answer circle, your answer will still be counted wrong, even if you knew what the correct answer was.**

Work until you come to the STOP sign at the bottom of the page. Fill in your answer circles with dark marks and completely erase any marks for answers that you change. Do you have any questions? Start working now.

Allow time for the students to do Numbers 1 through 8.

Say **It's time to stop. You have finished Lesson 1a.**

Review the answers with the students. Ask them if they remembered to look at all of the answer choices and take the best guess if they were unsure of the correct answer. Did they have any difficulty marking the circles in the answer rows? If any questions caused particular difficulty, work through each of the answer choices. It may be helpful to discuss with the students where they might have heard or read the underlined words.

Have the students indicate completion of the lesson by entering their score for this activity on the progress chart at the beginning of the book.

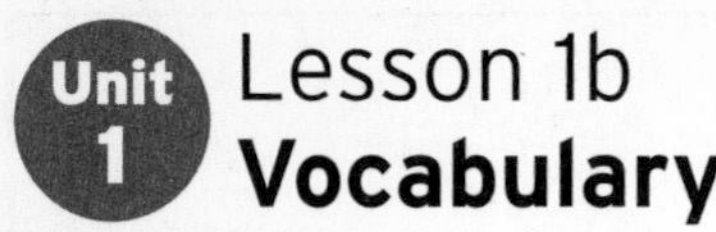

Lesson 1b Vocabulary

Focus

Reading Skill

- identifying synonyms

Test-taking Skills

- working methodically
- following printed directions
- noting lettering of answer choices
- considering every answer choice
- substituting answer choices
- taking the best guess when unsure of the answer

Vocabulary

Lesson 1b **Vocabulary**

Directions: Read the phrase and the answer choices. Choose the answer that means the same as the underlined word.

Sample A — Intend to stay
- * A desire
- B not like
- C resist
- D pay

Sample B — Walk through the mist
- J snow
- K archway
- * L fog
- M forest

- **It may help to substitute each answer for the underlined word.**

1 To squirm a little
- A stretch
- B bend over
- * C wiggle
- D sit down

2 Carry a lantern
- * J kind of lamp
- K backpack
- L wooden barrel
- M shovel

3 Storm the castle
- A own
- B tour
- C repair
- * D attack

4 A wooden pillar
- J bench
- K tool
- * L post
- M desk

5 A box of waste
- * A trash
- B gifts
- C coins
- D books

6 The snug shirt
- J soft
- K worn
- L new
- * M tight

7 To perch on a branch
- A sing
- * B sit
- C walk along
- D fall from

8 The initial idea
- J worst
- K best
- L last
- * M first

2 Answer rows A ● B C D 1 A B ● D 3 A B C ● 5 ● B C D 7 A ● C D
B J K ● M 2 ● K L M 4 J K ● M 6 J K L ● 8 J K L ●

Samples A and B

Say Turn to Lesson 1b on page 2. The page number is at the bottom of the page on the left.

Check to see that the students have found the right page.

Say In this lesson you will find more words that have the same or nearly the same meaning as another word used in a phrase. Read the directions at the top of the page to yourself while I read them out loud to you.

Read the directions to the students.

Say Read the phrase with the underlined word for Sample A. Think about what the word means as it is used in the phrase. Now, look at the four answer choices below the phrase. Which of the four answers means about the same as the underlined word? *(pause)* The answer is A, *desire*. In this phrase, *intend* and *desire* mean the same thing. Fill in the circle for answer A in the answer rows at the bottom of the page. Be sure your answer circle is completely filled in with a dark mark and that you have marked the correct answer circle.

Check to see that the students have marked the correct circle.

Say Now do Sample B by yourself. Read the phrase and fill in the circle for the word that means the same as the underlined word. You may find it helpful to substitute each answer for the underlined word. *(pause)* Which answer choice is correct? *(answer L)* Yes, *mist* and *fog* mean about the same thing. Make sure that circle L for Sample B is completely filled in. Press your pencil firmly so your mark comes out dark.

Check to see that the students have marked the correct circle.

TIPS

Say Let's review the tip.

Read the tip aloud to the students.

Say A good strategy to use for vocabulary items is to substitute each answer choice for the underlined word in the phrase. This will help you decide which answer is correct.

Explain as thoroughly as is necessary how to substitute answer choices.

Practice

Say We are ready for the Practice items. Remember, the letters for the answer choices change from question to question. For odd-numbered questions, they are A-B-C-D. For even-numbered questions, they are J-K-L-M. You must pay careful attention to the letters for the answer choices and the circles in the answer rows at the bottom of the page. It's a good idea to double-check to be sure that you have filled in the circle for the answer choice you think is correct. Check both the item number and the answer letter. If you make a mistake when you fill in the answer circle, your answer will still be counted wrong, even if you knew what the correct answer was. And remember, if you aren't sure which answer is correct, take your best guess.

Work until you come to the STOP sign at the bottom of the page. Fill in your answer circles with dark marks and completely erase any marks for answers that you change. Do you have any questions? Start working now.

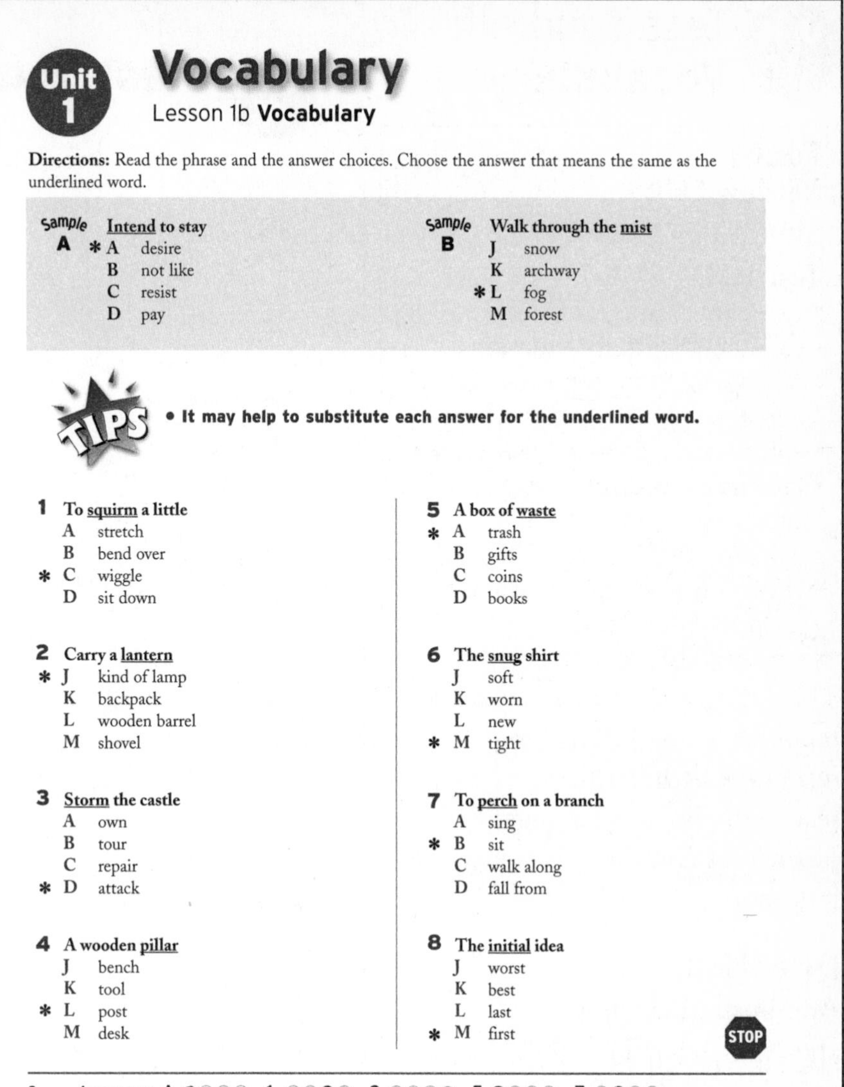

Unit 1 **Vocabulary**

Lesson 1b **Vocabulary**

Directions: Read the phrase and the answer choices. Choose the answer that means the same as the underlined word.

Sample A **Intend to stay**
* * A desire
* B not like
* C resist
* D pay

Sample B **Walk through the mist**
* J snow
* K archway
* * L fog
* M forest

TIPS • It may help to substitute each answer for the underlined word.

1 To squirm a little
* A stretch
* B bend over
* * C wiggle
* D sit down

2 Carry a lantern
* * J kind of lamp
* K backpack
* L wooden barrel
* M shovel

3 Storm the castle
* A own
* B tour
* C repair
* * D attack

4 A wooden pillar
* J bench
* K tool
* * L post
* M desk

5 A box of waste
* * A trash
* B gifts
* C coins
* D books

6 The snug shirt
* J soft
* K worn
* L new
* * M tight

7 To perch on a branch
* A sing
* * B sit
* C walk along
* D fall from

8 The initial idea
* J worst
* K best
* L last
* * M first

STOP

2 Answer rows A ● B C D 1 A B ● D 3 A B C ● 5 ● B C D 7 A ● C D
B J K ● M 2 ● K L M 4 J K ● M 6 J K L ● 8 J K L ●

Allow time for the students to do Numbers 1 through 8.

Say It's time to stop. You have finished Lesson 1b.

Review the answers with the students. Ask them if they remembered to look at all the answer choices and take the best guess if they were unsure of the correct answer. If any questions caused particular difficulty, work through each of the answer choices. You may want to practice substituting the answer choices for the underlined words in each item.

Have the students indicate completion of the lesson by entering their score for this activity on the progress chart at the beginning of the book.

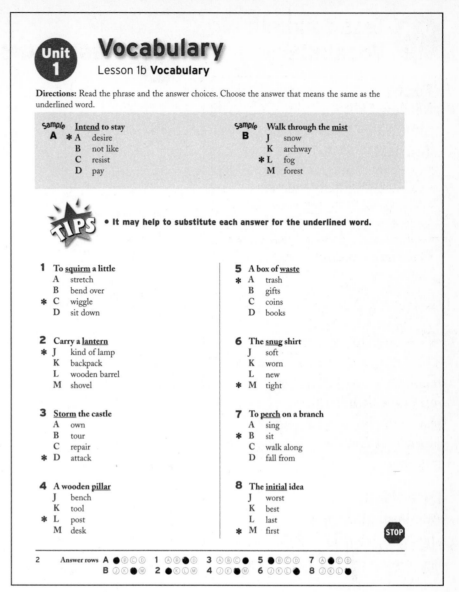

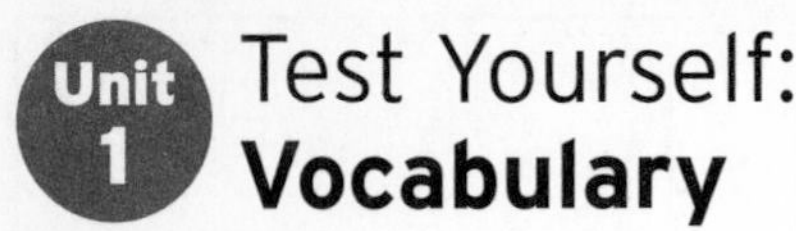

Test Yourself: Vocabulary

Focus

Reading Skill
- identifying synonyms

Test-taking Skills
- managing time effectively
- following printed directions
- noting the lettering of answer choices
- considering every answer choice
- recalling word meanings
- substituting answer choices
- working methodically
- taking the best guess when unsure of the answer

This lesson simulates an actual test-taking experience. Therefore, it is recommended that the directions be read verbatim and the suggested procedures and time allowances be followed.

Directions

Administration Time: approximately 15 minutes

Say **Turn to the Test Yourself lesson on page 3.**

Test Yourself: Vocabulary

Directions: Read the phrase and the answer choices. Choose the answer that means the same as the underlined word.

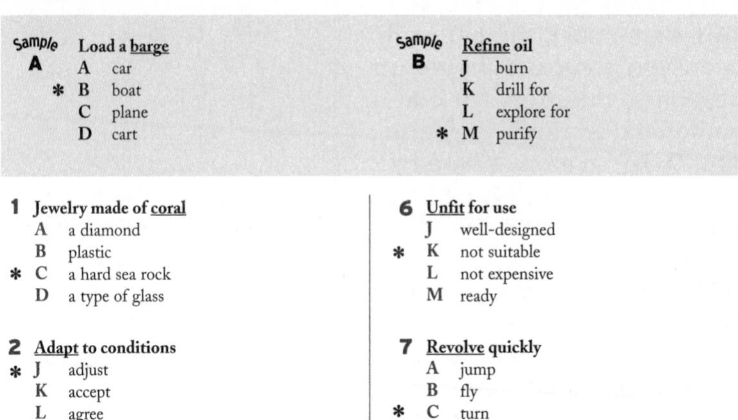

Sample A Load a barge
A car
* B boat
C plane
D cart

Sample B Refine oil
J burn
K drill for
L explore for
* M purify

1 Jewelry made of coral
A a diamond
B plastic
* C a hard sea rock
D a type of glass

2 Adapt to conditions
* J adjust
K accept
L agree
M allow

3 A large portion
A package
* B serving
C table
D chair

4 Vivid dream
J frightening
K short
L long
* M lifelike

5 A lively party
A important
B boring
* C exciting
D long

6 Unfit for use
J well-designed
* K not suitable
L not expensive
M ready

7 Revolve quickly
A jump
B fly
* C turn
D fall

8 Limp flowers
* J not stiff
K not cut
L beautiful
M unusual

9 Conduct a meeting
* A direct
B attend
C leave
D permit

10 The president's escort
J good friends
K group of enemies
* L group of guards
M people who vote

Answer rows A Ⓐ●ⒸⒹ 1 ⒶⒷ●Ⓓ 3 Ⓐ●ⒸⒹ 5 ⒶⒷ●Ⓓ 7 ⒶⒷ●Ⓓ 9 ●ⒷⒸⒹ 3
B ⒿⓀⓁ● 2 ●ⓀⓁⓂ 4 ⒿⓀⓁ● 6 Ⓙ●ⓁⓂ 8 ●ⓀⓁⓂ 10 ⒿⓀ●Ⓜ

Check to be sure the students have found the right page. Point out to the students that this Test Yourself lesson is timed like a real test, but that they will score it themselves to see how well they are doing. Explain that it is important to work quickly and to answer as many questions as possible.

Say **This lesson will check how well you understand word meanings. Remember to make sure that the circles for your answer choices are completely filled in. Press your pencil firmly so that your marks come out dark. Completely erase any marks for answers that you change. Do not write anything except your answer choices in your books.**

Look at Sample A. Read the phrase and fill in the circle for the word that means the same as the underlined word. Mark your answer in the row for Sample A at the bottom of the page.

Allow time for the students to read the item and mark their answers.

Say **You should have filled in answer circle B because a *barge* is a kind of *boat*. If you did not fill in answer B, erase your answer and fill in answer B now.**

Check to see that the students have filled in the correct answer circle.

Say **Do Sample B now. Read the phrase and fill in the circle for the word or words that means the same as the underlined word. Mark the circle for the answer you think is correct for Sample B in the answer rows at the bottom of the page.**

Allow time for the students to read the item and mark their answers.

Say **You should have filled in answer circle M because *refine* means about the same as *purify*. If you did not fill in answer M, erase your answer and fill in answer M now.**

Check to see that the students have filled in the correct answer circle.

Say **Now you will answer more questions. Fill in the spaces for your answers in the rows at the bottom of the page. When you come to the GO sign at the bottom of the page, turn to the next page and continue working. Work until you come to the STOP sign at the bottom of page 4. When you have finished, you can check over your answers to this test. Then wait for the rest of the group to finish. Any questions?**

Answer any questions that the students have.

Say **Start working now. You have 10 minutes.**

Allow 10 minutes. Most students should finish in a shorter amount of time.

Say **It's time to stop. You have completed the Test Yourself lesson. Check to see that you have completely filled in your answer circles with dark marks. Make sure that any marks for answers that you changed have been completely erased. Now you may close your books.**

Have the students indicate completion of the lesson by entering their score for this activity on the progress chart at the beginning of the book. Collect the students' books if this is the end of the testing session.

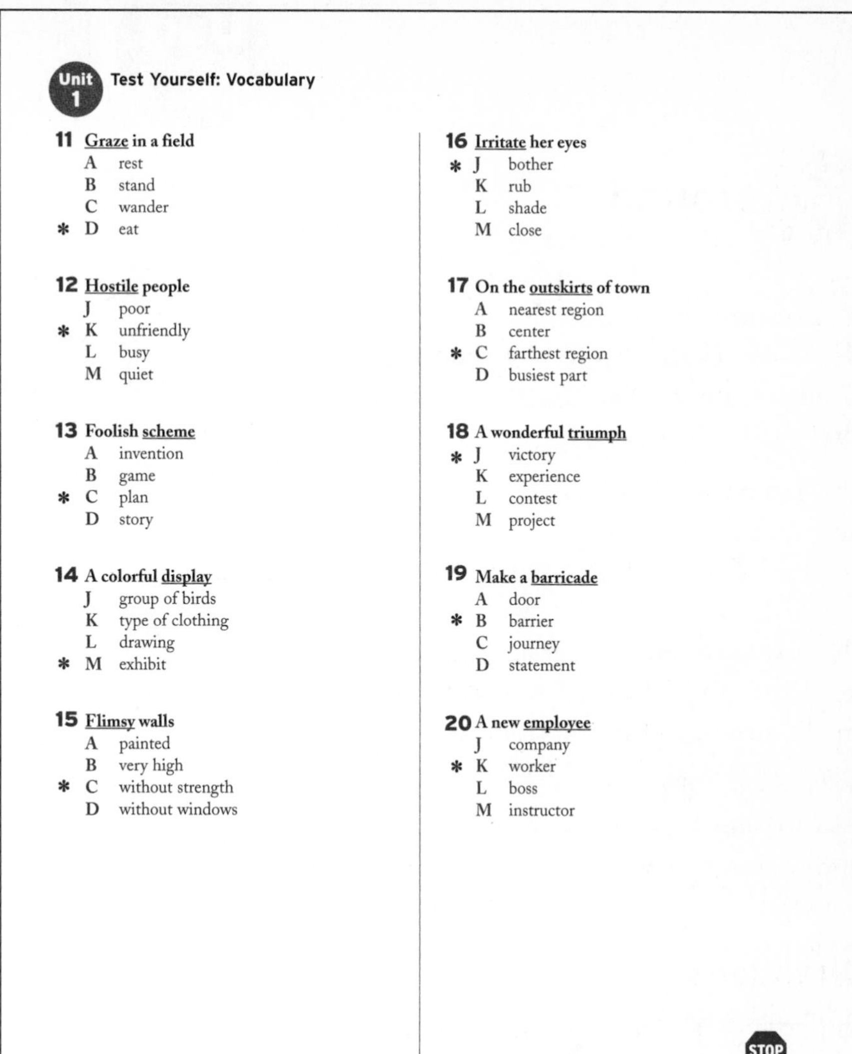

Unit 1 **Test Yourself: Vocabulary**

11 Graze in a field
A rest
B stand
C wander
* D eat

12 Hostile people
J poor
* K unfriendly
L busy
M quiet

13 Foolish scheme
A invention
B game
* C plan
D story

14 A colorful display
J group of birds
K type of clothing
L drawing
* M exhibit

15 Flimsy walls
A painted
B very high
* C without strength
D without windows

16 Irritate her eyes
* J bother
K rub
L shade
M close

17 On the outskirts of town
A nearest region
B center
* C farthest region
D busiest part

18 A wonderful triumph
* J victory
K experience
L contest
M project

19 Make a barricade
A door
* B barrier
C journey
D statement

20 A new employee
J company
* K worker
L boss
M instructor

STOP

4 Answer rows 11 Ⓐ Ⓑ Ⓒ ● 13 Ⓐ Ⓑ ● Ⓓ 15 Ⓐ Ⓑ ● Ⓓ 17 Ⓐ Ⓑ ● Ⓓ 19 Ⓐ ● Ⓒ Ⓓ
12 Ⓙ ● Ⓛ Ⓜ 14 Ⓙ Ⓚ Ⓛ ● 16 ● Ⓚ Ⓛ Ⓜ 18 ● Ⓚ Ⓛ Ⓜ 20 Ⓙ ● Ⓛ Ⓜ

Background

This unit contains three lessons that deal with reading comprehension skills. Students answer questions about stories they read.

- **In Lesson 2a,** students read a passage and answer questions based on the content of the passage. Students are encouraged to skim a passage and refer to the passage to answer questions. They use key words to find the answer, work methodically, and reason from facts and evidence.

- **In Lesson 2b,** students read a passage and answer questions based on the content of the passage. In addition to reviewing the test-taking skills introduced in Lesson 2a, students learn the importance of analyzing answer choices.

- **In the Test Yourself lesson,** the reading skills and test-taking skills introduced and used in Lessons 2a and 2b are reinforced and presented in a format that gives students the experience of taking an achievement test. Techniques for managing time effectively when taking a standardized test are reinforced.

Instructional Objectives

Lesson 2a	**Reading Comprehension**	Given a written passage and a literal or inferential question based on the passage, the student identifies which of four answer choices is correct.
Lesson 2b	**Reading Comprehension**	
	Test Yourself	Given questions similar to those in Lessons 2a and 2b, the student utilizes reading skills and test-taking strategies on achievement test formats.

Lesson 2a Reading Comprehension

Focus

Reading Skills

- understanding reasons
- identifying feelings
- drawing conclusions
- making inferences
- deriving word meanings
- making predictions
- recognizing details
- recognizing an author's technique

Test-taking Skills

- skimming a passage
- referring to a passage to answer questions
- using key words to find the answer
- working methodically
- reasoning from facts and evidence

Reading

Lesson 2a **Reading Comprehension**

Directions: Read the passage and the answer choices. Choose the best answer.

Sample A

Bees can't talk, but they can communicate with one another. If a bee finds a field of flowers, it tells the other bees where the field is by performing a dance. Scientists have studied these bee dances and have discovered that they are very accurate.

Why do bees dance?

A To warn of danger
* B To communicate directions
C To warn of bad weather
D To communicate with scientists

- **Skim the passage quickly to get an idea of what it is about.**
- **Read the question and answer choices carefully. Look for key words in the question and answer choices. Refer back to the passage to find the answer.**

"Do you really think you'll be ready for the race?" Carrie breathed heavily as she spoke to her friend, Nadia.

"I'm not sure. I haven't run much since I hurt my knee, and it still doesn't feel very strong. Even so, I'd like to give it a try."

The girls turned a corner and headed up a steep hill. About halfway up the hill, Nadia had to stop.

"Let's walk to the top. My knee doesn't feel so good. I can't believe I'm wimping out on this hill."

"Sure. I'm kind of tired too."

When they reached the top, Nadia said her knee was feeling better, and they started running again. The two girls ran for another mile until they reached Carrie's house.

"Come on in. My mother is home, and she can fix an ice pack. That will keep your knee from swelling."

Carrie was worried about her friend. Nadia had been a great runner until she had fallen while they were skating. Nadia didn't think much of it at the time, but the next day, Nadia's knee was terribly swollen. She went to the emergency room at the hospital, and a few days later she had surgery.

1 How did Nadia feel right after she hurt her knee?

A Worried
B Disappointed
C Angry
* D Unconcerned

2 From the passage, it appears that

* J Nadia had no trouble running up the hill before the accident.
K the hill had always been a problem for Nadia.
L Carrie was the one who really wanted to walk up the hill.
M both girls had hurt their knees.

3 Why did Carrie probably say she was tired after the girls had run up the hill?

A She was out of shape.
B She had hurt her knee.
* C So Nadia wouldn't feel bad.
D So she would be ready for the race.

Answer rows A Ⓐ●ⒸⒹ 1 ⒶⒷⒸ● 2 ●ⓀⓁⓂ 3 ⒶⒷ●Ⓓ

5

Sample A

Say Turn to Lesson 2a on page 5. In this lesson you will answer questions about passages that you read. Begin by reading the directions at the top of the page to yourself while I read them out loud.

Read the directions to the students.

Say Now we'll do Sample A. Skim the passage to yourself. *(pause)* **Now, read the question next to the passage. To find the correct answer, look back at the passage. What is the correct answer?** *(answer B)* **You can tell from the story that bees dance** ***to communicate directions*****. Fill in answer circle B for Sample A in the answer rows at the bottom of the page. Make sure the circle is completely filled in. Press your pencil firmly so that your mark comes out dark.**

Check to see that the students have marked the correct answer circle.

TIPS

Say Now let's look at the tips. Who will read them?

Have a volunteer read the tips aloud.

Say The best way to answer reading comprehension questions is to skim the passage quickly and then read the questions. Refer back to the passage to answer the questions, but don't reread the story for each question. Key words in the question will tell you where in the passage to look for the correct answer. If you can find the same key words in the passage, you can usually find the correct answer nearby.

Have a volunteer explain how to answer the sample question based on the information in the story.

Practice

Say **Now we are ready for Practice. You will read four more passages and answer questions about them in the same way that we did the Sample. Work as quickly as you can. Skim the passage and then read the questions. Use the meaning of the passage to find the answers. Use key words in the question to find the part of the passage that contains the answer. Fill in your answers in the circles at the bottom of the page. When you see a GO sign, turn the page and continue working. Work until you come to the STOP sign at the bottom of page 9. Remember to make sure that your answer circles are filled in with dark marks. Completely erase any marks for answers that you change. Do you have any questions? Start working now.**

Allow time for the students to read the stories and answer the questions.

Lesson 2a **Reading Comprehension**

"Look at those beautiful balloons, Annette!" Papa Joe shouted over the noise of the burner that was filling their balloon with hot air.

Annette looked around at the hot air balloon rally. A clear blue sky was a contrast to the many colors of the balloon. Papa Joe was right—the balloons were beautiful. Annette's face reflected Papa Joe's grin back to him.

Suddenly the balloon shifted a little. Annette huddled into a corner of the basket and squeezed her eyes shut.

Papa Joe was humming as he checked the anchor ropes, but Annette couldn't hear it over the roaring burner. A breeze picked up just then and pushed Annette's hair across her face. "This isn't so bad," Annette thought, convinced they were taking off. "With my eyes closed, I can't see the ground drop away underneath us."

Just as Annette started to relax, Papa Joe untied the anchor ropes. The basket of the balloon swung sideways and bumped along the ground a few times. "Look out!" Annette shouted, sure they had crashed into a tree. Then she heard Papa Joe chuckle, and she opened her eyes. The balloon was only a few feet off the ground, rising slowly. Realizing her mistake, Annette managed a shaky laugh and decided to keep her eyes open for the rest of the rally.

4 How does Annette's face reflect Papa Joe's grin back to him?

J She pays no attention to him.
K She looks at him closely.
L She holds up a mirror.
* M She smiles.

5 Papa Joe hums while he works on the balloon because

* A he enjoys flying hot air balloons.
B he thinks Annette is happy to be there.
C he is trying to set a good example for Annette.
D he is bored with the hot air balloon rally.

6 Why did Annette think the balloon had taken off?

J Other balloons are in the air.
K The burner stops roaring.
L She sees the ground fall away.
* M The wind begins to blow.

7 Annette's scream is funny because the reader knows that

A Annette is only pretending to be scared.
B Papa Joe is playing a trick on Annette.
* C the bumps are from the balloon's takeoff.
D hot air balloon crashes are not dangerous.

8 The description of Annette as "huddled" in the balloon's basket suggests that she

* J is nervous.
K feels sleepy.
L does not like Papa Joe.
M wants the balloon to take off.

6 Answer rows 4  5  6  7  8 

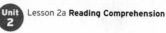

Thousands of years ago, people learned to tame horses. The Scythians, a tribe living north of the Black Sea, were among the first to make full use of horses. Scythians and their horses flourished from roughly 1000 B.C. to A.D. 1000.

Scythians were nomads who didn't have permanent homes or settlements. They traveled on horseback. Some Scythians, probably women with young children, traveled in wagons pulled by horses. Scythians, both men and women, became very good riders and were feared as warriors. They even learned to shoot accurately with a bow and arrow while riding.

To the Scythians, horses were more than just transportation. Horses were also an important source of food. Scythians hunted and fished, but their diets also included milk from horses and cheese made from the milk. Perhaps because horses were important to them in so many ways, Scythians often used images of horses in their decorations.

Because the Scythians did not often use written language, much of what we know about Scythians and their relationship with horses comes from Scythian graves. When Scythians died, valuable and important things were buried with them. Scythians probably believed that the dead would need these things in the next world. Along with clothing and gold ornaments, their graves usually contained things that were important for riding horses.

9 Which of these would most likely decorate a Scythian warrior's saddle?

* A A carving of a horse
B A picture of a bow and arrow
C The warrior's name
D Colored beads

10 According to the author, why did Scythians bury horse-related things in people's graves?

J As a sign of respect
* K For use in the next world
L To show the person had good friends
M As a substitute for gold ornaments

11 In the second paragraph, what are "nomads"?

A Arrowheads
B Clumsy, slow wagons
C Large herds of wild horses
* D People who move from place to place

12 Which of the following does the author emphasize in this passage?

J How wealthy the Scythians were
* K How important horses were to Scythians
L The difficulty of taming wild horses
M The equality of men and women in Scythian tribes

Answer rows 9 ● B C D 10 J ● L M 11 A B C ● 12 J ● L M

As her mother began to unload the car, Bailey sat for a moment. She rolled down the window and listened. Before she even saw the waves, she imagined their frothy tips rolling in and out over the sand like a baker rolling dough on a counter.

Bailey and her mother carried towels, sunscreen, snacks, chairs, and other necessities for settling into a day at the beach. Bailey almost hated to walk over the peak of the hill with her hands full like any other tourist. She wanted her first sight of the ocean to be different from the rest of the moments in her ordinary life. She was sure that she would be changed by this strange and wondrous encounter.

"Mom, do you remember your first trip to the ocean?" Bailey asked as they chose a spot on the sand. Bailey's mother stopped her unpacking.

"I couldn't forget it. For my brothers and sister it was just another vacation. But for me, going to the beach was like discovering a sound and a sight that called me back again and again."

As Bailey's mother looked out, she saw the same picture and heard the same song that called her so many years ago. She looked at Bailey, wiping a stray hair from her eyes. "And now I'm sharing my memory and this place with you," she said.

Bailey decided to begin by enjoying the sand in her toes. The sun baked the top of the white, dry sand. It looked liked tons of salt scattered for miles. As she dug in her toes, the sand became cool and damp.

After making her way across the sand, she decided it was time to test the water. She planted herself at the place where the tide stopped its climb onto the bank. Bailey squatted, watching where water met sky in one wide path of blue. "Forever must look like this," she thought to herself.

As the waves grew, they looked like gallons of gurgling milk thrust up into the sky. Though they changed shape, they seemed to stay in one spot, lapping over themselves again and again.

After what seemed like hours, she walked back to their spot on the beach. "I think I know exactly how you felt, Mom," Bailey said.

GO

Say **It's time to stop. You have finished Lesson 2a.**

Review the answers with the students. Ask them if they remembered to look back at the passage to find the answers to the questions. If any questions caused particular difficulty, work through the story, questions, and answer choices. Ask the students which key words helped them find the answers and discuss any strategies they used.

Have the students indicate completion of the lesson by entering their score for this activity on the progress chart at the beginning of the book.

Lesson 2a **Reading Comprehension**

13 How did Bailey's mother feel about the ocean before they came to visit?

A Her memory of the beach faded.
B Her brothers and sister made her afraid.
C She liked to swim and play in the water.
* D She had good memories.

14 When Bailey's mother said the beach "called me back again and again," she probably meant

J driving to the beach was easier because she had been there before.
K the waves crashed into her over and over again.
* L seeing the ocean for the first time made her want to return.
M the water sounded like a person speaking to her.

15 What does it mean that the sun "baked the top of the dry, white sand"?

A The sand felt like baked bread.
* B The sun made the sand hot.
C The sand changed its color.
D The sun hurt Bailey's eyes.

16 When Bailey says, "Forever must look like this," she suggests that

J the sun cannot go down.
K the sky does not resemble the water.
* L she cannot see the end of the water.
M the water does not move.

17 What makes Bailey say that she knows how her mother felt?

A They both noticed the same things about the sand.
B Bailey wanted to paint a picture and sing a song.
C Her feet were cold in the water and warm on the sand.
* D She saw the beauty of the ocean like her mother did.

18 Before she goes down to the beach, what does Bailey think about the ocean?

* J She thinks of it as beautiful and mysterious.
K She imagines it as frightening and dark.
L Thinking of the ocean makes her feel wild and free.
M The ocean sounds dangerous and strange to her.

Answer rows 13 Ⓐ Ⓑ Ⓒ ● 15 Ⓐ ● Ⓒ Ⓓ 17 Ⓐ Ⓑ Ⓒ ●
14 Ⓙ Ⓚ ● Ⓜ 16 Ⓙ Ⓚ ● Ⓜ 18 ● Ⓚ Ⓛ Ⓜ

9

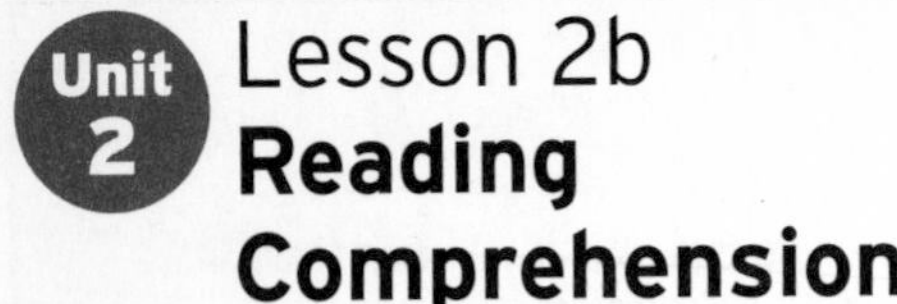

Lesson 2b Reading Comprehension

Focus

Reading Skills

- making inferences
- understanding literary devices
- deriving word meanings
- recognizing an author's technique
- recognizing details
- comparing and contrasting
- understanding reasons
- making predictions
- understanding the main idea
- drawing conclusions
- recognizing genre or text source

Test-taking Skills

- analyzing answer choices
- working methodically

Reading

Lesson 2b **Reading Comprehension**

Directions: Read the passage and the answer choices. Choose the best answer.

Sample A

The tallest tree in the forest grew at the bottom of a valley. This may have saved it from the woodcutters. They might not have noticed how tall it was. Other trees may have seemed much taller.

The tall tree was not cut because
- A other trees had more wood.
- B other trees were taller.
- C it was hard to cut.
- * D it grew in a valley.

- **Remember, the correct choice must answer the question, not just come from the poem or story.**

The Frog

A green blur of legs
Flies from the water's edge.
There it will sit,
Eyes blinking, chin bulging, "Brrrribbitt!"
A moment of quiet
Then again through the air
Another long leap
With a plop, to the pond, diving deep.

1 The poet describes the sound the frog makes with
- A a word that is hard to say.
- B a word that is like a loud scream.
- * C a word that sounds like a frog's croak.
- D a word that forms a sentence.

2 The words "A green blur of legs" describe
- * J what the frog looks like as it leaps through the air.
- K how the frog looks when it is far away.
- L where the frog goes when it is tired.
- M why a frog needs such long hind legs to leap.

3 The word "deep" in the eighth line is a good choice because it
- A shows what the pond is like.
- B imitates the sound of a frog.
- C describes how the frog is moving through the water.
- * D rhymes with the last word of line 7.

4 How does the frog move about?
- J By bulging and running
- * K By hopping and swimming
- L By crawling and walking
- M By diving and paddling

GO

10 Answer rows A Ⓐ Ⓑ Ⓒ ● 1 Ⓐ Ⓑ ● Ⓓ 2 ● Ⓚ Ⓛ Ⓜ 3 Ⓐ Ⓑ Ⓒ ● 4 Ⓙ ● Ⓛ Ⓜ

Sample A

Say **Turn to Lesson 2b on page 10. In this lesson you will answer questions about passages that you read. Begin by reading the directions at the top of the page to yourself while I read them out loud.**

Read the directions to the students.

Say **Now we'll do Sample A. Skim the passage to yourself.** *(pause)* **Now, read the question next to the passage. To find the correct answer, look back at the passage. What is the correct answer?** *(answer D)* **Even though the story doesn't say so directly, you can infer that the tall tree was not cut because** ***it grew in a valley.*** **Fill in answer circle D for Sample A in the answer rows at the bottom of the page. Make sure the circle is completely filled in. Press your pencil firmly so that your mark comes out dark.**

Check to see that the students have marked the correct answer circle.

Say **Now let's look at the tip. Who will read it?**

Have a volunteer read the tip aloud.

Say **Sometimes an answer choice will be from the story, but it won't answer the question. Think about the question and choose the answer that goes best with the question.**

Explain the tip further, if necessary. Point out that the answer choices for some items will come from the story, so they are accurate. Only one answer, however, will match the question.

Practice

Say Now we are ready for Practice. You will read four more passages and answer questions about them in the same way that we did the Sample. Work as quickly as you can. Skim the passage and then read the questions. Use the meaning of the passage to find the answers. Use key words in the question to find the part of the passage that contains the answer. Fill in your answers in the circles at the bottom of the page. When you see a GO sign, turn the page and continue working. Work until you come to the STOP sign at the bottom of page 14. Remember to make sure that your answer circles are filled in with dark marks. Completely erase any marks for answers you change. Do you have any questions? Start working now.

Allow time for the students to read the stories and answer the questions.

Unit 2 Lesson 2b **Reading Comprehension**

The raven is a black bird that looks much like its relative, the crow. Ravens can be two feet tall with a wingspan that is double their height. These adaptable birds live all over the world, in places as different as Arctic islands and the North African desert. They are especially common in wooded areas, but ravens rarely live in cities. Part of the reason ravens are so widespread is that they can eat just about anything. Ravens feast on insects, seeds, berries, dead animals, eggs, small mammals, and human garbage.

Many experts think ravens are as smart as human children. Some experiments show that ravens can count to seven, and the big birds are expert problem solvers. Ravens in Yellowstone Park have even learned to open the compartments on snowmobiles where people often store food. One scientist says ravens have a strong sense of curiosity that helps them compete with other predators like wolves.

5 What makes ravens so unusual?
A Their size
B Their coloring
C Their wingspan
* D Their intelligence

6 Why are ravens able to live in so many places?
* J They eat a wide variety of foods.
K Their coloring helps them blend in.
L Their ability to count helps them find nests.
M They are often tamed and kept as pets.

7 What probably happens when ravens find a new kind of latch on snowmobile compartments?
A The ravens avoid the latch because it is new.
B The ravens are not interested in opening the latch.
C The ravens try to open the latch but give up quickly.
* D The ravens try to figure out how to open it.

8 What is the main topic of the last paragraph?
J How to tell if a black bird is a raven
K How ravens live in many different places
* L How ravens are both smart and curious
M How to keep your food safe from ravens

GO

Answer rows 5 Ⓐ Ⓑ Ⓒ ● 6 ● Ⓚ Ⓛ Ⓜ 7 Ⓐ Ⓑ Ⓒ ● 8 Ⓙ Ⓚ ● Ⓜ

11

In 1879, a group of explorers made an incredible find. They discovered paintings of remarkable beauty on the walls of a cave in Spain. Some scientists believed that these paintings were created by early humans from the Stone Age, between ten and thirty thousand years ago. Other scientists and the public did not believe the claim, but over the years, it was proven correct. Our ancestors had incredible artistic talents.

Most of the cave art that has been discovered has been found in Spain and France. Other caves with art are located in Italy, Portugal, Russia, and other countries. Scientists believe many more caves will be discovered in the coming years and are concentrating their efforts on Africa and the area between Europe and Asia. These two regions of the world were the first populated by humans.

Cave art was carved or painted on the walls and roofs of caves, usually near the entrance. The entrance area was probably chosen to take advantage of daylight and to allow many people to view the paintings. In some cases, the art is located much deeper in caves and would have required artificial light to be used as the art was created. Evidence suggests that the artists used torches or shallow bowls in which animal fat was burned.

Primitive artists were able to create with a wide variety of colors, including yellow, red, brown, green, and black. These colors came from minerals that were ground and mixed with animal fat, vegetable juice, water, or blood. The colors were applied with sticks or brushes made of animal hair. One of the most unusual means of applying color was to blow it through a hollow reed.

The most popular subject of cave art was animals. The art included mammoths, horses, deer, bison, cave lions, wild cattle, and wooly rhinoceroses. Many of the animals shown in cave paintings are now extinct. Scientists are not sure why early humans made cave paintings, but some of the paintings appear to show successful hunts, while others might have been intended to bring good luck during upcoming hunts. Other popular subjects include human figures, battles, and, surprisingly, human hands. The outlines of human hands have been found on every continent where humans created cave art.

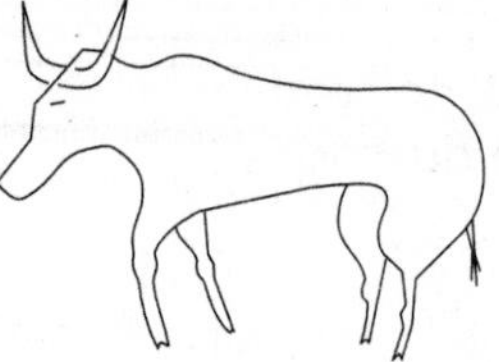

GO

Lesson 2b **Reading Comprehension**

9 **What was the response of the general public to the discovery of cave art made by Stone Age people?**
- A They believed it at first.
- ✱ B They did not believe it.
- C They thought it was beautiful.
- D They ignored it.

10 **From cave paintings, scientists learned that**
- J Stone Age people thought caves were sacred places.
- K animals were not hunted for food during the Stone Age.
- ✱ L some animals that are extinct now were alive during the Stone Age.
- M the temperature was much warmer during the Stone Age.

11 **Based on the passage, what can you conclude about animal fat?**
- A It does not burn.
- B Stone Age artists used it to preserve their paintings.
- ✱ C It can be burned to produce light.
- D Stone Age artists mixed it with their food.

12 **Where do scientists expect to find more cave paintings?**
- J In Central and South America
- K In Spain and France
- L In places where there are caves with large openings
- ✱ M In regions of the world first populated by humans

13 **In the fourth paragraph, what does the word "primitive" mean?**
- A Amusing
- B Talented
- C Untalented
- ✱ D Early in history

14 **Paintings that were created deep inside caves**
- J could be viewed easily by daylight.
- K were always made using the juice from plants.
- ✱ L were probably seen by fewer people than paintings near the entrance.
- M usually show more animals than paintings near the entrance.

15 **What can you conclude about minerals?**
- A Primitive humans knew how to turn minerals into metal.
- ✱ B Different types of minerals can be used to make different colors.
- C Different types of minerals were used to represent different animals.
- D The minerals used for paintings were always found in caves.

16 **Where would this passage be most likely to appear?**
- ✱ J In a textbook about early human history
- K In a textbook about modern art
- L In a dictionary
- M In an encyclopedia entry about caves

GO

Answer rows 9  

9 A ● C D 11 A B ● D 13 A B C ● 15 A ● C D
10 J K ● M 12 J K L ● 14 J K ● M 16 ● K L M

13

Say It's time to stop. You have finished Lesson 2b.

Review the answers with the students. Ask them if they remembered to look back at the passage to find the answers to the questions. If any questions caused particular difficulty, work through the story, questions, and answer choices. Ask the students which key words helped them find the answers and discuss any strategies they used.

Have the students indicate completion of the lesson by entering their score for this activity on the progress chart at the beginning of the book.

 Lesson 2b **Reading Comprehension**

June 12, Boiler Bay, Oregon

Dear Greg,

I'm at marine biology camp and it's great. You wouldn't believe the things we see at the beach here. The beach isn't sandy. Instead, it's all rocky tide pools. We went down at low tide so we could climb around on the rocks. I saw starfish, mussels, and sea anemones. Sea anemones can be green or pink, and they have lots of little "fingers" that close around their food. My favorites were the sea urchins because they're all spiny and colorful. I wanted to bring one home to show you, but I found out it's illegal to collect things in tide pools.

Last night, one of the counselors told us about a tsunami that hit the coast here in 1964. (Tsunamis are caused by earthquakes and can flood really far inland.) After that story, I made sure I knew where the high ground is.

See you soon,
Marvin

17 Why is it probably illegal to collect things from tide pools?
- A Boiler Bay wants people to collect shells on the beach instead.
- B Collecting might bring too many tourists to Boiler Bay.
- C The creatures that live in tide pools are poisonous to people.
- * D Overcollecting could cause the animals to disappear.

18 Which of these does Marvin say he sees in the tide pools?
- J Clams
- * K Mussels
- L Barnacles
- M Sea cucumbers

19 Why does Marvin look for high ground near the camp?
- * A He wants to be prepared for a flood.
- B The view of the ocean is better from up high.
- C He is looking for a place to hide from the other campers.
- D The tide pools with the sea urchins are on high ground.

20 How did "tide pools" probably get their name?
- J The rocks are worn away by the tides.
- K People swim in them when the tide is out.
- * L They are filled by the water at high tide.
- M Even the highest tide cannot reach them.

21 A "tsunami" must be a kind of
- * A giant wave.
- B sand dune.
- C shallow, sloping beach.
- D storm far out in the ocean.

14 Answer rows 17 Ⓐ Ⓑ Ⓒ ● 18 Ⓙ ● Ⓛ Ⓜ  19 ● Ⓑ Ⓒ Ⓓ  20 Ⓙ Ⓚ ● Ⓜ  21 ● Ⓑ Ⓒ Ⓓ

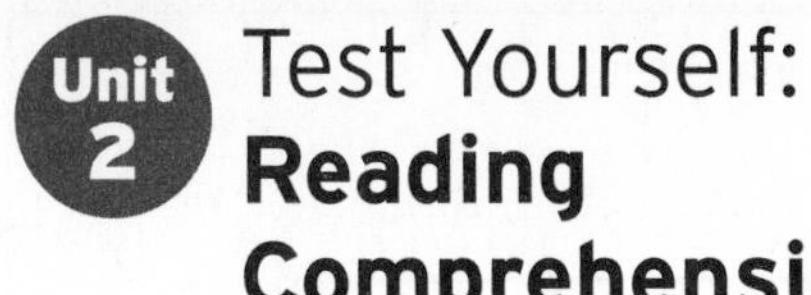

Test Yourself: Reading Comprehension

Focus

Reading Skills

- recognizing details
- comparing and contrasting
- analyzing characters
- making inferences
- deriving word meanings
- recognizing genre or text source
- drawing conclusions
- recognizing an author's purpose
- identifying feelings
- recognizing an author's technique
- understanding the main idea
- understanding reasons

Test-taking Skills

- managing time effectively
- following printed directions
- noting the lettering of answer choices
- skimming a passage
- referring to a passage to answer questions
- using key words to find the answer
- working methodically
- reasoning from facts and evidence
- analyzing answer choices

Test Yourself: Reading Comprehension

Directions: Read the passage and the answer choices. Choose the best answer.

Sample **A** Antonio and his sister, Annette, waited in the principal's office. Their father stood at the counter and filled in the forms that the secretary had given him. The family had just moved to Mountainview.

Why do you think the children are in the principal's office?

A They are late for school.
B They are getting report cards.
* C They are new in school.
D They are going on a class trip.

Walt Disney was perhaps the most famous cartoonist in history. In the 1920s, he produced several films where he made cartoon characters move as if by magic. The technique Disney used was painstaking. He made hundreds or even thousands of repeated drawings of the same character. In each drawing, the character was changed just a bit. A film was taken of the series of drawings, and when it was shown, the characters appeared to move. The process, called animation, is still used today, although computers have made the process much easier.

In 1928, Disney created his most famous character, Mortimer Mouse, who we know today as Mickey. The list of Disney's animation successes is long and memorable. It includes *Pinocchio, Dumbo, Bambi, Cinderella*, and *Peter Pan*. Perhaps his most remarkable animated film was *Snow White and the Seven Dwarfs*, created in 1937. Today, more than fifty years later, it is still one of the most popular films for children.

1 What is one of the chief differences between animation today and in Walt Disney's early years?

A More people like animated movies.
B Fewer people like animated movies.
* C Computers have made the job easier.
D Computers have made the job harder.

2 Which of these words best describes Walt Disney?

* J Creative
K Athletic
L Exciting
M Quiet

3 Which of these words best describes what makes the film *Snow White* so remarkable?

A It was a great success.
B It took more than a year to make.
C It was made at a time when there were no computers.
* D It has remained popular for more than fifty years.

4 In the first paragraph, what is the meaning of the word "painstaking"?

J Something that hurts because it involves hard work
* K Something that takes a long time and involves much hard work
L Requiring a lot of effort, like running a marathon
M Requiring many fine tools, such as pens and pencils

Answer rows A Ⓐ Ⓑ ● Ⓓ 1 Ⓐ Ⓑ ● Ⓓ 2 ● Ⓚ Ⓛ Ⓜ 3 Ⓐ Ⓑ Ⓒ ● 4 Ⓙ ● Ⓛ Ⓜ

This lesson simulates an actual test-taking experience. Therefore, it is recommended that the directions be read verbatim and the suggested procedures and time allowances be followed.

Directions

Administration Time: approximately 25 minutes

Say Turn to the Test Yourself lesson on page 15.

Check to be sure the students have found the right page. Point out to the students that this Test Yourself lesson is timed like a real test, but that they will score it themselves to see how well they are doing. Explain that it is important to work quickly and to answer as many questions as possible.

Say This lesson will check how well you understand what you read. Remember to make sure that the circles for your answer choices are completely filled in. Press your pencil firmly so that your marks come out dark. Completely erase any marks for answers that you change. Do not write anything except your answer choices in your books.

Look at Sample A. Read the passage and answer the question about it. The answer rows are at the bottom of the page.

Allow time for the students to fill in their answers.

Say The correct answer is C. The story says the family just moved to the town. If you chose another answer, erase yours and fill in answer C now.

Check to see that the students have correctly filled in their answer circles with a dark mark.

Say **Now you will do more items like Sample A. There are three different passages for this part of the lesson. When you come to the GO sign at the bottom of a page, turn the page and continue working. Work until you come to the STOP sign at the bottom of page 19. Fill in your answers in the rows at the bottom of the page. Make sure you fill in the circles completely with dark marks. Completely erase any marks for answers you change. You will have 20 minutes. You may begin.**

Allow 20 minutes.

Test Yourself: Reading Comprehension

The cat that purrs sweetly when you scratch its chin is a close cousin of the lions that roam the plains of Africa and other great cats. All cats belong to the Felidae family, whose members can be found in every region of the globe except Antarctica. They are skilled hunters, and even the tamest cat will fall into a crouch if a mouse or other small animal is nearby.

Scientists believe that small, wild cats were captured and kept as pets by people as long as 10,000 years ago. The Egyptians were the first to breed cats, and for a time cats were thought by Egyptians to be holy. As civilization spread from the Middle East to other parts of the world, cats followed. Today, cats are the most popular pet in both America and Western Europe. They are less popular in other parts of the world, and are often thought of as being pests.

The body temperature of a cat is about 101°, which is a few degrees warmer than humans. Cats are very sensitive to the temperature around them, and as the temperature rises above 95°, they pant to keep cool.

Cats have keen eyesight and have developed the ability to see well in the dark. They also have a good sense of hearing and can hear sounds beyond the range of humans. Unlike a dog's, a cat's sense of smell is not particularly good.

Anyone who is familiar with both cats and dogs knows that dogs are more easily trained and seem to be more loyal. These differences can be traced to the origins of both animals. The wild ancestors of dogs were pack animals in which loyalty to the group and cooperative behavior were important for survival. The ancestors of cats were more solitary and independent, so the domestic cats of today seem less affectionate than dogs.

Another important difference between cats and dogs is that there are fewer breeds of cats. In addition, the differences among breeds are smaller than among breeds of dogs. For example, a small breed of dog may be one tenth the size of a large breed and may have much different features. Cats are all about the same size and their ears, coats, tails, and other features are very similar.

GO

16

Test Yourself: Reading Comprehension

5 Where would a passage like this be most likely to appear?

A In an almanac
B In a dictionary
C In a book about history
* D In an encyclopedia

6 What does it mean to say that a cat will "fall into a crouch"?

J It is tired.
* K It is ready to hunt.
L It is ready to purr.
M It is afraid.

7 How did cats get from the Middle East to Europe?

* A They followed people as they moved or they were brought by people.
B They were there before the people moved from the Middle East.
C The Egyptians bred them.
D Cats originated in Europe.

8 What happens to cats if the temperature gets too high?

J They sweat just like people.
K Their body temperature falls.
* L They begin breathing heavily.
M They become sensitive to the temperature.

9 What is the author's purpose in writing this passage?

A To describe some of the history and characteristics of pets
B To explain the differences between cats and dogs
C To explain the advantages of owning a cat
* D To describe some of the history and characteristics of cats

10 In the fifth paragraph, what does the phrase "pack animals" mean?

* J Animals that stay in groups
K Good hunters
L Animals that carry things
M Animals that hunt by themselves

11 When compared to dogs, cats have

A poor vision.
B good vision.
* C a poor sense of smell.
D a keen sense of smell.

12 Who belongs to the Felidae family?

J Only domestic cats
* K All cats
L Only wild cats
M All cats and dogs

Answer rows

17

Test Yourself: Reading Comprehension

Reina hated walking home from school. Even though it was just a few blocks, it was disgusting. Trash was everywhere, graffiti was all over the walls, and junked cars lined the streets. She couldn't understand how people could live that way. It was wonderful when she got home to her neat house and yard that stood out like a picture on a dingy wall.

"Mom, was our neighborhood always so terrible?"

"Not at all, honey. Why ten years ago, this was one of the most wonderful neighborhoods in the city. People took care of their houses and had beautiful gardens. It was so nice that people came from all over to walk through the neighborhood and look at the houses." Mrs. Chavez sighed and looked away.

"I wish it were like that now. I hate being outside. It's such a mess it makes me feel dirty."

Mrs. Chavez thought about what Reina had said. That night, after Reina was asleep, she and her husband talked it over. They decided Reina was right, and that since the city wasn't going to do anything about the neighborhood, they would have to.

On Saturday morning, Mr. Chavez knocked on his neighbor's door. He explained his idea to Mr. Jackson, who, despite being over seventy years old, agreed to help. The Chavez family and Mr. Jackson spent the morning cleaning up the trash in the tiny "pocket park" on the corner.

About noon some of the other neighbors came out to lend a hand even though no one had asked them. Before they knew it, there were more than twenty people working in the park. There were so many in fact, that some of them decided to pick up the trash on the sidewalks and in the street.

Mrs. Alioto, who lived adjacent to the park, called her son and asked him to come and pick up the trash in his truck. By Saturday afternoon, the park was spotless, and the truckload of trash they had picked up was on its way to a city landfill.

For the next few weeks the neighbors came out each evening and tackled another job. They planted flowers, continued to pick up the trash that thoughtless people kept throwing on the ground and convinced the city to tow the junked cars away. Little by little, the neighborhood started to look better.

Reina noticed that something else was happening, too. Some of the unpleasant people who had been hanging out on her street weren't around as much. The children in the neighborhood were also playing outside more. And she didn't mind the walk home from school at all.

GO

Say **It's time to stop. You have completed the Test Yourself lesson.**

Check to see that the students have correctly filled in their answer circles. At this point, go over the answers with the students. Did they have enough time to complete the lesson? Did they remember to skim the passage and to look for key words in the questions? Did they take the best guess when they were unsure of the answer?

Work through any questions that caused difficulty. It may be helpful to discuss the strategies students used to answer the comprehension items. You may also want to have the students identify the specific part of a passage that helped them find the right answer.

Have the students indicate completion of the lesson by entering their score for this activity on the progress chart at the beginning of the book.

Unit 2 Test Yourself: Reading Comprehension

13 Which problem will the neighbors find most difficult to solve?
A Finding a way to move the trash they pick up to the landfill
* B Convincing thoughtless people to stop throwing trash on the ground
C Getting started
D Planting flowers

14 In the beginning of the story, how does Reina feel about her neighborhood?
J Happy
K Excited
L Determined
* M Disgusted

15 The reaction of the other neighbors to seeing the park cleaned up shows that
* A they wanted to help solve the problem.
B they didn't think there was much of a problem to solve.
C they enjoyed sleeping late.
D they wanted to clean up their own yards first.

16 In the eighth paragraph, what do the words "adjacent to" mean?
* J Next to
K Far from
L Across the street from
M On the next block

17 Why does the writer mention Mr. Jackson's age?
A Because it is unusual for a person to be that old
B Because he was Reina's grandfather
C Because he lived adjacent to the park
* D To show that older people are willing to help clean up the neighborhood

18 What is a "pocket park"?
J A park on a corner
* K A small park
L A large park
M A park with small flowers

19 What is the main point of this story?
A Young people are more likely to solve problems than old people.
B Parents should listen to their children more often.
* C People sometimes have to take action to solve neighborhood problems.
D Trash is a major problem in many city neighborhoods.

20 Why does Mrs. Chavez sigh and look away when Reina asks her about the neighborhood?
J She is ignoring Reina.
K She is thinking about work.
L She is thinking about another neighborhood.
* M She is remembering how it used to be.

Answer rows 13 (A) ● (C) (D) 15 ● (B) (C) (D) 17 (A) (B) (C) ● 19 (A) (B) ● (D)
14 (J) (K) (L) ● 16 ● (K) (L) (M) 18 (J) ● (L) (M) 20 (J) (K) (L) ●

19

Background

This unit contains three lessons that deal with spelling skills. Students are asked to identify a misspelled word in isolation.

- **In Lesson 3a,** students identify an incorrectly spelled word. Students work methodically, take the best guess when unsure of the answer, and indicate that an item has no mistakes.
- **In Lesson 3b,** students identify an incorrectly spelled word. In addition to reviewing the test-taking skills introduced in Lesson 3a, students learn about recalling error types.
- **In the Test Yourself lesson,** the spelling skills and test-taking skills introduced and used in Lessons 3a and 3b are reinforced and presented in a format that gives students the experience of taking an achievement test. Techniques for managing time effectively when taking a standardized test are reinforced.

Instructional **Objectives**

Lesson 3a **Spelling** Lesson 3b **Spelling**	Given four words, the student identifies which of the four is misspelled or indicates that there are no mistakes.
Test Yourself	Given questions similar to those in Lessons 3a and 3b, the student utilizes spelling skills and test-taking strategies on achievement test formats.

Lesson 3a Spelling

Focus

Spelling Skill
- identifying spelling errors

Test-taking Skills
- managing time effectively
- working methodically
- taking the best guess when unsure of the answer
- indicating that an item has no mistakes

Samples A and B

Say **Turn to Lesson 3a on page 20. In this lesson you will find misspelled words. Read the directions at the top of the page to yourself while I read them out loud.**

Read the directions out loud to the students.

Say **Let's look at Sample A. Look at the answer choices. Find the word that has a spelling mistake. If none of the words has a mistake, choose the last answer. Which answer did you choose?** *(answer A, t-r-e-s-u-r-e)* **Mark circle A for Sample A in the answer rows at the bottom of the page. Make sure the circle is completely filled in. Press your pencil firmly so that your mark comes out dark.**

Check to see that the students have filled in the correct answer circle. Review the correct spelling of the word *treasure*.

Say **Do Sample B yourself. Find the word that has a spelling mistake. If none of the words has a mistake, choose the last answer.** *(pause)* **Which answer should you choose?** *(answer N, No mistakes)* **What should you do now?** *(mark the circle for answer N in the answer rows)* **Make sure the circle is completely filled in with a dark mark.**

Check to see that the students have filled in the correct answer circle.

Spelling

Lesson 3a **Spelling**

Directions: Fill in the space for any word that has a spelling mistake. If there is no mistake, fill in the last answer space.

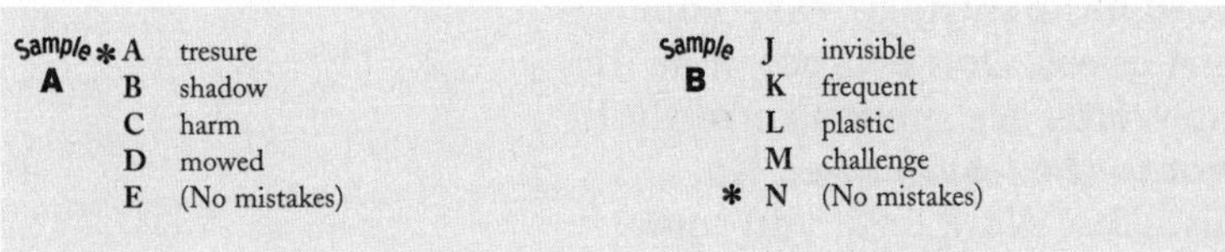

Sample A
* A tresure
B shadow
C harm
D mowed
E (No mistakes)

Sample B
J invisible
K frequent
L plastic
M challenge
* N (No mistakes)

- **Remember, you are looking for the word that has a spelling mistake.**
- **If you are not sure which answer to choose, take your best guess.**

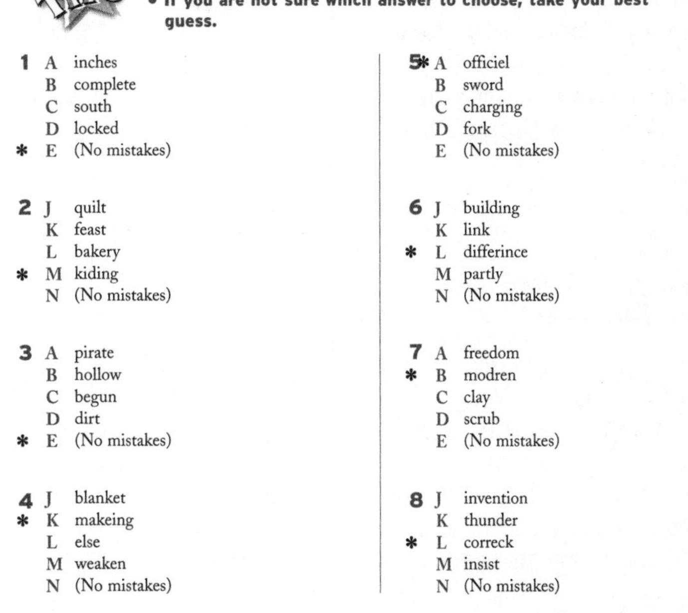

1 A inches
B complete
C south
D locked
* E (No mistakes)

2 J quilt
K feast
L bakery
* M kiding
N (No mistakes)

3 A pirate
B hollow
C begun
D dirt
* E (No mistakes)

4 J blanket
* K makeing
L else
M weaken
N (No mistakes)

5 * A officiel
B sword
C charging
D fork
E (No mistakes)

6 J building
K link
* L differince
M partly
N (No mistakes)

7 A freedom
* B modren
C clay
D scrub
E (No mistakes)

8 J invention
K thunder
* L correck
M insist
N (No mistakes)

STOP

20 Answer rows A ● B C D E 1 A B C D ● 3 A B C D ● 5 ● B C D E 7 A ● C D E
B J K L M ● 2 J K L ● N 4 J ● L M N 6 J K ● M N 8 J K ● M N

TIPS

Say **Now let's look at the tips.**

Have a volunteer read the tips aloud.

Say **Don't forget, you are looking for the word that is spelled wrong. Sometimes you may not be able to figure out which word has a mistake. When this happens, take your best guess. Choose the word that looks a little unusual and move on to the next item. Guessing when you are not sure keeps you from wasting too much time.**

Practice

Say Now we are ready for Practice. Do Numbers 1 through 8 in the same way that we did the samples. Work as quickly as you can, and if you aren't sure which word has a mistake, take your best guess. Don't forget, if all of the words are spelled correctly, choose the last answer, No mistakes. Work until you come to the STOP sign at the bottom of the page. Remember to make sure that your answer circles are completely filled in with dark marks. Completely erase any marks for answers that you change. Any questions? Start working now.

Allow time for the students to mark their answers.

Say It's time to stop. You have finished Lesson 3a.

Review the answers with the students. If any items caused particular difficulty, work through each of the answer choices. Do an informal item analysis to determine which items were most difficult. Discuss with the students the words that gave them the most difficulty, including the misspelled words and the distractors that are spelled correctly and that the students identify as wrong.

Have the students indicate completion of the lesson by entering their score for this activity on the progress chart at the beginning of the book.

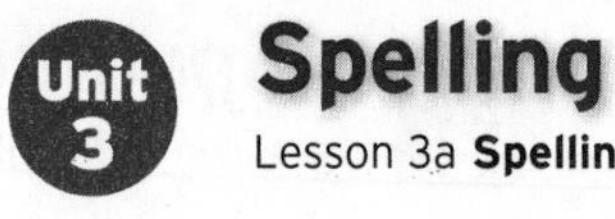

Lesson 3a **Spelling**

Directions: Fill in the space for any word that has a spelling mistake. If there is no mistake, fill in the last answer space.

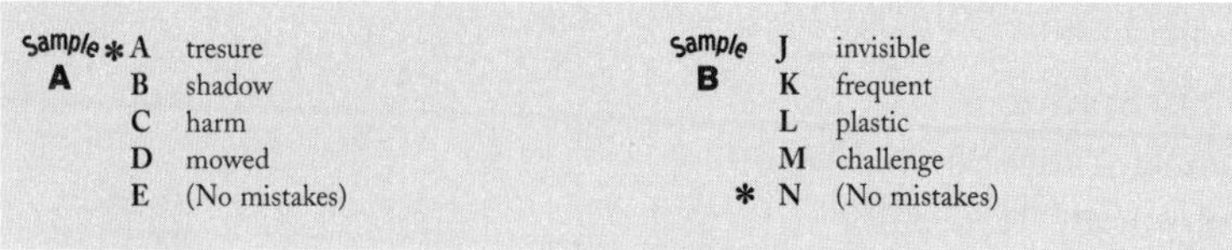

Sample A
* A tresure
B shadow
C harm
D mowed
E (No mistakes)

Sample B
J invisible
K frequent
L plastic
M challenge
* N (No mistakes)

- **Remember, you are looking for the word that has a spelling mistake.**
- **If you are not sure which answer to choose, take your best guess.**

1
A inches
B complete
C south
D locked
* E (No mistakes)

2
J quilt
K feast
L bakery
* M kiding
N (No mistakes)

3
A pirate
B hollow
C begun
D dirt
* E (No mistakes)

4
J blanket
* K makeing
L else
M weaken
N (No mistakes)

5
* A officiel
B sword
C charging
D fork
E (No mistakes)

6
J building
K link
* L differince
M partly
N (No mistakes)

7
A freedom
* B modren
C clay
D scrub
E (No mistakes)

8
J invention
K thunder
* L correck
M insist
N (No mistakes)

STOP

20 Answer rows A ● B C D E 1 A B C D ● 3 A B C D ● 5 ● B C D E 7 A ● C D E
B J K L M ● 2 J K L ● N 4 J ● L M N 6 J K ● M N 8 J K ● M N

Unit 3 Lesson 3b Spelling

Focus

Spelling Skill
- identifying spelling errors

Test-taking Skills
- recalling error types
- working methodically
- indicating that an item has no mistakes

Samples A and B

Say **Turn to Lesson 3b on page 21. In this lesson you will find misspelled words. Read the directions at the top of the page to yourself while I read them out loud.**

Read the directions out loud to the students.

Say **Find Sample A at the top of the page. Look at the answer choices. Find the word that has a spelling mistake. If none of the words has a mistake, choose the last answer. Which answer did you choose?** *(answer C, s-a-i-d-n-e-s-s)* **Mark circle C for Sample A in the answer rows at the bottom of the page. Make sure the circle is completely filled in. Press your pencil firmly so that your mark comes out dark.**

Check to see that the students have filled in the correct answer circle. Review the correct spelling of the word *sadness*.

Say **Do Sample B yourself. Find the word that has a spelling mistake. If none of the words has a mistake, choose the last answer.** *(pause)* **Which answer should you choose?** *(answer N, No mistakes)* **What should you do now?** *(mark the circle for answer N in the answer rows)* **Make sure the circle is completely filled in with a dark mark.**

Check to see that the students have filled in the correct answer circle.

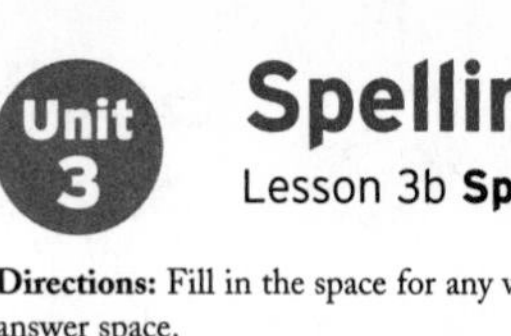

Spelling

Lesson 3b **Spelling**

Directions: Fill in the space for any word that has a spelling mistake. If there is no mistake, fill in the last answer space.

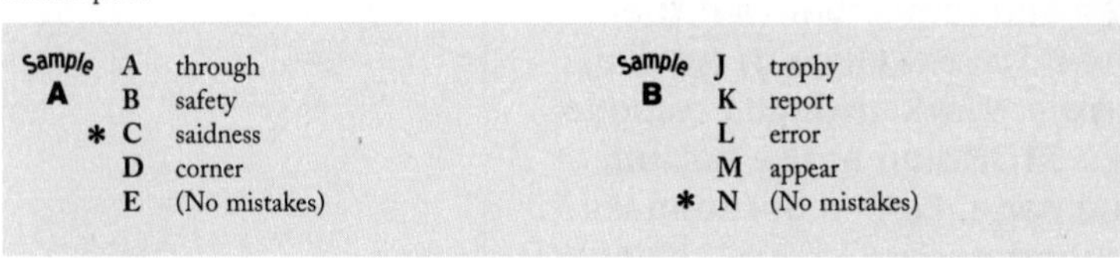

Sample A
A through
B safety
* C saidness
D corner
E (No mistakes)

Sample B
J trophy
K report
L error
M appear
* N (No mistakes)

- **Spelling mistakes can be missing letters, extra letters, or incorrect letters.**

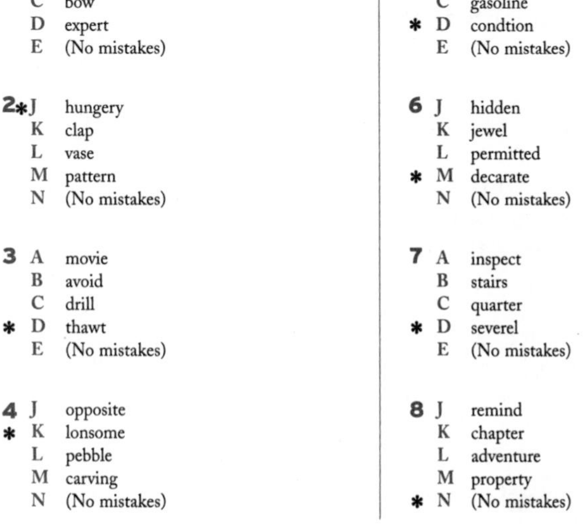

1
A snack
* B maching
C bow
D expert
E (No mistakes)

2
* J hungery
K clap
L vase
M pattern
N (No mistakes)

3
A movie
B avoid
C drill
* D thawt
E (No mistakes)

4
J opposite
* K lonsome
L pebble
M carving
N (No mistakes)

5
A unite
B north
C gasoline
* D condtion
E (No mistakes)

6
J hidden
K jewel
L permitted
* M decarate
N (No mistakes)

7
A inspect
B stairs
C quarter
* D severel
E (No mistakes)

8
J remind
K chapter
L adventure
M property
* N (No mistakes)

STOP

Answer rows A Ⓐ Ⓑ ● Ⓓ Ⓔ 1 Ⓐ ● Ⓒ Ⓓ Ⓔ 3 Ⓐ Ⓑ Ⓒ ● Ⓔ 5 Ⓐ Ⓑ Ⓒ ● Ⓔ 7 Ⓐ Ⓑ Ⓒ ● Ⓔ
B Ⓙ Ⓚ Ⓛ Ⓜ ● 2 ● Ⓚ Ⓛ Ⓜ Ⓝ 4 Ⓙ ● Ⓛ Ⓜ Ⓝ 6 Ⓙ Ⓚ Ⓛ ● Ⓝ 8 Ⓙ Ⓚ Ⓛ Ⓜ ●

21

TIPS

Say **Now let's look at the tip.**

Have a volunteer read the tip aloud.

Say **There are many different kinds of spelling mistakes. They include incorrect letters, extra letters, and missing letters. When you look at the answer choices, look for all of these mistakes.**

Demonstrate, as an option, various misspellings of the words in the sample items, errors such as *trofy* or *safty*. Point out that the error in sample A is the extra letter *i* in the word *saidness*.

Practice

Say **Now we are ready for Practice. Do Numbers 1 through 8 in the same way that we did the samples. Work as quickly as you can and remember that there are different kinds of spelling errors. Work until you come to the STOP sign at the bottom of the page. Remember to make sure that your answer circles are completely filled in with dark marks. Completely erase any marks for answers that you change. Any questions? Start working now.**

Allow time for the students to mark their answers.

Say **It's time to stop. You have finished Lesson 3b.**

Review the answers with the students. If any items caused particular difficulty, work through each of the answer choices.

Have the students indicate completion of the lesson by entering their score for this activity on the progress chart at the beginning of the book.

Spelling

Lesson 3b **Spelling**

Directions: Fill in the space for any word that has a spelling mistake. If there is no mistake, fill in the last answer space.

Sample **A**
A through
B safety
* C saidness
D corner
E (No mistakes)

Sample **B**
J trophy
K report
L error
M appear
* N (No mistakes)

- **Spelling mistakes can be missing letters, extra letters, or incorrect letters.**

1
A snack
* B maching
C bow
D expert
E (No mistakes)

2
* J hungery
K clap
L vase
M pattern
N (No mistakes)

3
A movie
B avoid
C drill
* D thawt
E (No mistakes)

4
J opposite
* K lonsome
L pebble
M carving
N (No mistakes)

5
A unite
B north
C gasoline
* D condtion
E (No mistakes)

6
J hidden
K jewel
L permitted
* M decarate
N (No mistakes)

7
A inspect
B stairs
C quarter
* D severel
E (No mistakes)

8
J remind
K chapter
L adventure
M property
* N (No mistakes)

Answer rows **A** Ⓐ Ⓑ ● Ⓓ Ⓔ **1** Ⓐ ● Ⓒ Ⓓ Ⓔ **3** Ⓐ Ⓑ Ⓒ ● Ⓔ **5** Ⓐ Ⓑ Ⓒ ● Ⓔ **7** Ⓐ Ⓑ Ⓒ ● Ⓔ
B Ⓙ Ⓚ Ⓛ Ⓜ ● **2** ● Ⓚ Ⓛ Ⓜ Ⓝ **4** Ⓙ ● Ⓛ Ⓜ Ⓝ **6** Ⓙ Ⓚ Ⓛ ● Ⓝ **8** Ⓙ Ⓚ Ⓛ Ⓜ ●

21

Unit 3 Test Yourself: Spelling

Focus

Spelling Skill
- identifying spelling errors

Test-taking Skills
- working methodically
- taking the best guess when unsure of the answer
- indicating that an item has no mistakes
- recalling error types

This lesson simulates an actual test-taking experience. Therefore it is recommended that the directions be read verbatim and that the suggested procedures and time allowances be followed.

Directions

Administration Time: approximately 20 minutes

Say **Turn to the Test Yourself lesson on page 22.**

Point out to the students that this Test Yourself lesson is timed like a real test, but that they will score it themselves to see how well they are doing. Remind the students to work quickly and to mark the answer as soon as they are sure which word is misspelled.

Say **This lesson will check how well you can find words with spelling errors. Remember to make sure that the circles for your answer choices are completely filled in. Press your pencil firmly so that your marks come out dark. Completely erase any answers that you change. Do not write anything except your answer choices in your books.**

Look at the answer choices for Sample A. Find the answer choice that has a spelling error. If there is no error, choose the last answer choice. Mark the circle for your answer.

Allow time for the students to mark their answers.

Say **The circle for answer C should have been marked because it is the incorrect spelling of *d-a-i-r-y*. If you chose another answer, erase yours and fill in circle C now.**

Check to see that the students have correctly marked their answer circles for Sample A.

Say **Do Sample B yourself. Mark the circle for the answer choice that has a spelling mistake. If there is no error, choose the last answer choice. Mark the circle for your answer.**

Allow time for the students to fill in their answers.

Say **You should have filled in the circle for answer N because none of the words has a spelling error. If you chose another answer, erase yours and fill in circle N now.**

Check to see that the students have correctly marked their answer circles for Sample B.

Unit 3 Test Yourself: Spelling

Directions: Fill in the space for any word that has a spelling mistake. If there is no mistake, fill in the last answer space.

Sample A
A indoor
B board
* C darey
D clump
E (No mistakes)

Sample B
J file
K aunt
L girl
M hinge
* N (No mistakes)

1
A horse
B microphone
C ruin
D shelter
* E (No mistakes)

2
* J apearance
K industry
L mistaken
M popular
N (No mistakes)

3
A length
B disagree
C against
* D realise
E (No mistakes)

4
J crawl
* K journel
L difficult
M hammer
N (No mistakes)

5
A junior
B believe
* C districk
D vanish
E (No mistakes)

6
J mighty
K quality
L glue
* M powdre
N (No mistakes)

7
A important
B excuse
C contract
* D throte
E (No mistakes)

8
J shift
K wave
L quit
M supper
* N (No mistakes)

9
A foolish
B celery
* C hansome
D advantage
E (No mistakes)

10
J size
K medal
L spring
* M carear
N (No mistakes)

GO

22 Answer rows A Ⓐ Ⓑ ● Ⓓ Ⓔ B Ⓙ Ⓚ Ⓛ Ⓜ ● 1 Ⓐ Ⓑ Ⓒ Ⓓ ● 2 ● Ⓚ Ⓛ Ⓜ Ⓝ 3 Ⓐ Ⓑ Ⓒ ● Ⓔ 4 Ⓙ ● Ⓛ Ⓜ Ⓝ 5 Ⓐ Ⓑ ● Ⓓ Ⓔ 6 Ⓙ Ⓚ Ⓛ ● Ⓝ 7 Ⓐ Ⓑ Ⓒ ● Ⓔ 8 Ⓙ Ⓚ Ⓛ Ⓜ ● 9 Ⓐ Ⓑ ● Ⓓ Ⓔ 10 Ⓙ Ⓚ Ⓛ ● Ⓝ

Say Now you will do Numbers 1 through 22 in the same way that we did the samples. When you come to the GO sign at the bottom of the page, continue working. Work until you come to the STOP sign at the bottom of page 23. When you have finished, you can check over your answers to this lesson. Then wait for the rest of the group to finish. Any questions? You will have 15 minutes. Begin working now.

Allow 15 minutes.

Say It's time to stop. You have completed the Test Yourself lesson. Check to see that you have completely filled in your answer circles with dark marks. Make sure that any marks for answers that you changed have been completely erased.

Go over the lesson with the students. Ask them if they had enough time to finish the lesson. Ask for volunteers to identify the spelling errors in each item.

Work through any questions that caused difficulty. Discuss any rules the students used to determine whether or not a word is spelled correctly. If necessary, provide additional practice questions similar to the ones in this unit.

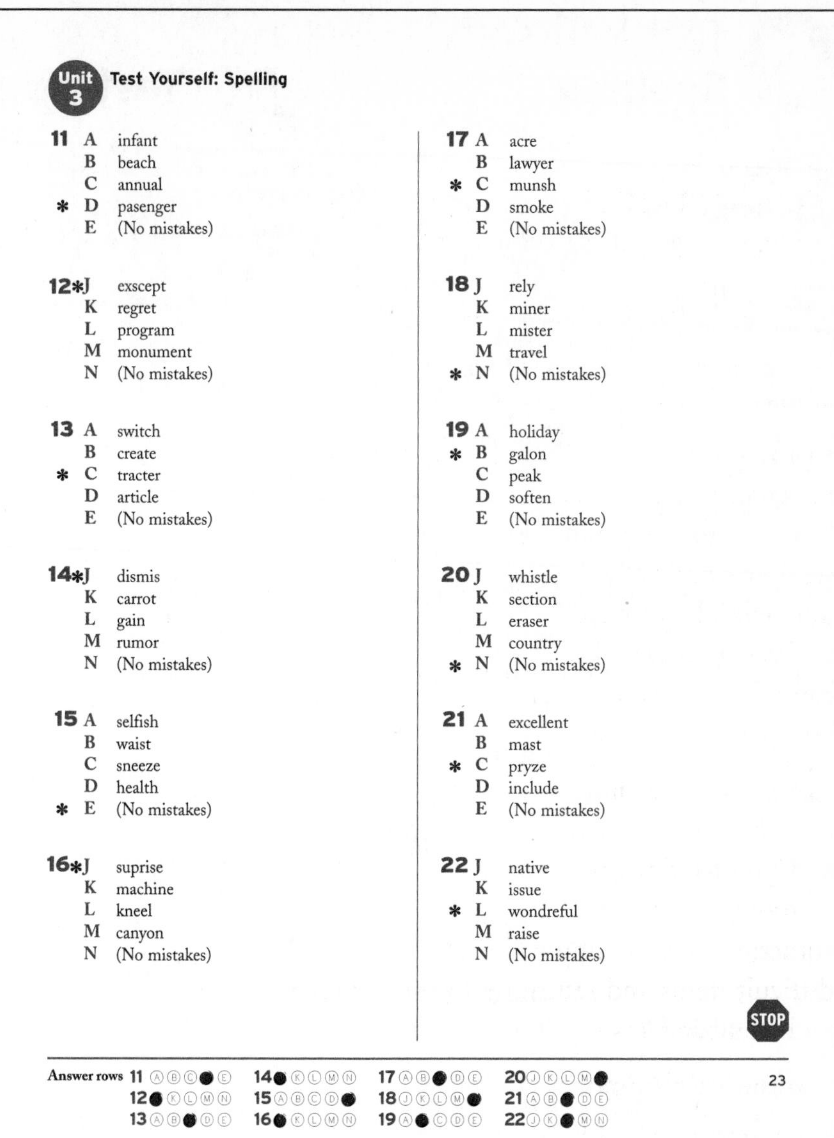

Unit 3 **Test Yourself: Spelling**

11 A infant
B beach
C annual
* D pasenger
E (No mistakes)

12*J exscept
K regret
L program
M monument
N (No mistakes)

13 A switch
B create
* C tracter
D article
E (No mistakes)

14*J dismis
K carrot
L gain
M rumor
N (No mistakes)

15 A selfish
B waist
C sneeze
D health
* E (No mistakes)

16*J suprise
K machine
L kneel
M canyon
N (No mistakes)

17 A acre
B lawyer
* C munsh
D smoke
E (No mistakes)

18 J rely
K miner
L mister
M travel
* N (No mistakes)

19 A holiday
* B galon
C peak
D soften
E (No mistakes)

20 J whistle
K section
L eraser
M country
* N (No mistakes)

21 A excellent
B mast
* C pryze
D include
E (No mistakes)

22 J native
K issue
* L wondreful
M raise
N (No mistakes)

STOP

Answer rows 11 A B C ● E 14 ● K L M N 17 A B ● D E 20 J K L M ●
12 ● K L M N 15 A B C D ● 18 J K L M ● 21 A B ● D E
13 A B ● D E 16 ● K L M N 19 A ● C D E 22 J K ● M N

23

Have the students indicate completion of the lesson by entering their score for this activity on the progress chart at the beginning of the book.

Background

This unit contains five lessons that deal with capitalization and punctuation skills.

- **In Lessons 4a and 4b,** students identify mistakes in capitalization in written text. Students follow printed directions and work methodically. They practice understanding unusual item formats, analyzing answer choices, recalling special capitalization rules, and indicating that an item has no mistakes.
- **In Lessons 5a and 5b,** students identify mistakes in punctuation in written text. In addition to reviewing the test-taking skills introduced in the two previous lessons, students learn the importance of skipping difficult items and returning to them later and analyzing answer choices.
- **In the Test Yourself lesson,** the capitalization and punctuation skills and test-taking skills introduced in Lessons 4a through 5b are reinforced and presented in a format that gives students the experience of taking an achievement test. Techniques for managing time effectively when taking a standardized test are reinforced.

Instructional Objectives

Lesson	Objective
Lesson 4a **Capitalization** Lesson 4b **Capitalization**	Given text divided into three parts, the student identifies which part has a capitalization mistake or indicates that there is no mistake.
Lesson 5a **Punctuation** Lesson 5b **Punctuation**	Given text divided into three parts, the student identifies which part has a punctuation mistake or indicates that there is no mistake.
Test Yourself	Given questions similar to those in Lessons 4a through 5b, the student utilizes capitalization, punctuation, and test-taking strategies on achievement test formats.

Unit 4 Lesson 4a Capitalization

Focus

Language Skill
- identifying capitalization errors

Test-taking Skills
- following printed directions
- working methodically
- understanding unusual item formats
- analyzing answer choices
- indicating that an item has no mistakes

Samples A and B

Say **Turn to Lesson 4a on page 24. In this lesson you will look for capitalization in sentences. Read the directions at the top of the page to yourself while I read them out loud.**

Read the directions out loud to the students.

Say **Let's begin with Sample A. It is two sentences divided into three parts. You are to find the part that has a mistake in capitalization. If there is no mistake, choose the last answer, No mistakes. Read the answer choices to yourself. Does one of them have a mistake in capitalization?** *(yes, answer C)* **Answer C has a mistake because *time* should not begin with a capital letter. Fill in circle C for Sample A in the answer rows at the bottom of the page. Check to make sure your answer circle is completely filled in with a dark mark.**

Check to see that the students have filled in the correct answer circle.

Say **Do Sample B yourself. Mark the circle for the answer choice that has a capitalization mistake. If there is no error, choose the last answer choice. Mark the circle for your answer.**

Allow time for the students to fill in their answers.

Say **You should have filled in the circle for answer M, *No mistakes*. If you chose another answer, erase yours and fill in circle M now.**

Capitalization and Punctuation

Lesson 4a **Capitalization**

Directions: Fill in the space for the answer that has a capitalization mistake. Fill in the last answer space if there is no mistake.

Sample A
A The mall was very crowded.
B Thomas could not see his friends,
* C and it was almost Time to leave.
D (No mistakes)

Sample B
J Corrie's dog waits for her
K every day when she comes
L home on the school bus.
* M (No mistakes)

- **Remember, you are looking for the answer that has a mistake in capitalization.**
- **The first word of a sentence and important words in a sentence are capitalized. Look for those words.**

1
A Jackson's school dismisses
* B early on martin luther king day
C to watch a play about the man's life.
D (No mistakes)

2
* J The Avenue was filled with people
K from the neighborhood who gathered
L to watch the meteor shower.
M (No mistakes)

3
A Jada's mother is president of the
* B parent teacher organization at
C Rockwood Elementary School.
D (No mistakes)

4
J When I go to sleep at night,
* K ellie, my kitten, likes to curl up
L in a ball beside my pillow.
M (No mistakes)

5
A Mr. and Mrs. Sanders came to
B my birthday party at the El Rancho
C Restaurant last November.
* D (No mistakes)

6
J "The Star-Spangled Banner" was
K written after Francis Scott Key
* L watched a battle in the war of 1812.
M (No mistakes)

7
* A Jesse leaves for camp on august 14.
B He plans to take canoe lessons
C and swimming lessons while there.
D (No mistakes)

8
* J Jody read the poem patterns
K by Amy Lowell for the poetry
L reading contest held at her school.
M (No mistakes)

24 **Answer rows** A Ⓐ Ⓑ ● Ⓓ 1 Ⓐ ● Ⓒ Ⓓ 3 Ⓐ ● Ⓒ Ⓓ 5 Ⓐ Ⓑ Ⓒ ● 7 ● Ⓑ Ⓒ Ⓓ
B Ⓙ Ⓚ Ⓛ ● 2 ● Ⓚ Ⓛ Ⓜ 4 Ⓙ ● Ⓛ Ⓜ 6 Ⓙ Ⓚ ● Ⓜ 8 ● Ⓚ Ⓛ Ⓜ

Check to see that the students have filled in the correct answer circle.

TIPS

Say **Now let's look at the tips.**

Have a volunteer read the tips aloud.

Say **Look at each word in the sentence. Be sure the first word in a sentence and important words in a sentence are capitalized. And don't forget, sometimes the mistake will be a word that begins with a capital letter when it should not.**

Discuss with the students the error types they should be looking for. Be sure to review the different types of proper nouns with which the students have had experience.

Practice

Say Now you will do the Practice items. Remember to look carefully at all of the answer choices for a capitalization mistake. Make sure you fill in the circles in the answer rows with dark marks. Do not write anything except your answer choices in your books. Completely erase any marks for answers that you change. Work until you come to the STOP sign at the bottom of the page. Any questions? Start working now.

Allow time for the students to fill in their answers.

Say It's time to stop. You have finished Lesson 4a.

Review the answers with the students. It will be helpful to discuss the errors in the items and the capitalization rules with which the errors are associated. If any questions caused particular difficulty, work through each of the answer choices.

Have the students indicate completion of the lesson by entering their score for this activity on the progress chart at the beginning of the book.

Capitalization and Punctuation

Lesson 4a **Capitalization**

Directions: Fill in the space for the answer that has a capitalization mistake. Fill in the last answer space if there is no mistake.

Sample A
A The mall was very crowded.
B Thomas could not see his friends,
* C and it was almost Time to leave.
D (No mistakes)

Sample B
J Corrie's dog waits for her
K every day when she comes
L home on the school bus.
* M (No mistakes)

- **Remember, you are looking for the answer that has a mistake in capitalization.**
- **The first word of a sentence and important words in a sentence are capitalized. Look for those words.**

1
A Jackson's school dismisses
* B early on martin luther king day
C to watch a play about the man's life.
D (No mistakes)

2 * J The Avenue was filled with people
K from the neighborhood who gathered
L to watch the meteor shower.
M (No mistakes)

3
A Jada's mother is president of the
* B parent teacher organization at
C Rockwood Elementary School.
D (No mistakes)

4
J When I go to sleep at night,
* K ellie, my kitten, likes to curl up
L in a ball beside my pillow.
M (No mistakes)

5
A Mr. and Mrs. Sanders came to
B my birthday party at the El Rancho
C Restaurant last November.
* D (No mistakes)

6
J "The Star-Spangled Banner" was
K written after Francis Scott Key
* L watched a battle in the war of 1812.
M (No mistakes)

7 * A Jesse leaves for camp on august 14.
B He plans to take canoe lessons
C and swimming lessons while there.
D (No mistakes)

8 * J Jody read the poem patterns
K by Amy Lowell for the poetry
L reading contest held at her school.
M (No mistakes)

24 Answer rows A Ⓐ Ⓑ ● Ⓓ 1 Ⓐ ● Ⓒ Ⓓ 3 Ⓐ ● Ⓒ Ⓓ 5 Ⓐ Ⓑ Ⓒ ● 7 ● Ⓑ Ⓒ Ⓓ
B Ⓙ Ⓚ Ⓛ ● 2 ● Ⓚ Ⓛ Ⓜ 4 Ⓙ ● Ⓛ Ⓜ 6 Ⓙ Ⓚ ● Ⓜ 8 ● Ⓚ Ⓛ Ⓜ

Unit 4

Lesson 4b Capitalization

Focus

Language Skill
- identifying capitalization errors

Test-taking Skills
- following printed directions
- working methodically
- understanding unusual item formats
- recalling special capitalization rules
- indicating that an item has no mistakes

Capitalization and Punctuation

Lesson 4b **Capitalization**

Directions: Fill in the space for the answer that has a capitalization mistake. Fill in the last answer space if there is no mistake.

Sample A
A My sister went to the
*B university of iowa. She
C studied biology there.
D (No mistakes)

Sample B
J The hockey game was
K exciting. We sat right
L behind the home team.
*M (No mistakes)

- **Remember, letters need special punctuation.**

1 *A Oregon's timberline lodge was
B built during the Depression by
C the Works Progress Administration.
D (No mistakes)

2 J The first airline began when
K blimps carried people between
*L german cities in 1909.
M (No mistakes)

3 A New Seasons sells organic
*B foods. It is a Supermarket on
C the south side of town.
D (No mistakes)

4 J The first time the comic
*K strip l'il abner appeared in
L newspapers was 1934.
M (No mistakes)

5 *A Larry visited france last
B year with a group of
C students from our school.
D (No mistakes)

6 *J 38554 Sea mist way
K Ridgefield, WA 98644
L September 18, 2006
M (No mistakes)

7 *A dear Ben,
B I really enjoyed visiting
C with you in your new home.
D (No mistakes)

8 J The town of Harperville
K is great. I never thought a
L small town could be fun.
*M (No mistakes)

Answer rows A Ⓐ●ⒸⒹ 1 ●ⒷⒸⒹ 3 Ⓐ●ⒸⒹ 5 ●ⒷⒸⒹ 7 ●ⒷⒸⒹ
B ⒿⓀⓁ● 2 ⒿⓀ●Ⓜ 4 Ⓙ●ⓁⓂ 6 ●ⓀⓁⓂ 8 ⒿⓀⓁ●

25

Samples A and B

Say Turn to Lesson 4b on page 25. This is another lesson about capitalization. Read the directions at the top of the page to yourself while I read them out loud.

Read the directions out loud to the students.

Say Let's do Sample A. It is two sentences divided into three parts. You are to find the part that has a mistake in capitalization. If there is no mistake, choose the last answer, No mistakes. Does one of the answer choices have a mistake in capitalization? *(yes, answer B)* Answer B has a mistake because the words *University* and *Iowa* should begin with a capital letter. They form a proper noun. Fill in circle B for Sample A in the answer rows at the bottom of the page. Check to make sure your answer circle is completely filled in with a dark mark.

Check to see that the students have filled in the correct answer circle.

Say Do Sample B yourself. Mark the circle for the answer choice that has a capitalization mistake. If there is no error, choose the last answer choice. Mark the circle for your answer.

Allow time for the students to fill in their answers.

Say You should have filled in the circle for answer M. None of the answer choices has a mistake in capitalization. If you chose another answer, erase yours and fill in circle M now.

Check to see that the students have filled in the correct answer circle.

TIPS

Say Now let's look at the tip.

Have a volunteer read the tip aloud.

Say Some of the items in this lesson are parts of a letter. Keep in mind that the parts of a letter need special capitalization. You should look at these items very carefully and think about how they should be capitalized.

Remind the students that street names, city names, state abbreviations, dates, and the greeting and closing of a letter have special capitalization.

Practice

Say **Now you will do the Practice items. Remember to look carefully at all the answer choices for a capitalization mistake, especially the items that involve parts of a letter. Make sure you fill in the circles in the answer rows with dark marks. Do not write anything except your answer choices in your books. Completely erase any marks for answers that you change. Work until you come to the STOP sign at the bottom of the page. Any questions? Start working now.**

Allow time for the students to fill in their answers.

Say **It's time to stop. You have finished Lesson 4b.**

Review the answers with the students. It will be helpful to discuss the errors in the items and the rules for capitalization. If any questions caused particular difficulty, work through each of the answer choices.

Have the students indicate completion of the lesson by entering their score for this activity on the progress chart at the beginning of the book.

Capitalization and Punctuation

Lesson 4b **Capitalization**

Directions: Fill in the space for the answer that has a capitalization mistake. Fill in the last answer space if there is no mistake.

Sample A
A My sister went to the
*B university of iowa. She
C studied biology there.
D (No mistakes)

Sample B
J The hockey game was
K exciting. We sat right
L behind the home team.
*M (No mistakes)

• **Remember, letters need special punctuation.**

1 *A Oregon's timberline lodge was
B built during the Depression by
C the Works Progress Administration.
D (No mistakes)

2 J The first airline began when
K blimps carried people between
*L german cities in 1909.
M (No mistakes)

3 A New Seasons sells organic
*B foods. It is a Supermarket on
C the south side of town.
D (No mistakes)

4 J The first time the comic
*K strip l'il abner appeared in
L newspapers was 1934.
M (No mistakes)

5 *A Larry visited france last
B year with a group of
C students from our school.
D (No mistakes)

6 *J 38554 Sea mist way
K Ridgefield, WA 98644
L September 18, 2006
M (No mistakes)

7 *A dear Ben,
B I really enjoyed visiting
C with you in your new home.
D (No mistakes)

8 J The town of Harperville
K is great. I never thought a
L small town could be fun.
*M (No mistakes)

Answer rows A Ⓐ●ⒸⒹ 1 ●ⒷⒸⒹ 3 Ⓐ●ⒸⒹ 5 ●ⒷⒸⒹ 7 ●ⒷⒸⒹ
B ⒿⓀⓁ● 2 ⒿⓀ●Ⓜ 4 Ⓙ●ⓁⓂ 6 ●ⓀⓁⓂ 8 ⒿⓀⓁ●

25

Unit 4 Lesson 5a
Punctuation

Focus

Language Skill
- identifying punctuation errors

Test-taking Skills
- following printed directions
- working methodically
- understanding unusual item formats
- skipping difficult items and returning to them later
- indicating that an item has no mistakes

Capitalization and Punctuation

Lesson 5a **Punctuation**

Directions: Fill in the space for the answer that has a punctuation mistake. Fill in the last answer space if there is no mistake.

Sample A
A Each morning, our friend
* B Mrs Howe drops by to take
C our dog for a walk with hers.
D (No mistakes)

Sample B
J Mountains are formed by
K movements of Earth's surface.
L This process takes millions of years.
* M (No mistakes)

- **Remember, you are looking for the word that has a mistake in punctuation.**
- **Check for punctuation at the end of the sentence. Then look for a missing comma, apostrophe, or question mark in the sentence.**

1 A "This is really hard work,
* B Bob" my friend Alex said.
C "How do you do this every day?"
D (No mistakes)

2 J Skateboards were invented in
K America by surfers. The skateboard
L has been around for over sixty years.
* M (No mistakes)

3 A My great-grandmother was
* B born on August 12 1901.
C She has been alive for a century.
D (No mistakes)

4* J John P Garcia likes
K to use his middle name
L instead of his first name.
M (No mistakes)

5 A Jack loved his horse.
B He brushed its hair and
* C fed it juicy red, apples.
D (No mistakes)

6 J The phone rang as we
K walked through the door.
* L It was my sisters friend.
M (No mistakes)

7* A We found three cats two
B dogs, and a bunny rabbit
C in the barn we bought.
D (No mistakes)

8 J Sometimes I think about
* K what. my future will hold.
L I am looking forward to it.
M (No mistakes)

26 Answer rows A Ⓐ●ⒸⒹ 1 Ⓐ●ⒸⒹ 3 Ⓐ●ⒸⒹ 5 ⒶⒷ●Ⓓ 7 ●ⒷⒸⒹ
B ⒿⓀⓁ● 2 ⒿⓀⓁ● 4 ●ⓀⓁⓂ 6 ⒿⓀ●Ⓜ 8 Ⓙ●ⓁⓂ

Samples A and B

Say Turn to Lesson 5a on page 26. In this lesson you will look for punctuation mistakes in sentences. Read the directions at the top of the page to yourself while I read them out loud.

Read the directions out loud to the students.

Say Let's begin with Sample A. It is one sentence divided into three parts. You are to find the part that has a mistake in punctuation. If there is no mistake, choose the last answer. Read the answer choices to yourself. Does one of them have a mistake in punctuation? *(yes, the second one)* The second answer has a mistake because the abbreviation *Mrs* should end with a period. Fill in circle B for Sample A in the answer rows at the bottom of the page. Check to make sure your answer circle is completely filled in with a dark mark.

Check to see that the students have filled in the correct answer circle.

Say Now do Sample B yourself. Read the answer choices and look for a mistake in punctuation. Choose the last answer if the punctuation is correct. *(pause)* Which answer did you choose? *(the last one, M)* Yes, the punctuation in this item is correct. Fill in circle M for Sample B in the answer rows at the bottom of the page. Check to make sure that answer circle M is completely filled in with a dark mark.

Check to see that the students have filled in the correct answer circle.

TIPS

Say Now let's look at the tips.

Have a volunteer read the tips aloud.

Say Always begin by looking for missing or wrong end punctuation. Then read the sentence again and look for missing or wrong punctuation inside the sentence. Be sure to work carefully. It is easy to miss a punctuation mistake.

Discuss with the students the error types they should be looking for. The punctuation marks they should look for are the period, question mark, exclamation mark, comma, apostrophe, and quotation mark.

Practice

Say **Now you will do some Practice items. If an item seems difficult, skip it and come back to it later. This will save you time on a real achievement test. Make sure you fill in the circles in the answer rows with dark marks. Do not write anything except your answer choices in your books. Completely erase any marks for answers that you change. Work until you come to the STOP sign at the bottom of the page. Any questions? Start working now.**

Allow time for the students to fill in their answers.

Say **It's time to stop. You have finished Lesson 5a.**

Review the answers with the students. It will be helpful to discuss the punctuation errors in the items. If any questions caused particular difficulty, work through each of the answer choices.

Have the students indicate completion of the lesson by entering their score for this activity on the progress chart at the beginning of the book.

Capitalization and Punctuation

Lesson 5a **Punctuation**

Directions: Fill in the space for the answer that has a punctuation mistake. Fill in the last answer space if there is no mistake.

Sample A
A Each morning, our friend
* B Mrs Howe drops by to take
C our dog for a walk with hers.
D (No mistakes)

Sample B
J Mountains are formed by
K movements of Earth's surface.
L This process takes millions of years.
* M (No mistakes)

- **Remember, you are looking for the word that has a mistake in punctuation.**
- **Check for punctuation at the end of the sentence. Then look for a missing comma, apostrophe, or question mark in the sentence.**

1
A "This is really hard work,
* B Bob" my friend Alex said.
C "How do you do this every day?"
D (No mistakes)

2
J Skateboards were invented in
K America by surfers. The skateboard
L has been around for over sixty years.
* M (No mistakes)

3
A My great-grandmother was
* B born on August 12 1901.
C She has been alive for a century.
D (No mistakes)

4
* J John P Garcia likes
K to use his middle name
L instead of his first name.
M (No mistakes)

5
A Jack loved his horse.
B He brushed its hair and
* C fed it juicy red, apples.
D (No mistakes)

6
J The phone rang as we
K walked through the door.
* L It was my sisters friend.
M (No mistakes)

7
* A We found three cats two
B dogs, and a bunny rabbit
C in the barn we bought.
D (No mistakes)

8
J Sometimes I think about
* K what. my future will hold.
L I am looking forward to it.
M (No mistakes)

26 Answer rows A Ⓐ ● Ⓒ Ⓓ 1 Ⓐ ● Ⓒ Ⓓ 3 Ⓐ ● Ⓒ Ⓓ 5 Ⓐ Ⓑ ● Ⓓ 7 ● Ⓑ Ⓒ Ⓓ
B Ⓙ Ⓚ Ⓛ ● 2 Ⓙ Ⓚ Ⓛ ● 4 ● Ⓚ Ⓛ Ⓜ 6 Ⓙ Ⓚ ● Ⓜ 8 Ⓙ ● Ⓛ Ⓜ

Lesson 5b Punctuation

Focus

Language Skill

- identifying punctuation errors

Test-taking Skills

- following printed directions
- working methodically
- analyzing answer choices
- understanding unusual item formats
- indicating that an item has no mistakes

Capitalization and Punctuation

Lesson 5b **Punctuation**

Directions: Fill in the space for the answer that has a punctuation mistake. Fill in the last answer space if there is no mistake.

Sample A
A This is my first visit
* B to New York I don't know
C what to do first.
D (No mistakes)

Sample B
J Barry likes to study with
K the radio on. I don't like any
L noise at all.
* M (No mistakes)

- **Sometimes the error will be the wrong punctuation mark in a place that needs different punctuation.**

1 * A Some large kangaroos can hop.
B as fast as 30 miles per hour. They
C can also jump as high as six feet.
D (No mistakes)

2 J Louis J. M. Daguerre found a way to
K reproduce images. These images were
L the beginning of the modern photograph.
* M (No mistakes)

3 * A Sharks eels, and squid
B are three of the creatures
C that can be found in the ocean.
D (No mistakes)

4 J Janice does not like the
* K new shopping center? She
L says it is an eyesore.
M (No mistakes)

5 A 19662 Dogwood Trail
B Portales, NM 88130
* C Nov, 28, 2006
D (No mistakes)

6 * J Dear Peter
K How did your birthday party
L go? I'm so sorry I missed it.
M (No mistakes)

7 A I had to go to a family reunion.
B It was really fun. My cousins
* C were there I don't see them often.
D (No mistakes)

8 J I can't wait to see you again.
* K Yours truly
L Knox
M (No mistakes)

Answer rows A Ⓐ●ⒸⒹ 1 ●ⒷⒸⒹ 3 ●ⒷⒸⒹ 5 ⒶⒷ●Ⓓ 7 ⒶⒷ●Ⓓ
B ⒿⓀⓁ● 2 ⒿⓀⓁ● 4 Ⓙ●ⓁⓂ 6 ●ⓀⓁⓂ 8 Ⓙ●ⓁⓂ

27

Samples A and B

Say **Turn to Lesson 5b on page 27. In this lesson you will look for punctuation mistakes in sentences. Read the directions at the top of the page to yourself while I read them out loud.**

Read the directions out loud to the students.

Say **Find Sample A at the top of the page. Read the answer choices and look for a mistake in punctuation. Choose the last answer if the punctuation is correct.** *(pause)* **Which answer did you choose?** *(the second one, B)* **There should be a period after *New York* because it is the end of a sentence. Fill in circle B for Sample A in the answer rows at the bottom of the page. Check to make sure that answer circle B is completely filled in with a dark mark.**

Check to see that the students have filled in the correct answer circle.

Say **Now do Sample B yourself. Fill in the space for the answer that has a mistake in punctuation. Choose the last answer if the punctuation is correct.** *(pause)* **The last answer is correct because none of the answer choices has a punctuation mistake. Fill in circle M for Sample B in the answer rows at the bottom of the page. Check to make sure your answer circle is completely filled in with a dark mark.**

Check to see that the students have filled in the correct answer circle.

TIPS

Say **Now let's look at the tip.**

Have a volunteer read the tip aloud.

Say **One of the mistakes you should look for is the wrong punctuation in a place that needs a punctuation mark. This kind of mistake is easy to miss if you are not paying attention.**

Discuss some possible error types with the students, such as a question mark being placed where a period should be or a period where a comma should be.

Practice

Say Now you will do some Practice items. Remember to look carefully at all of the answer choices. Look for missing punctuation, too many punctuation marks, and the wrong punctuation mark. Make sure you fill in the circles in the answer rows with dark marks. Do not write anything except your answer choices in your books. Completely erase any marks for answers that you change. Work until you come to the STOP sign at the bottom of the page. Any questions? Start working now.

Allow time for the students to fill in their answers.

Say It's time to stop. You have finished Lesson 5b.

Review the answers with the students. It will be helpful to discuss the punctuation errors in the items. If any questions caused particular difficulty, work through each of the answer choices.

Have the students indicate completion of the lesson by entering their score for this activity on the progress chart at the beginning of the book.

Capitalization and Punctuation

Lesson 5b **Punctuation**

Directions: Fill in the space for the answer that has a punctuation mistake. Fill in the last answer space if there is no mistake.

Sample **A**
A This is my first visit
* B to New York I don't know
C what to do first.
D (No mistakes)

Sample **B**
J Barry likes to study with
K the radio on. I don't like any
L noise at all.
* M (No mistakes)

- **Sometimes the error will be the wrong punctuation mark in a place that needs different punctuation.**

1 *A Some large kangaroos can hop.
B as fast as 30 miles per hour. They
C can also jump as high as six feet.
D (No mistakes)

2 J Louis J. M. Daguerre found a way to
K reproduce images. These images were
L the beginning of the modern photograph.
* M (No mistakes)

3 *A Sharks eels, and squid
B are three of the creatures
C that can be found in the ocean.
D (No mistakes)

4 J Janice does not like the
* K new shopping center? She
L says it is an eyesore.
M (No mistakes)

5 A 19662 Dogwood Trail
B Portales, NM 88130
* C Nov, 28, 2006
D (No mistakes)

6 *J Dear Peter
K How did your birthday party
L go? I'm so sorry I missed it.
M (No mistakes)

7 A I had to go to a family reunion.
B It was really fun. My cousins
* C were there I don't see them often.
D (No mistakes)

8 J I can't wait to see you again.
* K Yours truly
L Knox
M (No mistakes)

Answer rows A Ⓐ ● Ⓒ Ⓓ 1 ● Ⓑ Ⓒ Ⓓ 3 ● Ⓑ Ⓒ Ⓓ 5 Ⓐ Ⓑ ● Ⓓ 7 Ⓐ Ⓑ ● Ⓓ
B Ⓙ Ⓚ Ⓛ ● 2 Ⓙ Ⓚ Ⓛ ● 4 Ⓙ ● Ⓛ Ⓜ 6 ● Ⓚ Ⓛ Ⓜ 8 Ⓙ ● Ⓛ Ⓜ

27

Test Yourself: Capitalization and Punctuation

Focus

Language Skills
- identifying capitalization errors
- identifying punctuation errors

Test-taking Skills
- managing time effectively
- following printed directions
- working methodically
- understanding unusual item formats
- analyzing answer choices
- indicating that an item has no mistakes
- recalling special capitalization rules
- skipping difficult items and returning to them later

This lesson simulates an actual test-taking experience. Therefore, it is recommended that the directions be read verbatim and the suggested procedures and time allowances be followed.

Unit 4 Test Yourself: Capitalization and Punctuation

Directions: Fill in the space for the answer that has a capitalization or punctuation mistake. Fill in the last answer space if there is no mistake.

Sample A
A Candace shouted to Kevin,
B "Hurry up and close the door
C before the cat gets out."
* D (No mistakes)

Sample B
J The game was almost
* K over Brad was the only
L one who could save it.
M (No mistakes)

1
* A The wind in march is very strong.
B Sometimes it blows the chairs
C off our deck onto the lawn.
D (No mistakes)

2
J Last week, my brother broke his
K arm. The physician who treated him
* L at County Hospital was dr. Proctor.
M (No mistakes)

3
A The book I bought is called
* B waiting for winter. It is about a
C girl who lives in North Dakota.
D (No mistakes)

4
J The teacher asked the children,
K "How many of you would like to
L go to the aquarium next week?"
* M (No mistakes)

5
A The sale on plants will end
* B on friday. We should buy some
C for the yard and the garden.
D (No mistakes)

6
J When Tiffany got to the airport,
K she was surprised to see a
* L Restaurant in the terminal.
M (No mistakes)

7
A The train arrived in Chicago
B at eight in the morning. The
C weather there was terrible.
* D (No mistakes)

8
J The sporting goods store was
* K just bought by linda fuller. She
L also owns the bakery next door.
M (No mistakes)

9
A After you clean up the living
B room, remember to put the vacuum
* C cleaner back in the Closet.
D (No mistakes)

10
J In January, it got so cold that
K the pipes in our kitchen froze.
L Luckily, they didn't break.
* M (No mistakes)

28 Answer rows A Ⓐ Ⓑ Ⓒ ● 1 ● Ⓑ Ⓒ Ⓓ 3 Ⓐ ● Ⓒ Ⓓ 5 Ⓐ ● Ⓒ Ⓓ 7 Ⓐ Ⓑ Ⓒ ● 9 Ⓐ Ⓑ ● Ⓓ
B Ⓙ ● Ⓛ Ⓜ 2 Ⓙ Ⓚ ● Ⓜ 4 Ⓙ Ⓚ Ⓛ ● 6 Ⓙ Ⓚ ● Ⓜ 8 Ⓙ ● Ⓛ Ⓜ 10 Ⓙ Ⓚ Ⓛ ●

Directions

Administration Time: approximately 20 minutes

Say Turn to the Test Yourself lesson on page 28.

Point out to the students that this Test Yourself lesson is timed like a real test, but that they will score it themselves to see how well they are doing. Remind the students to pace themselves and to check the clock after they have finished the capitalization items to see how much time is left. This is about the halfway point in the lesson. Encourage the students to avoid spending too much time on any one item and to take the best guess if they are unsure of the answer.

Say There are two types of items in the Test Yourself lesson, so you will have to read the directions for each section and pay close attention to what you are doing. Remember to make sure that the circles in the answer rows are completely filled in. Press your pencil firmly so that your marks come out dark. Completely erase any marks for answers that you change. Do not write anything except your answer choices in your books.

Look at Sample A and listen carefully. Read the answer choices to yourself. Mark the circle for the answer that has a mistake in capitalization. Choose the last answer, No mistakes, if none of the answer choices has a mistake. Mark the circle for your answer.

Allow time for the students to fill in their answers.

Say The circle for answer D should be filled in because all of the answer choices are correct. If you chose another answer, erase yours and fill in the circle for answer D now.

Check to see that the students have filled in the correct answer circle.

Say **Now do Sample B. Read the answer choices to yourself. Mark the circle for the answer that has a mistake in punctuation. Choose the last answer, No mistakes, if none of the answer choices has a mistake in punctuation. Mark the circle for your answer.**

Allow time for the students to fill in their answers.

Say **The circle for answer K should be filled in. There should be a period before the word *Brad* to end the sentence. If you chose another answer, erase yours and fill in the circle for answer K now.**

Check to see that the students have filled in the correct answer circle.

Say **Now you will do more items. Read the directions for each section. When you come to the GO sign at the bottom of the page, continue working. Work until you come to the STOP sign on page 29. If you are not sure of an answer, fill in the circle for the answer you think might be right. Do you have any questions?**

Answer any questions the students have.

Say **You may begin working. You will have 15 minutes.**

Allow 15 minutes.

Say **It's time to stop. You have finished the Test Yourself lesson. Check to see that you have completely filled in your answer circles with dark marks. Make sure that any marks for answers that you changed have been completely erased.**

Go over the lesson with the students. Ask the students if they read the directions for each section. Did they have enough time to finish all the items? Which items were most difficult?

Work through any questions that caused difficulty. Have the students indicate completion of the lesson by entering their score for this activity on the progress chart at the beginning of the book.

Test Yourself: Capitalization and Punctuation

Directions: For questions 11–20, fill in the space for the answer that has a punctuation mistake. Fill in the last answer space if there is no mistake.

11
A The problem is the time. My
B father thinks that we won't
* C be home until around 1030.
D (No mistakes)

12
J You can catch trout, bass,
* K and, sunfish in this lake.
L We like to fish here.
M (No mistakes)

13
* A The hotel room was small.
B but I didn't mind. It was
C quiet, and I only slept there.
D (No mistakes)

14
J We like to go skiing in
K Utah. This year, our trip
* L will begin on Jan 7.
M (No mistakes)

15
A Until this year, we never
B had any trouble growing
C corn in our garden.
* D (No mistakes)

16
J 2336 Columbus Rd.
* K Fellertown PA 19965
L October 6, 2006
M (No mistakes)

17
* A Alsto Manufacturing Co
B Stowe, VT
C Dear Mrs. Mosley:
D (No mistakes)

18
J I recently bought a bicycle pump
K made by your company. When I got
L it home, I found that it was broken.
* M (No mistakes)

19
A The store where I bought the pump
* B said I should write to you? Will you
C please send me a replacement pump?
D (No mistakes)

20
J I hope to hear from you soon.
K Sincerely yours,
* L Lisa V Martinez
M (No mistakes)

Answer rows 11 Ⓐ Ⓑ ● Ⓓ 13 ● Ⓑ Ⓒ Ⓓ 15 Ⓐ Ⓑ Ⓒ ● 17 ● Ⓑ Ⓒ Ⓓ 19 Ⓐ ● Ⓒ Ⓓ
12 Ⓙ ● Ⓛ Ⓜ 14 Ⓙ Ⓚ ● Ⓜ 16 Ⓙ ● Ⓛ Ⓜ 18 Ⓙ Ⓚ Ⓛ ● 20 Ⓙ Ⓚ ● Ⓜ

29

Background

This unit contains five lessons that deal with usage and expression skills.

- **In Lessons 6a and 6b,** students identify usage mistakes in written text. Students work methodically, use context to find an answer, and skim text. They indicate that an item has no mistakes, subvocalize answer choices, and recall usage errors.
- **In Lesson 7a,** students identify the correct word to fit in a sentence, identify which paragraph best suits a stated purpose, and answer questions about a paragraph. They learn the importance of following printed directions and understanding unusual item formats. They subvocalize answer choices, work methodically, and skim answer choices.
- **In Lesson 7b,** students identify correctly formed sentences, identify which paragraph best suits a stated purpose, and identify the correct word to fit in a sentence. In addition to reviewing the test-taking skills learned in previous lessons, they practice analyzing answer choices.
- **In the Test Yourself lesson,** the usage and expression skills and test-taking skills introduced in Lessons 6a through 7b are reinforced and presented in a format that gives students the experience of taking an achievement test. Techniques for managing time effectively when taking a standardized test are reinforced.

Instructional **Objectives**

Lesson 6a **Usage** Lesson 6b **Usage**	Given text divided into three parts, the student identifies which part has a usage mistake or indicates that there is no mistake.
Lesson 7a **Expression** Lesson 7b **Expression**	Given a sentence with an underlined word or words, the student identifies which of three answer choices should replace the word or words or indicates that there should be no change. Given four paragraphs, the student identifies which paragraph best suits a stated purpose. Given a paragraph and questions about it, the student identifies which of four answer choices is correct. Given four sentences, the student identifies the best way to express the underlying idea.
Test Yourself	Given questions similar to those in Lessons 6a through 7b, the student utilizes English skills and test-taking strategies on achievement test formats.

Lesson 6a Usage

Focus

Language Skill
- identifying mistakes in usage

Test-taking Skills
- using context to find an answer
- skimming text
- indicating that an item has no mistakes
- subvocalizing answer choices

Samples A and B

Say Turn to Lesson 6a on page 30. In this lesson you will look for mistakes in the correct use of English. Read the directions at the top of the page to yourself while I read them out loud.

Read the directions out loud to the students.

Say Let's begin with Sample A. It is a sentence divided into three parts. You are to find the part that has a mistake in English. If there is no mistake, choose the last answer, No mistakes. Read the answer choices to yourself. Does one of them have a mistake? *(yes, the second one)* The second answer choice has a mistake. The word *flied* should be *flew*. Fill in circle B for Sample A in the answer rows at the bottom of the page. Check to make sure your answer circle is completely filled in with a dark mark.

Check to see that the students have filled in the correct answer circle.

Say Now do Sample B. Read the answer choices and look for a mistake in English. Choose the last answer if there is no mistake. *(pause)* Which answer did you choose? *(answer J)* The first answer choice has a mistake. The word *she* should be *her*. Fill in circle J for Sample B in the answer rows at the bottom of the page. Check to make sure the answer circle is completely filled in with a dark mark.

Check to see that the students have filled in the correct answer circle.

Usage and Expression

Lesson 6a **Usage**

Directions: Fill in the space for the answer that has a mistake in usage. Fill in the last answer space if there is no mistake.

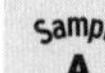

Sample A
A After the plane took off, it
* B flied over the mountain and
C headed toward the ocean.
D (No mistakes)

Sample B
* J Corrie's dog waits for she
K every day when she comes
L home on the school bus.
M (No mistakes)

- **Say the answer choices to yourself carefully. The part that has the mistake will usually sound wrong to you.**
- **Use the meaning of the text to help you find the answer.**

1
A In August, our family goes
B to the county fair. This year,
* C my brother and me worked there.
D (No mistakes)

2
* J A flock of geese were eating
K in the corn field. In a little while,
L they took off and flew to a lake.
M (No mistakes)

3
A Janelle's mother wants to learn
B how to golf, but she is so busy
* C that she doesn't have no time.
D (No mistakes)

4
J Manny wants to be in the
K school play. His mother says he
* L hasta improve his grades first.
M (No mistakes)

5
A The pilot walked around the
B plane and looked it over. She
C had a long flight ahead of her.
* D (No mistakes)

6
J Because it is Saturday, we should
* K get their early. The beach is always
L crowded on weekends in August.
M (No mistakes)

7
A I thought I could catch the
* B pass, but Pat through it too
C hard and I dropped it.
D (No mistakes)

8
J My mother tried a new way
* K to go to work, but it wasn't no
L faster than her usual way.
M (No mistakes)

30 **Answer rows** A Ⓐ ● Ⓒ Ⓓ 1 Ⓐ Ⓑ ● Ⓓ 3 Ⓐ Ⓑ ● Ⓓ 5 Ⓐ Ⓑ Ⓒ ● 7 Ⓐ ● Ⓒ Ⓓ
B ● Ⓚ Ⓛ Ⓜ 2 ● Ⓚ Ⓛ Ⓜ 4 Ⓙ Ⓚ ● Ⓜ 6 Ⓙ ● Ⓛ Ⓜ 8 Ⓙ ● Ⓛ Ⓜ

★TIPS

Say Now let's look at the tips.

Have a volunteer read the tips aloud.

Say Begin by skimming the answer choices and then look at each one more carefully. You might find it helpful to say the answer choices to yourself and choose the one that has a part that sounds incorrect. Think about the meaning of the answer choices. Their meaning will help you choose the correct answer.

Practice

Say **Let's do the Practice items now. Say the answer choices to yourself and listen for the one that sounds incorrect. Make sure you fill in the circles in the answer rows with dark marks. Do not write anything except your answer choices in your books. Completely erase any marks for answers that you change. Work until you come to the STOP sign at the bottom of the page. Any questions? Start working now.**

Allow time for the students to fill in their answers.

Say **It's time to stop. You have finished Lesson 6a.**

Review the answers with the students. It will be helpful to discuss the error types that appear in the lesson and have the students read aloud the correct form of the sentences. If any questions caused particular difficulty, work through each of the answer choices.

Have the students indicate completion of the lesson by entering their score for this activity on the progress chart at the beginning of the book.

Usage and Expression

Lesson 6a **Usage**

Directions: Fill in the space for the answer that has a mistake in usage. Fill in the last answer space if there is no mistake.

Sample A
A After the plane took off, it
* B flied over the mountain and
C headed toward the ocean.
D (No mistakes)

Sample B
* J Corrie's dog waits for she
K every day when she comes
L home on the school bus.
M (No mistakes)

- **Say the answer choices to yourself carefully. The part that has the mistake will usually sound wrong to you.**
- **Use the meaning of the text to help you find the answer.**

1 A In August, our family goes
B to the county fair. This year,
* C my brother and me worked there.
D (No mistakes)

2 * J A flock of geese were eating
K in the corn field. In a little while,
L they took off and flew to a lake.
M (No mistakes)

3 A Janelle's mother wants to learn
B how to golf, but she is so busy
* C that she doesn't have no time.
D (No mistakes)

4 J Manny wants to be in the
K school play. His mother says he
* L hasta improve his grades first.
M (No mistakes)

5 A The pilot walked around the
B plane and looked it over. She
C had a long flight ahead of her.
* D (No mistakes)

6 J Because it is Saturday, we should
* K get their early. The beach is always
L crowded on weekends in August.
M (No mistakes)

7 A I thought I could catch the
* B pass, but Pat through it too
C hard and I dropped it.
D (No mistakes)

8 J My mother tried a new way
* K to go to work, but it wasn't no
L faster than her usual way.
M (No mistakes)

30 Answer rows A Ⓐ ● Ⓒ Ⓓ 1 Ⓐ Ⓑ ● Ⓓ 3 Ⓐ Ⓑ ● Ⓓ 5 Ⓐ Ⓑ Ⓒ ● 7 Ⓐ ● Ⓒ Ⓓ
B ● Ⓚ Ⓛ Ⓜ 2 ● Ⓚ Ⓛ Ⓜ 4 Ⓙ Ⓚ ● Ⓜ 6 Ⓙ ● Ⓛ Ⓜ 8 Ⓙ ● Ⓛ Ⓜ

Unit 5 Lesson 6b Usage

Focus

Language Skill
- identifying mistakes in usage

Test-taking Skills
- working methodically
- recalling usage errors
- indicating that an item has no mistakes
- subvocalizing answer choices

Usage and Expression

Lesson 6b **Usage**

Directions: Fill in the space for the answer that has a mistake in usage. Fill in the last answer space if there is no mistake.

Sample A
A This bridge was built
B long ago. The city is
* C gonna repair it soon.
D (No mistakes)

Sample B
J The Shawn family went
K to Indiana for a family
L wedding last week.
* M (No mistakes)

- **Look for errors in subject-verb agreement, plurals, negative forms, and other usage errors.**

1
A If you go into the garage,
B be careful when you open the
* C door. The knob is broke.
D (No mistakes)

2
J Long ago, this ghost town was
K a busy place in which thousands
L of people lived and worked.
* M (No mistakes)

3
A Sometimes people flying in
B planes are surprised to see
* C gooses flying nearby.
D (No mistakes)

4
J At the end of the road is an
K old house. People say it is
L haunted, but I don't believe it.
* M (No mistakes)

5
*A My sister she made the varsity
B softball team. They practice
C two hours every day after school.
D (No mistakes)

6
J Jeanne and Eddie caught four
* K fish, and they mighta caught more
L but they ran out of bait before lunch.
M (No mistakes)

7
*A My friends and I was late
B for school because our bus
C got a flat tire on Elm Street.
D (No mistakes)

8
J Jack is a good player, but
* K he don't have time to study
L and get to soccer practice.
M (No mistakes)

9
A My cousin has an unusual
B hobby. She collects postcards
C from cities around the world.
* D (No mistakes)

10
J My grandmother lives on a
K farm. In the morning, you can
* L see deers on her lawn.
M (No mistakes)

Answer rows A Ⓐ Ⓑ ● Ⓓ 1 Ⓐ Ⓑ ● Ⓓ 3 Ⓐ Ⓑ ● Ⓓ 5 ● Ⓑ Ⓒ Ⓓ 7 ● Ⓑ Ⓒ Ⓓ 9 Ⓐ Ⓑ Ⓒ ●
B Ⓙ Ⓚ Ⓛ ● 2 Ⓙ Ⓚ Ⓛ ● 4 Ⓙ Ⓚ Ⓛ ● 6 Ⓙ ● Ⓛ Ⓜ 8 Ⓙ ● Ⓛ Ⓜ 10 Ⓙ Ⓚ ● Ⓜ

31

Samples A and B

Say **Turn to Lesson 6b on page 31. This is another lesson in which you will look for mistakes in the correct use of English. Read the directions at the top of the page to yourself while I read them out loud.**

Read the directions out loud to the students.

Say **Sample A is two sentences divided into three parts. You are to find the part that has a mistake in English. If there is no mistake, choose the last answer, No mistakes.** *(pause)* **Answer C has a mistake. The word *gonna* should be *going to*. Fill in answer circle C for Sample A in the answer rows at the bottom of the page. Check to make sure that the answer circle is completely filled in with a dark mark.**

Check to see that the students have filled in the correct answer circle.

Say **Now do Sample B. Read the answer choices and look for a mistake in English usage. Choose the last answer if there is no mistake.** *(pause)* **Which answer did you choose?** *(M, No mistakes)* **Yes, there are no mistakes in Sample B. Fill in circle M for Sample B in the answer rows at the bottom of the page. Make sure the circle is completely filled in with a dark mark.**

Check to see that the students have filled in the correct answer circle.

★TIPS

Say **Now let's look at the tip.**

Have a volunteer read the tip aloud.

Say **When you read the answers, think about the different kinds of errors there might be. Look for errors in subject-verb agreement, plurals, negative forms, and other usage errors.**

Be sure that the students understand what a usage error is and that they are familiar with the various types of usage errors. Remind them that there is a difference between informal, spoken language and the items on a test, as shown in Sample A.

Practice

Say **Let's do the Practice items now. Look for the answer that has a mistake in English usage, and remember the different kinds of mistakes we talked about. Mark your answers in the rows at the bottom of the page. Make sure you fill in the circles in the answer rows with dark marks. Do not write anything except your answer choices in your books. Completely erase any marks for answers that you change. Work until you come to the STOP sign at the bottom of the page. Any questions? Start working now.**

Allow time for the students to fill in their answers.

Say **It's time to stop. You have finished Lesson 6b.**

Review the answers with the students. It will be helpful to discuss the error types that appear in the lesson and have the students read aloud the correct form of the sentences. If any questions caused particular difficulty, work through each of the answer choices.

Have the students indicate completion of the lesson by entering their score for this activity on the progress chart at the beginning of the book.

Usage and Expression

Lesson 6b **Usage**

Directions: Fill in the space for the answer that has a mistake in usage. Fill in the last answer space if there is no mistake.

Sample A
A This bridge was built
B long ago. The city is
* C gonna repair it soon.
D (No mistakes)

Sample B
J The Shawn family went
K to Indiana for a family
L wedding last week.
* M (No mistakes)

- **Look for errors in subject-verb agreement, plurals, negative forms, and other usage errors.**

1
A If you go into the garage,
B be careful when you open the
* C door. The knob is broke.
D (No mistakes)

2
J Long ago, this ghost town was
K a busy place in which thousands
L of people lived and worked.
* M (No mistakes)

3
A Sometimes people flying in
B planes are surprised to see
* C gooses flying nearby.
D (No mistakes)

4
J At the end of the road is an
K old house. People say it is
L haunted, but I don't believe it.
* M (No mistakes)

5
* A My sister she made the varsity
B softball team. They practice
C two hours every day after school.
D (No mistakes)

6
J Jeanne and Eddie caught four
* K fish, and they mighta caught more
L but they ran out of bait before lunch.
M (No mistakes)

7
* A My friends and I was late
B for school because our bus
C got a flat tire on Elm Street.
D (No mistakes)

8
J Jack is a good player, but
* K he don't have time to study
L and get to soccer practice.
M (No mistakes)

9
A My cousin has an unusual
B hobby. She collects postcards
C from cities around the world.
* D (No mistakes)

10
J My grandmother lives on a
K farm. In the morning, you can
* L see deers on her lawn.
M (No mistakes)

Answer rows A Ⓐ Ⓑ ● Ⓓ 1 Ⓐ Ⓑ ● Ⓓ 3 Ⓐ Ⓑ ● Ⓓ 5 ● Ⓑ Ⓒ Ⓓ 7 ● Ⓑ Ⓒ Ⓓ 9 Ⓐ Ⓑ Ⓒ ●
B Ⓙ Ⓚ Ⓛ ● 2 Ⓙ Ⓚ Ⓛ ● 4 Ⓙ Ⓚ Ⓛ ● 6 Ⓙ ● Ⓛ Ⓜ 8 Ⓙ ● Ⓛ Ⓜ 10 Ⓙ Ⓚ ● Ⓜ

31

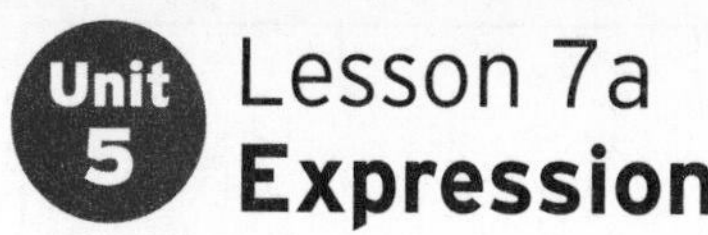

Lesson 7a Expression

Focus

Language Skills
- choosing the best word to complete a sentence
- choosing the best paragraph for a given purpose
- identifying the best closing sentence for a paragraph
- identifying the sentence that does not fit in a paragraph
- identifying the best location for a sentence in a paragraph

Test-taking Skills
- following printed directions
- understanding unusual item formats
- skimming answer choices
- subvocalizing answer choices
- working methodically

Usage and Expression

Lesson 7a **Expression**

Directions: Fill in the space for the answer you think is correct.

Sample A Bandar ordered roast chicken <u>**because**</u> the restaurant was out of steamed crab.
A but B and C however * D (No change)

Sample B We found that <u>**walked**</u> to the mall was faster than driving or taking the bus.
J should walk * K walking L was walking M (No change)

- **Read all the answers before making your choice. The answer that sounds better than the others is correct.**
- **There are several different kinds of items in this section. Be sure you understand what you are supposed to do before choosing an answer.**

Directions: For questions 1 and 2, choose the best way to write the underlined part of the sentence.

1 <u>To feel tired,</u> Uncle Jorge decided to take a nap.
A Have to feel tired B Felt tired * C Feeling tired D (No change)

2 We ate our lunch under a bridge <u>**while**</u> we waited for the storm to pass.
J during K before L after * M (No change)

3 Which of these would be most appropriate in a letter to the local newspaper?

A Your article in Sunday's paper was really great. I'm thinking of becoming a writer myself. Would you mind if I suggested some stories sometime? Anyway, you guys had a great story idea.

C On the front page of the newspaper you had this really great article. I also liked the picture underneath it, though the picture didn't go with the article. You should make the pictures go with the articles.

* B I enjoyed the article on the front page of the Sunday paper. The information was valuable to the public. It was also very informative. Thank you for making your readers aware of what is happening in the community.

D I love reading the Sunday paper more than anything. I usually make a bowl of oatmeal and curl up in my favorite chair. Then I read the front page first. There was a story there that I really liked.

GO

32 Answer rows A Ⓐ Ⓑ Ⓒ ● B Ⓙ ● Ⓛ Ⓜ 1 Ⓐ Ⓑ ● Ⓓ 2 Ⓙ Ⓚ Ⓛ ● 3 Ⓐ ● Ⓒ Ⓓ

Samples A and B

Say **Turn to Lesson 7a on page 32. In this lesson you will work with sentences and paragraphs. There are directions for each section of this lesson, so read them carefully before you answer questions.**

Look at Sample A. Read the sentence with the underlined word. Then read each of the answer choices. Find the answer choice that is the best way to write the underlined part of the sentence. If the underlined part is already correct, choose answer D, *No change*. *(pause)* **Which answer choice is correct?** *(D, No change)* **The underlined part is correct as it is. Mark answer circle D for Sample A in the answer rows at the bottom of the page. Make sure the circle is completely filled in with a dark mark.**

Check to see that the students have filled in the correct answer circle.

Move down to Sample B. Find the answer choice that is the best way to write the underlined part of the sentence. If the underlined part is already correct, choose answer D, *No change*. *(pause)* **Which answer choice is correct?** *(answer K, walking)* **Mark circle K for Sample B in the answer rows at the bottom of the page. Make sure the circle is completely filled in with a dark mark.**

Check to see that the students have filled in the correct answer circle. Explain why answer K is better than the other answers.

TIPS

Say **Who will read the tips for us?**

Have a volunteer read the tips aloud.

Say **Read the answer choices carefully and say them to yourself. The correct answer for the first set of items will sound better than the others. You should also read the directions for each section of the lesson carefully. There are different kinds of items, and if you don't pay attention to the directions, you may make a mistake.**

Practice

Say Now we are ready for Practice. There are two types of items in this lesson, so be sure to read the directions for each section carefully. Choose the answer you think is correct for each item. When you come to the GO sign at the bottom of the page, continue working. Work until you come to the STOP sign at the bottom of page 33. Make sure your answer circles are completely filled in with dark marks. Do not write anything except your answer choices in your books. Completely erase any marks for answers that you change. Any questions? Start working now.

Allow time for the students to fill in their answers. Walk around the room to be sure the students know how to answer the different item types in the lesson.

Say It's time to stop. You have finished Lesson 7a.

Review the answers with the students. If any questions caused particular difficulty, work through each of the answer choices. It will be helpful to have the students read the items aloud in order to give them practice listening for the one that sounds best.

Have the students indicate completion of the lesson by entering their score for this activity on the progress chart at the beginning of the book.

Unit 5 Lesson 7a **Expression**

Directions: Use this paragraph to answer questions 4–9.

> [1]To enjoy a vacation, it is important to plan ahead. [2]You must decide where you want to go, how you will get there, and what you will do once you arrive. [3]It will also be helpful to think about what clothes you should pack. [4]If you put packing off to the last minute, you might forgetting something. [5]Vacations are an important part of life that should be enjoyed.

4 What is the best way to write the underlined part of sentence 1?
- J planning
- K plans
- L will plan
- * M (No change)

5 What is the best way to write the underlined part of sentence 4?
- * A forget
- B forgotten
- C will forget
- D (No change)

6 Choose the best concluding sentence to add to this paragraph.
- J Most people enjoy one good vacation each year.
- K California and Florida are among the most popular vacation destinations.
- * L The better you plan, the more enjoyable your vacation will be.
- M Nothing is more relaxing than a pleasant vacation.

7 Which sentence should be left out of this paragraph?
- A Sentence 1
- B Sentence 3
- C Sentence 4
- * D Sentence 5

8 What is the best way to write the underlined part of sentence 2?
- J did
- K are doing
- L to do
- * M (No change)

9 What is the best place for sentence 4?
- * A Where it is now
- B Between sentences 1 and 2
- C After sentence 5
- D Before sentence 1

STOP

Answer rows 4 Ⓙ Ⓚ Ⓛ ● 6 Ⓙ Ⓚ ● Ⓜ 8 Ⓙ Ⓚ Ⓛ ●
5 ● Ⓑ Ⓒ Ⓓ 7 Ⓐ Ⓑ Ⓒ ● 9 ● Ⓑ Ⓒ Ⓓ

33

Lesson 7b Expression

Focus

Language Skills

- identifying correctly formed sentences
- choosing the best paragraph for a given purpose
- choosing the best word to complete a sentence

Test-taking Skills

- following printed directions
- understanding unusual item formats
- analyzing answer choices

Usage and Expression

Lesson 7b **Expression**

Directions: Fill in the space for the answer that you think is correct.

Sample A
A In their gardens on the weekend, many people enjoy working.
* B On the weekend, many people enjoy working in their gardens.
C Many people enjoy working. In their gardens on the weekend.
D Many people enjoy in their gardens. Working on the weekend.

- **Don't skim the answers. Read them carefully, word by word.**

Directions: For questions 1–6, choose the best way of writing the idea.

1 * A I enjoy watching my two hamsters play together.
B My two hamsters I enjoy watching play together.
C My two hamsters play together I enjoy watching.
D Watching my two hamsters play together I enjoy.

2 J In 1993 to the South Pole Ann Bancroft took a team of four women.
K A team of four women Ann Bancroft took in 1993 to the South Pole.
* L Ann Bancroft took a team of four women to the South Pole in 1993.
M To the South Pole Ann Bancroft took in 1993 a team of four women.

3 A Emile knocked at the door and was surprised. When she saw who opened it.
B Being surprised when she saw who opened it, Emile knocked at the door.
C When she saw who opened it, Emile was surprised knocking at the door.
* D Emile knocked at the door. She was surprised when she saw who opened it.

4 J Martina loves her job at a construction company, or it is hard work.
* K Martina's job at a construction company is hard work, but she loves it.
L Loving it, Martina's job at a construction company is hard work.
M Because she loves it, Martina's job at a construction company is hard work.

34 Answer rows A Ⓐ ● Ⓒ Ⓓ 1 ● Ⓑ Ⓒ Ⓓ 2 Ⓙ Ⓚ ● Ⓜ 3 Ⓐ Ⓑ Ⓒ ● 4 Ⓙ ● Ⓛ Ⓜ

Sample A

Say **Turn to Lesson 7b on page 34. In this lesson you will work with sentences and paragraphs. There are directions for each section of this lesson, so read them carefully before you answer questions.**

Let's look at Sample A. Read each of the answer choices. Find the one that expresses the meaning of the sentence better than the others. *(pause)* **Which answer choice is correct?** *(answer B)* **Mark answer circle B for Sample A in the answer rows at the bottom of the page. Make sure the circle is completely filled in with a dark mark.**

Check to see that the students have filled in the correct answer circle. If necessary, explain why the correct answer is better than the others.

★TIPS

Say **Who will read the tip for us?**

Have a volunteer read the tip aloud.

Say **In this lesson, you are looking for the answer choice that is correct, not a mistake. You should read the answer choices very carefully, word by word. Don't just skim the answer choices or you may make a mistake.**

Practice

Say **Now we are ready for Practice. There are three types of items in this lesson. Read the directions for each section of the lesson. Choose the answer you think is correct for each item. When you come to the GO sign at the bottom of the page, continue working. Work until you come to the STOP sign at the bottom of page 35. Make sure your answer circles are completely filled in with dark marks. Do not write anything except your answer choices in your books. Completely erase any marks for answers that you change. Any questions? Start working now.**

Allow time for the students to fill in their answers. Walk around the room to be sure the students know how to answer the different item types in the lesson.

Say **It's time to stop. You have finished Lesson 7b.**

Review the answers with the students. If any questions caused particular difficulty, work through each of the answer choices.

Have the students indicate completion of the lesson by entering their score for this activity on the progress chart at the beginning of the book.

Lesson 7b **Expression**

5 A In Europe is the longest river the Volga.
B In Europe the longest Volga River is.
C The longest river, the Volga is in Europe.
* D The Volga is the longest river in Europe.

6 J For activities such as climbing trees, balance its body a cat's tail helps.
* K A cat's tail helps balance its body for activities such as climbing trees.
L For activities, a cat's tail helps balance its body such as climbing trees.
M Its body for activities a cat's tail helps balance such as climbing trees.

7 **Which of these would be most appropriate in a letter asking for a job?**

* A Last summer, I worked for Parson's Market. I did many different jobs and worked about forty hours a week. Mrs. Parsons said she would be happy to write a letter of recommendation.

B This is not my first job. I have had another one. I worked hard and saved some money. The money I earned went for a bicycle. It's a great bike that I ride almost every day.

C Parson's Supermarket is on the corner of Mill Street and First Avenue. It is smaller than the Super Duper, but our prices are better. I worked at Parson's Supermarket before.

D One of my friends worked for you before. She said I might get a job there. I need a job because I want to buy a bicycle. My old bike is not very good any more.

Directions: For questions 8–10, choose the best way to write the underlined part of the sentence.

8 Rebecca learned <u>riding</u> a horse when she was in first grade.
J with riding K for a ride * L to ride M (No change)

9 Dillon <u>is going</u> to the store after practice.
A to be going B going C has gone * D (No change)

10 <u>Although</u> Shelley watches her mother flip pancakes, she thinks of frogs hopping.
J Until K In case * L When M (No change)

STOP

Answer rows 5 Ⓐ Ⓑ Ⓒ ● 7 ● Ⓑ Ⓒ Ⓓ 9 Ⓐ Ⓑ Ⓒ ●
6 Ⓙ ● Ⓛ Ⓜ 8 Ⓙ Ⓚ ● Ⓜ 10 Ⓙ Ⓚ ● Ⓜ

35

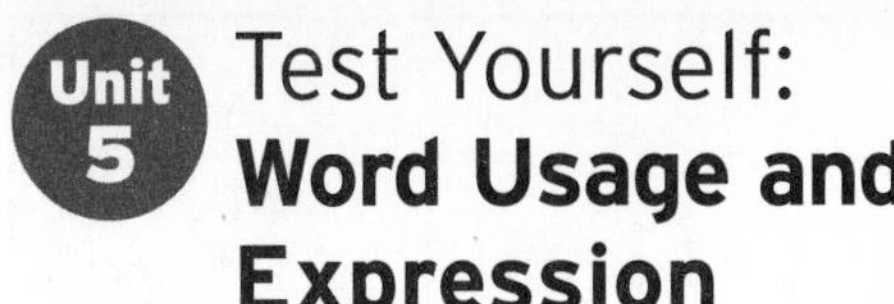

Focus

Language Skills

- identifying mistakes in usage
- choosing the best word to complete a sentence
- identifying correctly formed sentences
- identifying the best opening sentence for a paragraph
- identifying the sentence that does not fit in a paragraph
- identifying the best closing sentence for a paragraph
- choosing the best paragraph for a given purpose

Test-taking Skills

- managing time effectively
- following printed directions
- working methodically
- using context to find an answer
- skimming text
- indicating that an item has no mistakes
- subvocalizing answer choices
- recalling usage errors
- understanding unusual item formats
- skimming answer choices
- analyzing answer choices

Test Yourself: Usage and Expression

Directions: For Sample A, choose the best way to write the underlined part. For Sample B, choose the best way to express the idea.

Sample A The children enjoyed the picnic **in spite of** the rainy weather.
A although
B because of
C except
* D (No change)

Sample B
J It rained almost last week, every day.
*K Last week, it rained almost every day.
L Almost last week, it rained every day.
M Every day, it almost rained last week.

Directions: For questions 1–6, fill in the space for the answer that has a mistake in usage. Fill in the last answer space if there is no mistake.

1 A The game was good, but it
* B might of been better if Jowanda
C had been able to play longer.
D (No mistakes)

2 J We were careful when we moved,
K but later we discovered that a
* L box full of dishes were missing.
M (No mistakes)

3 A The space shuttle took off at
B five in the morning. Thousands of
C people were there to watch it.
* D (No mistakes)

4 J Salt Lake City is beautiful.
K It is located near a huge lake
L and is right beside the mountains.
* M (No mistakes)

5 A Last night, the moon was
* B full. It was the most brightest
C that I have ever seen it.
D (No mistakes)

6*J When we were showed the old
K pictures, we were surprised to
L see that one was of my mother.
M (No mistakes)

GO

36 Answer rows A Ⓐ Ⓑ Ⓒ ● 1 Ⓐ ● Ⓒ Ⓓ 3 Ⓐ Ⓑ Ⓒ ● 5 Ⓐ ● Ⓒ Ⓓ
B Ⓙ ● Ⓛ Ⓜ 2 Ⓙ Ⓚ ● Ⓜ 4 Ⓙ Ⓚ Ⓛ ● 6 ● Ⓚ Ⓛ Ⓜ

This lesson simulates an actual test-taking experience. Therefore, it is recommended that the directions be read verbatim and the suggested procedures and time allowances be followed.

Directions

Administration Time: approximately 25 minutes

Say Turn to the Test Yourself lesson on page 36.

Point out to the students that this Test Yourself lesson is timed like a real test, but that they will score it themselves to see how well they are doing. Remind the students to pace themselves and to check the clock after they have finished Number 12 to see how much time is left. This is about the halfway point in the lesson. Encourage the students to avoid spending too much time on any one item and to take the best guess if they are unsure of the answer.

Say There are different types of items in the Test Yourself lesson, so you will have to read the directions for each section and pay close attention to what you are doing. Remember to make sure that the circles in the answer rows are completely filled in. Press your pencil firmly so that your marks come out dark. Completely erase any marks for answers that you change. Do not write anything except your answer choices in your books.

y **Look at Sample A and listen carefully. Read the sentence with the underlined part and the answer choices. Mark the circle for the best way to write the underlined part. Choose the last answer, No change, if the underlined part is already correct. Mark the circle for your answer.**

Allow time for the students to fill in their answers.

Say The circle for answer D should be filled in because the underlined words are correct. If you chose another answer, erase yours and fill in the circle for answer D now.

Check to see that the students have filled in the correct answer circle.

Say Now do Sample B. Read each of the answer choices. Fill in the circle for the one that expresses the meaning of the sentence better than the others.

Allow time for the students to fill in their answers.

Say The circle for answer K should be filled in. If you chose another answer, erase yours and fill in the circle for answer K now.

Check to see that the students have filled in the correct answer circle.

Test Yourself: Usage and Expression

Directions: For questions 7–12, choose the best way to write the underlined part of the sentence.

7 Our class is **learned** about geometry this year.
A learn
* B learning
C learns
D (No change)

8 Kashani would have won the race, **but** her bike had a flat tire.
J yet
K or
L and
* M (No change)

9 Mort was surprised **to be discovered** he had won a science award.
* A when he discovered
B discovering
C while discovering
D (No change)

10 **While** you are home by nine, you can go to the movies.
J Although
K Unless
* L As long as
M (No change)

11 The town library **is located** on Elm Street.
A located
B locating
C to locate
* D (No change)

12 A bowl of apples **sit** on the kitchen counter by the door.
* J sits
K sitting
L are sitting
M (No change)

Answer rows 7 Ⓐ●ⒸⒹ 9 ●ⒷⒸⒹ 11 ⒶⒷⒸ●
8 ⒿⓀⓁ● 10 ⒿⓀ●Ⓜ 12 ●ⓀⓁⓂ

37

Say Now you will do more items. Read the directions for each section. When you come to the GO sign at the bottom of a page, turn the page and continue working. Work until you come to the STOP sign on page 40. If you are not sure of an answer, fill in the circle for the answer you think might be right. Do you have any questions?

Answer any questions the students have.

Say You may begin working. You will have 20 minutes.

Allow 20 minutes.

 **Test Yourself: Usage and Expression**

Directions: For questions 13–18, choose the best way to express the idea.

13 A As soon as you know call me when we will leave for camp.
* B Call me as soon as you know when we will leave for camp.
C When we will leave for camp call me as soon as you know.
D Leaving for camp call me as soon as you know.

14 J Overcoming cancer Lance Armstrong to win the Tour de France.
K The Tour de France won by Lance Armstrong overcoming cancer.
L Won by Lance Armstrong overcoming cancer the Tour de France.
* M Lance Armstrong overcame cancer to win the Tour de France.

15*A Desert plants can survive with very little water.
B Desert plants, they can survive with very little water.
C Desert plants with very little water can survive.
D Desert plants, that can survive with very little water.

16 J Migrating to Mexico from the United States, thousands of miles by some butterflies.
K To Mexico, some butterflies migrate thousands of miles from the United States.
* L Some butterflies migrate thousands of miles from the United States to Mexico.
M From the United States to Mexico, thousands of miles migrating some butterflies.

17 A Because of heavy snow, to the top of the mountain the road was closed.
* B The road to the top of the mountain was closed because of heavy snow.
C The road to the top of the mountain was closed. Because of heavy snow.
D To the top of the mountain, the road was closed because of heavy snow.

18*J Matthew or Felicia will be able to baby-sit for the Jacksons on Saturday night.
K On Saturday night for the Jacksons, Matthew or Felicia will be able to baby-sit.
L To baby-sit for the Jacksons, Matthew or Felicia will be able on Saturday night.
M Matthew or Felicia on Saturday night for the Jacksons will be able to baby-sit.

GO

38 Answer rows 13 Ⓐ ● Ⓒ Ⓓ 15 ● Ⓑ Ⓒ Ⓓ 17 Ⓐ ● Ⓒ Ⓓ
14 Ⓙ Ⓚ Ⓛ ● 16 Ⓙ Ⓚ ● Ⓜ 18 ● Ⓚ Ⓛ Ⓜ

Test Yourself: Usage and Expression

Directions: Use this paragraph to answer questions 19–24.

[1]Governor Maxine Harris runs in marathons, climbs mountains, and rides a bike everyday. [2]She also enjoys working with computers. [3]The governor visits schools often, because when she arrives, she heads right to the computer lab. [4]There she spends time with students learning about new programs. [5]More than sixty percent of the people voting for her in the last election.

19 Choose the best opening sentence to add to this paragraph.
- A The governor in our state is a woman.
- B Most governors are more interested in politics than other things.
- * C The new governor in our state has some unusual hobbies.
- D It is often difficult for politicians to stay in good physical shape.

20 What is the best way to write the underlined part of sentence 2?
- J to work
- K having worked
- L works
- * M (No change)

21 Which sentence should be left out of this paragraph?
- A Sentence 1
- B Sentence 3
- C Sentence 4
- * D Sentence 5

22 What is the best way to write the underlined part of sentence 3?
- J often, when
- * K often, and when
- L often, or when
- M (No change)

23 What is the best way to write the underlined part of sentence 5?
- * A voted
- B will vote
- C to vote
- D (No change)

24 Choose the best concluding sentence to add to this paragraph.
- J She hasn't visited our school yet, but I hope she will before I graduate.
- K Most people think that Governor Harris will run for office again.
- L Very few governors are as active as Governor Harris.
- * M It is clear that Governor Harris thinks computers are important in education.

Answer rows 19 Ⓐ Ⓑ ● Ⓓ 21 Ⓐ Ⓑ Ⓒ ● 23 ● Ⓑ Ⓒ Ⓓ
20 Ⓙ Ⓚ Ⓛ ● 22 Ⓙ ● Ⓛ Ⓜ 24 Ⓙ Ⓚ Ⓛ ●

39

Say **It's time to stop. You have finished the Test Yourself lesson. Check to see that you have completely filled in your answer circles with dark marks. Make sure that any marks for answers that you changed have been completely erased.**

Go over the lesson with the students. Ask the students if they read the directions for each section. Did they have enough time to finish all the items? Which items were most difficult?

Work through any questions that caused difficulty. Have the students indicate completion of the lesson by entering their score for this activity on the progress chart at the beginning of the book.

Test Yourself: Usage and Expression

Directions: Use this paragraph to answer questions 25 and 26.

> [1]Unlike other animals, the coyote is not threatened by humans moving into its territory. [2]Instead, coyotes have learned to adjust to the presence of humans. [3]They change their diet to include garbage and scraps that humans throw away. [4]In the last fifty years, coyotes have spread all over America. [5]Surprisingly, they have even been sighted in New York City.

25 **Choose the best opening sentence to add to this paragraph.**

A Coyotes are related to wolves and dogs.
* B Some animals have a hard time adapting to human development.
C The coyote is an adaptable animal.
D Coyotes make a strange noise.

26 **What is the best way to write the underlined part of sentence 4?**

J will spread
K to spread
L are spreading
* M (No change)

27 **Which of these would be most appropriate in a letter from a group of students to a town council asking for permission to use a town park?**

A Our fifth-grade class is raising funds for a camcorder. We think there are many good things we can do with it. One of them is to make tapes of school plays to send home to parents.

B Our class was thinking of ways to raise funds for a camcorder. One was to have a bake sale. We decided not to because everybody does that. Now we have another idea.

* C Our class is planning a picnic to raise funds for a camcorder. We would like permission to use Mill Run Park on Saturday, May 2, from noon until three in the afternoon.

D Mill Run Park is the perfect place for our class to have a picnic. It is in the center of town and people can get there easily. We want to use the park for part of the afternoon.

40 Answer rows 25 Ⓐ ● Ⓒ Ⓓ 26 Ⓙ Ⓚ Ⓛ ● 27 Ⓐ Ⓑ ● Ⓓ

Background

This unit contains five lessons that deal with math concepts and estimation skills.

- **In Lessons 8a and 8b,** students solve problems involving math concepts. Students identify and use key words, numbers, and pictures. They refer to a graphic, find the answer without computing, working methodically, evaluate answer choices, and reread questions.
- **In Lessons 9a and 9b,** students solve problems involving estimation. In addition to reviewing the test-taking skills introduced in the two previous lessons, students learn the importance of eliminating answer choices.
- **In the Test Yourself lesson,** the math concepts and estimation skills and test-taking skills introduced in Lessons 8a through 9b are reinforced and presented in a format that gives students the experience of taking an achievement test. Techniques for managing time effectively when taking a standardized test are reinforced.

Instructional Objectives

Lesson	Objective
Lesson 8a **Math Concepts** Lesson 8b **Math Concepts**	Given a problem involving math concepts, the student identifies which of four answer choices is correct.
Lesson 9a **Math Estimation** Lesson 9b **Math Estimation**	Given a problem involving estimation, the student identifies which of four answer choices is correct.
Test Yourself	Given questions similar to those in Lessons 8a through 9b, the student utilizes math concepts, estimation, and test-taking strategies on achievement test formats.

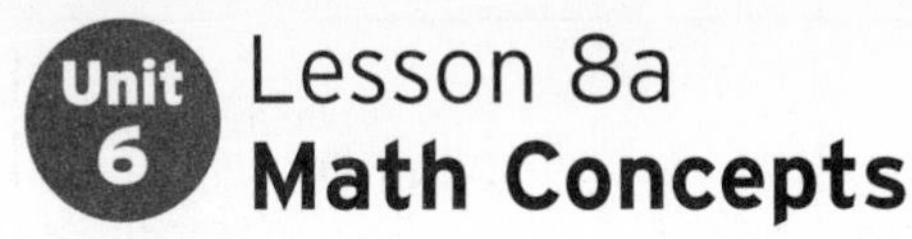

Lesson 8a Math Concepts

Focus

Mathematics Skills

- comparing and ordering whole numbers and fractions
- naming numerals
- understanding place value
- understanding number sentences
- finding area
- recognizing plane figures
- understanding average (mean)
- sequencing numbers
- understanding multiplication
- finding volume
- understanding elapsed time
- understanding simple probability
- identifying the best measurement unit
- identifying parts of a figure
- identifying multiples
- understanding ratio and proportion
- transforming plane to solid figures

Test-taking Skills

- identifying and using key words, numbers, and pictures
- referring to a graphic
- finding the answer without computing
- working methodically
- evaluating answer choices

Math Concepts and Estimation

Lesson 8a **Math Concepts**

Directions: Read each mathematics problem. Choose the best answer.

Sample A Which of the following numerals has a value between 1,695 and 1,705?

A 1,689
B 1,694
* C 1,699
D 1,709

Sample B What is another name for three thousand five?

* J 3,005
K 3,500
L 30,005
M 30,050

- **Use key words, numbers, or pictures to find the answer.**
- **Before you mark an answer, ask yourself: "Does this answer make sense?"**

1 Which numeral has the greatest value?

3,902 3,920 3,892 3,092

A 3,902
B 3,092
* C 3,920
D 3,892

2 What is the value of the 4 in 13.94?

J 4 tenths
K 4 ones
* L 4 hundredths
M 4 tens

3 Which numeral will make the number sentence true?

$(3x) - 4 = 14$

A 3
B 4
C 5
* D 6

4 The shaded portion of the figure below is $\frac{2}{5}$ of the total area. How much of the area is not shaded?

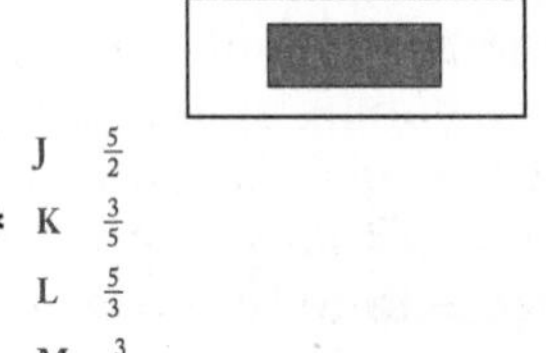

J $\frac{5}{2}$
* K $\frac{3}{5}$
L $\frac{5}{3}$
M $\frac{3}{10}$

5 Which of the figures below is a trapezoid?

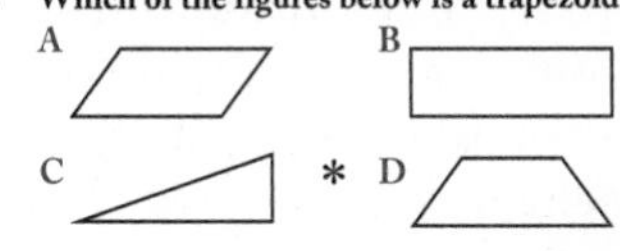

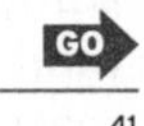

Answer rows A Ⓐ Ⓑ ● Ⓓ 1 Ⓐ Ⓑ ● Ⓓ 3 Ⓐ Ⓑ Ⓒ ● 5 Ⓐ Ⓑ Ⓒ ●
B ● Ⓚ Ⓛ Ⓜ 2 Ⓙ Ⓚ ● Ⓜ 4 Ⓙ ● Ⓛ Ⓜ

41

Samples A and B

Distribute scratch paper to the students.

Say **Turn to Lesson 8a on page 41. In this lesson you will work on math problems. Read the directions at the top of the page to yourself.**

Allow time for the students to read the directions.

Say **Find Sample A. Read the question to yourselves.** *(pause)* **What are you supposed to do?** *(find a number that is between 1,695 and 1,705)* **Now, which answer choice is correct?** *(answer C, 1,699)* **Yes, answer C is correct. Mark answer C for Sample A in the answer rows. Make sure the circle is completely filled in with a dark mark.**

Check to see that the students have filled in the correct answer circle.

Say **Now we'll do Sample B. Read the question to yourself.** *(pause)* **Think about the important words in the question that will help you find the answer. Now, which answer is correct?** *(answer J)* **Fill in answer J for Sample B in the answer rows at the bottom of the page. Be sure you fill in the circle with a dark mark.**

Check to see that the students have filled in the correct answer circle. If necessary, elaborate on the solutions to the sample items.

TIPS

Say **Now let's look at the tips.**

Have a volunteer read the tips aloud to the group.

Say You should look for key words, numbers, and pictures in a problem. They will help you find the answer. And before you mark your answer, be sure it makes sense. Compare it with the question and any graphic that is part of the question.

Practice

Say We are ready for Practice. You are going to do more problems in the same way that we did the samples. Do not write anything except your answer choices in your book. If you think it will help, you may do your work on the scratch paper I gave you. Remember to look for key words, numbers, and pictures in the problems. You should also remember that you don't have to compute to find some of the answers in this lesson. When you have finished working a problem, fill in the circle for your answer in the answer rows at the bottom of the page. Make sure that the circles for your answer choices are completely filled in with dark marks. Completely erase any marks for answers that you change. When you come to the GO sign at the bottom of a page, turn the page and continue working. Work until you come to the STOP sign at the bottom of page 43. Do you have any questions? Start working now.

Allow time for the students to fill in their answers.

Lesson 8a **Math Concepts**

6 Which set of numbers below has the greatest average (mean)?

J {2, 3, 4}
K {3, 4, 1}
L {3, 5, 1}
* M {2, 5, 8}

7 Which is the largest fraction?

A $\frac{2}{4}$
* B $\frac{2}{3}$
C $\frac{1}{3}$
D $\frac{1}{4}$

8 Which number is between 4,143 and 4,427?

J 4,126
K 4,136
* L 4,267
M 4,431

9 Isaac threw a baseball 40 feet and then threw another baseball 50 feet. What was the average distance of baseballs thrown?

A 40 feet
* B 45 feet
C 50 feet
D 90 feet

10 What should replace the Δ in the multiplication problem below?

$$\begin{array}{r} 44 \\ \times\ 272 \\ \hline 88 \\ 3\Delta8 \\ 88 \\ \hline \end{array}$$

* J 0
K 1
L 2
M 8

11 If the 3 in 9,324 is changed to a 1, how is the value of the number changed?

A The number increases by 100.
B The number increases by 200.
C The number decreases by 100.
* D The number decreases by 200.

12 How many blocks are needed to make the figure below?

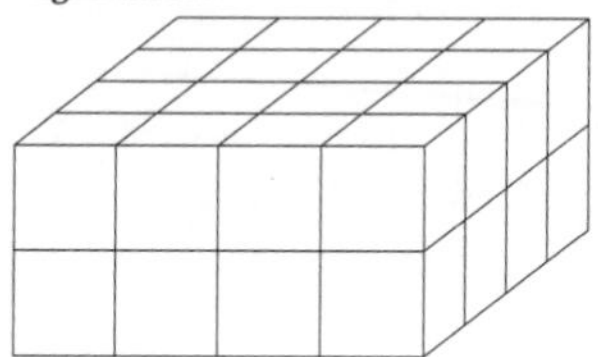

J 4
K 8
L 16
* M 32

13 Taylor's birthday party will start at 3:15 P.M., and it is 10:45 A.M. now. How long is it until the start of Taylor's party?

A 7 hours and 30 minutes
B 6 hours and 0 minutes
* C 4 hours and 30 minutes
D 4 hours and 15 minutes

42 Answer rows 6 Ⓙ Ⓚ Ⓛ ● 8 Ⓙ Ⓚ ● Ⓜ 10 ● Ⓚ Ⓛ Ⓜ 12 Ⓙ Ⓚ Ⓛ ●
7 Ⓐ ● Ⓒ Ⓓ 9 Ⓐ ● Ⓒ Ⓓ 11 Ⓐ Ⓑ Ⓒ ● 13 Ⓐ Ⓑ ● Ⓓ

Say **You may stop working now. You have finished Lesson 8a.**

Review the answers with the students. If any problems caused particular difficulty, work through each of the answer choices. It may be helpful to have the students identify the key words and numbers in each problem. It is also a good idea to have volunteers solve each problem at the chalkboard and discuss the strategy they used.

Have the students indicate completion of the lesson by entering their score for this activity on the progress chart at the beginning of the book.

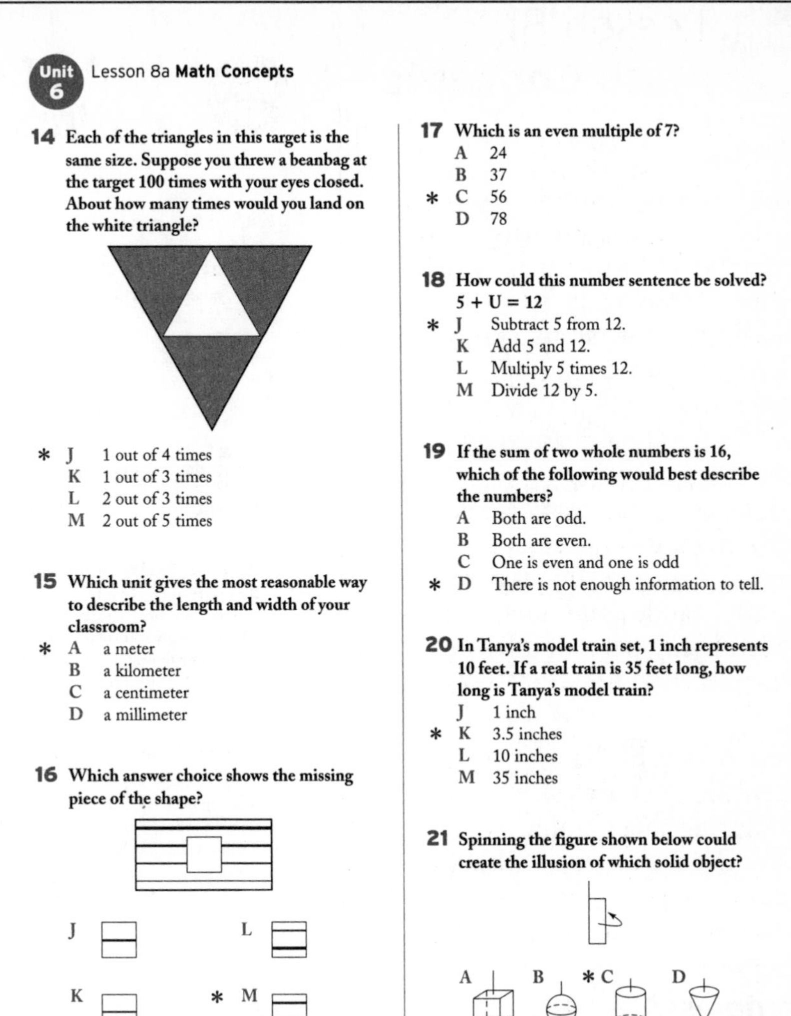

Unit 6 Lesson 8a **Math Concepts**

14 **Each of the triangles in this target is the same size. Suppose you threw a beanbag at the target 100 times with your eyes closed. About how many times would you land on the white triangle?**

* J 1 out of 4 times
K 1 out of 3 times
L 2 out of 3 times
M 2 out of 5 times

15 **Which unit gives the most reasonable way to describe the length and width of your classroom?**

* A a meter
B a kilometer
C a centimeter
D a millimeter

16 **Which answer choice shows the missing piece of the shape?**

J
L
K
* M

17 **Which is an even multiple of 7?**

A 24
B 37
* C 56
D 78

18 **How could this number sentence be solved?**
5 + U = 12

* J Subtract 5 from 12.
K Add 5 and 12.
L Multiply 5 times 12.
M Divide 12 by 5.

19 **If the sum of two whole numbers is 16, which of the following would best describe the numbers?**

A Both are odd.
B Both are even.
C One is even and one is odd
* D There is not enough information to tell.

20 **In Tanya's model train set, 1 inch represents 10 feet. If a real train is 35 feet long, how long is Tanya's model train?**

J 1 inch
* K 3.5 inches
L 10 inches
M 35 inches

21 **Spinning the figure shown below could create the illusion of which solid object?**

A B * C D

STOP

Answer rows 14 ● K L M 16 J K L ● 18 ● K L M 20 J ● L M
15 ● B C D 17 A B ● D 19 A B C ● 21 A B ● D

43

Unit 6 Lesson 8b Math Concepts

Focus

Mathematics Skills

- comparing and ordering whole numbers and fractions
- naming numerals
- understanding simple probability
- using a number line
- identifying a line of symmetry
- understanding factors and remainders
- understanding average (mean)
- finding area
- recognizing fractional parts
- understanding number sentences
- identifying parts of a figure
- sequencing numbers

Test-taking Skills

- rereading a question
- referring to a graphic
- finding the answer without computing
- working methodically

Math Concepts and Estimation

Lesson 8b **Math Concepts**

Directions: Read each mathematics problem. Choose the best answer.

Sample A Which of the following numerals has a value between 1,690 and 1,695?

A 1,689
* B 1,694
C 1,699
D 1,709

Sample B What is another name for thirty thousand five

J 3,005
K 3,500
* L 30,005
M 30,050

- **For many of the problems, you don't have to compute to find the answer.**

1 A box of 16 breakfast bars has 4 different flavors. If you reach into the box without looking, how many breakfast bars must you take out before you are certain you have 2 of the same flavor?

A 4
* B 5
C 8
D 12

2 Reading from left to right, which numerals are represented by the □, △, and ◇ on the number line below?

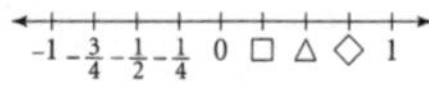

* J $\frac{1}{4}, \frac{1}{2}, \frac{3}{4}$
K $\frac{3}{4}, \frac{1}{2}, \frac{1}{4}$
L 1, 2, 3
M 3, 2, 1

3 What number is 1 less than 90,000?

A 8,999
B 9,000
C 80,000
* D 89,999

4 Which letter can be divided in half with a line of symmetry?

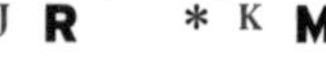

J **R** * K **M**

L **L** M **F**

5 Which of these will have a remainder when divided by 7?

* A 17
B 21
C 28
D 35

GO

44 Answer rows A Ⓐ●ⒸⒹ 1 Ⓐ●ⒸⒹ 3 ⒶⒷⒸ● 5 ●ⒷⒸⒹ
B ⒿⓀ●Ⓜ 2 ●ⓀⓁⓂ 4 Ⓙ●ⓁⓂ

Samples A and B

Distribute scratch paper to the students.

Say **Turn to Lesson 8b on page 44. In this lesson you will work on more mathematics problems. Read the directions at the top of the page to yourself.**

Allow time for the students to read the directions.

Say **Find Sample A. Read the question to yourselves.** *(pause)* **Which answer choice is correct?** *(answer B)* **Yes, answer B is correct because *1,694* is between 1,690 and 1,695. Mark answer B for Sample A in the answer rows. Make sure the circle is completely filled in with a dark mark.**

Check to see that the students have filled in the correct answer circle.

Say **Now we'll do Sample B. Read the question to yourself.** *(pause)* **Which answer is correct?** *(answer L)* **Fill in answer L for Sample B in the answer rows at the bottom of the page. Be sure you fill in the circle with a dark mark.**

Check to see that the students have filled in the correct answer circle. If necessary elaborate on the solutions to the sample items.

TIPS

Say **Now let's look at the tip.**

Have a volunteer read the tip aloud to the group.

Say **You don't have to compute to find the answer for many of the problems in this lesson. You can think through the problem using the numbers or picture that is part of the problem.**

Practice

Say We are ready for Practice. You are going to do more problems in the same way that we did the samples. Do not write anything except your answer choices in your book. If you think it will help, you may do your work on scratch paper. When you have finished working a problem, fill in the circle for your answer in the answer rows at the bottom of the page. Make sure that the circles for your answer choices are completely filled in with dark marks. Completely erase any marks for answers that you change. When you come to the GO sign at the bottom of a page, continue working. Work until you come to the STOP sign at the bottom of page 45. Do you have any questions? Start working now.

Allow time for the students to fill in their answers.

Say You may stop working now. You have finished Lesson 8b.

Review the answers with the students. If any problems caused particular difficulty, work through each of the answer choices. It may be helpful to have volunteers solve each problem at the chalkboard and discuss the strategy they used.

Have the students indicate completion of the lesson by entering their score for this activity on the progress chart at the beginning of the book.

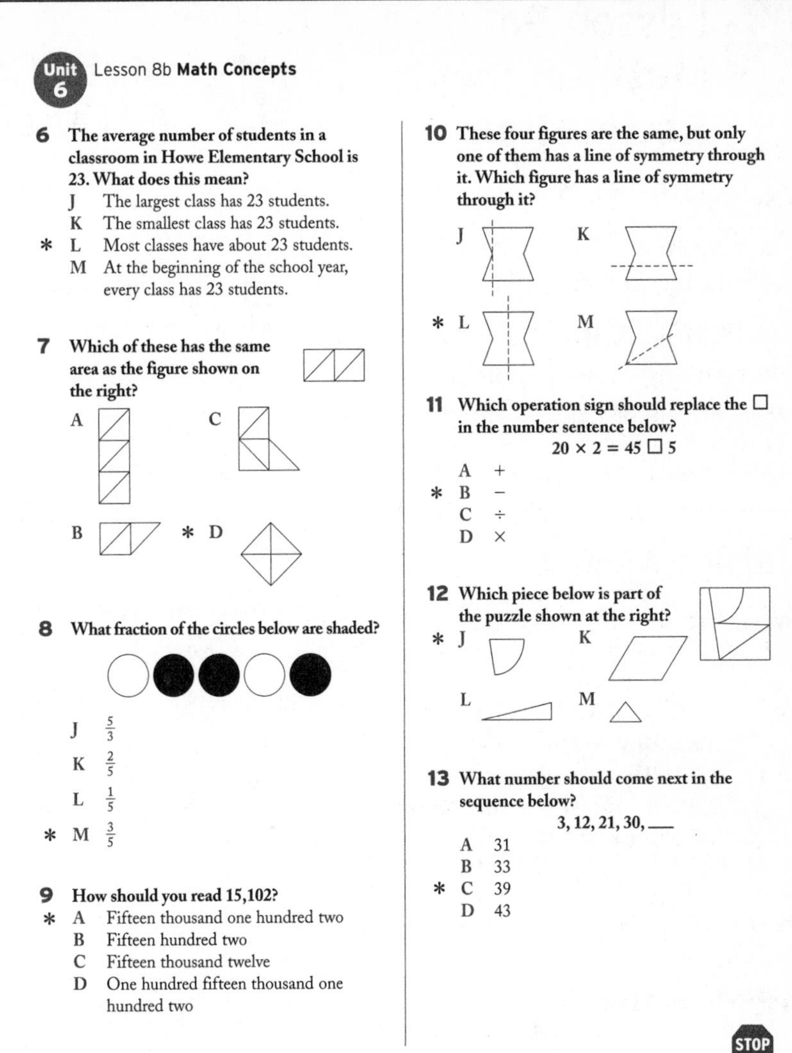

Unit 6 Lesson 8b **Math Concepts**

6 The average number of students in a classroom in Howe Elementary School is 23. What does this mean?
J The largest class has 23 students.
K The smallest class has 23 students.
* L Most classes have about 23 students.
M At the beginning of the school year, every class has 23 students.

7 Which of these has the same area as the figure shown on the right?
A
C
B
* D

8 What fraction of the circles below are shaded?
J $\frac{5}{3}$
K $\frac{2}{5}$
L $\frac{1}{5}$
* M $\frac{3}{5}$

9 How should you read 15,102?
* A Fifteen thousand one hundred two
B Fifteen hundred two
C Fifteen thousand twelve
D One hundred fifteen thousand one hundred two

10 These four figures are the same, but only one of them has a line of symmetry through it. Which figure has a line of symmetry through it?
J
K
* L
M

11 Which operation sign should replace the □ in the number sentence below?
$20 \times 2 = 45 \square 5$
A +
* B −
C ÷
D ×

12 Which piece below is part of the puzzle shown at the right?
* J
K
L
M

13 What number should come next in the sequence below?
3, 12, 21, 30, ___
A 31
B 33
* C 39
D 43

STOP

Answer rows 6 Ⓙ Ⓚ ● Ⓜ 7 Ⓐ Ⓑ Ⓒ ● 8 Ⓙ Ⓚ Ⓛ ● 9 ● Ⓑ Ⓒ Ⓓ 10 Ⓙ Ⓚ ● Ⓜ 11 Ⓐ ● Ⓒ Ⓓ 12 ● Ⓚ Ⓛ Ⓜ 13 Ⓐ Ⓑ ● Ⓓ

45

Lesson 9a Math Estimation

Focus

Mathematics Skill
- estimating and rounding

Test-taking Skills
- eliminating answer choices
- finding the answer without computing
- working methodically

Math Concepts and Estimation

Lesson 9a **Math Estimation**

Directions: Choose the answer that is the best estimate of the exact answer.

Sample A The closest estimate of 19 + 48 is _____.
A 40
B 50
C 60
* D 70

Sample B If one bagel costs 59¢, the closest estimate of the cost of 7 bagels is _____.
J $3.00
* K $4.00
L $5.00
M $6.00

- **Remember, you aren't supposed to find the exact answer, just the best estimate.**
- **If a question is too difficult, skip it and come back to it later.**

1 The closest estimate of 3,992 + 2,958 is _____.
A 3,000 + 2,000
B 3,000 + 3,000
* C 4,000 + 3,000
D 4,000 + 4,000

2 It takes 270 passengers to fill a jet airplane. The closest estimate of the number of passengers needed to fill 42 jet airplanes is _____.
J 120
K 1,200
* L 12,000
M 120,000

3 The closest estimate of $8.79 – $2.88 is _____.
A $4
B $5
* C $6
D $7

4 The state capital building is 512 feet high, and the legislative building is 197 feet high. The closest estimate of the difference in height of the 2 buildings is _____.
J 250 feet
* K 300 feet
L 350 feet
M 400 feet

46 Answer rows A Ⓐ Ⓑ Ⓒ ● 1 Ⓐ Ⓑ ● Ⓓ 3 Ⓐ Ⓑ ● Ⓓ
B Ⓙ ● Ⓛ Ⓜ 2 Ⓙ Ⓚ ● Ⓜ 4 Ⓙ ● Ⓛ Ⓜ

Samples A and B

Distribute scratch paper to the students.

Say **Turn to Lesson 9a on page 46. In this lesson you will solve mathematics problems involving estimation. Read the directions at the top of the page to yourself.**

Allow time for the students to read the directions.

Say **Find Sample A. Read the question to yourselves.** *(pause)* **Think about how to solve the problem. Which answer choice is correct?** *(answer D)* **Yes, answer D is correct. If you round the numbers in the problem and solve it, the answer is** ***70.*** **Mark answer D for Sample A in the answer rows. Make sure the circle is completely filled in with a dark mark.**

Check to see that the students have filled in the correct answer circle.

Say **Now we'll do Sample B. Read the question to yourself. Remember to round before you solve the problem.** *(pause)* **Which answer is correct?** *(answer K)* **Fill in answer K for Sample B in the answer rows at the bottom of the page. Be sure you fill in the circle with a dark mark.**

Check to see that the students have filled in the correct answer circle. If necessary elaborate on the solutions to the sample items and review the rules for rounding numbers.

★TIPS

Say **Now let's look at the tips.**

Have a volunteer read the tips aloud to the group.

Say **Estimation problems are different from other math problems because you do not have to find an exact answer. In the problems in this lesson, you will round numbers to come up with an estimate of the answer or a solution strategy. And remember, if a problem seems difficult, skip it and come back to it later. This strategy is especially important in math problems that involve estimation because it gives you a chance to try all the items.**

Practice

Say We are ready for Practice. You are going to do more problems in the same way that we did the samples. Do not write anything except your answer choices in your book. If you think it will help, you may do your work on scratch paper. Remember that you do not have to find an exact answer to the problems, and you should skip difficult items and come back to them later. When you have finished working a problem, fill in the circle for your answer in the answer rows at the bottom of the page. Make sure that the circles for your answer choices are completely filled in with dark marks. Completely erase any marks for answers that you change. When you come to the GO sign, continue working. Work until you come to the STOP sign at the bottom of page 47. Do you have any questions? Start working now.

Allow time for the students to fill in their answers.

Say You may stop working now. You have finished Lesson 9a.

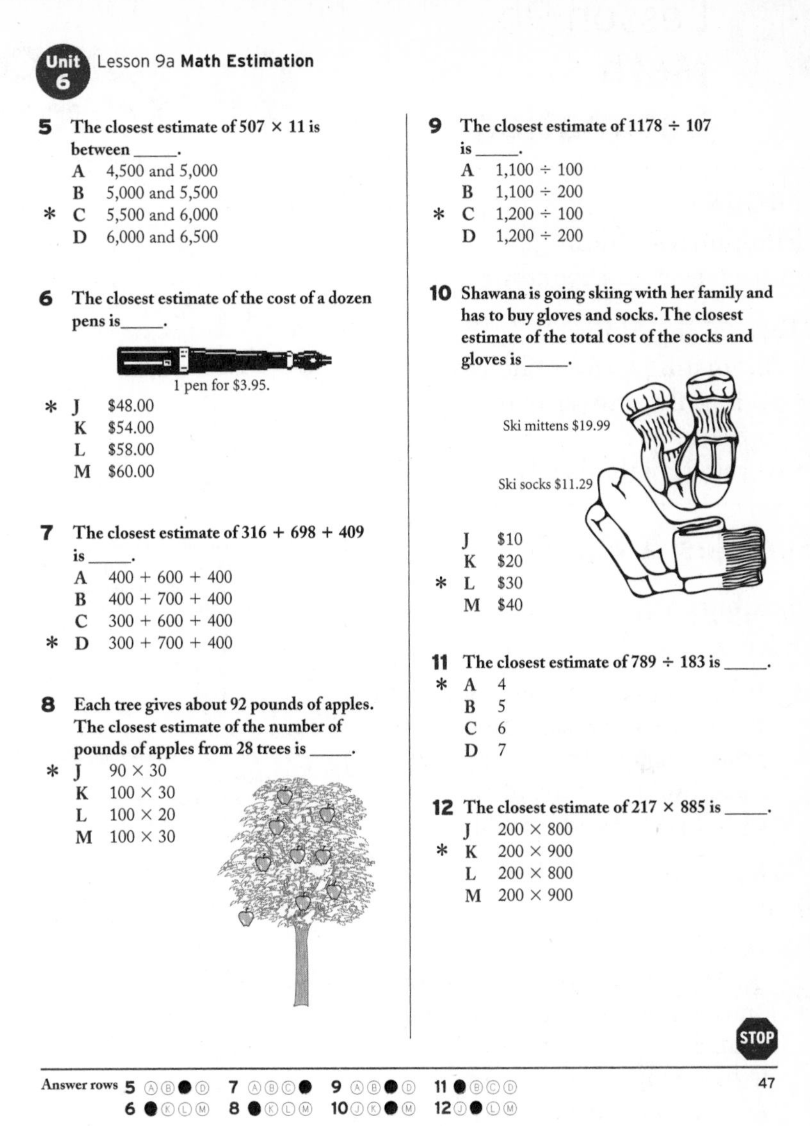
Unit 6 Lesson 9a **Math Estimation**

5 The closest estimate of 507 × 11 is between _____.
A 4,500 and 5,000
B 5,000 and 5,500
* C 5,500 and 6,000
D 6,000 and 6,500

6 The closest estimate of the cost of a dozen pens is_____.

1 pen for $3.95.

* J $48.00
K $54.00
L $58.00
M $60.00

7 The closest estimate of 316 + 698 + 409 is_____.
A 400 + 600 + 400
B 400 + 700 + 400
C 300 + 600 + 400
* D 300 + 700 + 400

8 Each tree gives about 92 pounds of apples. The closest estimate of the number of pounds of apples from 28 trees is _____.
* J 90 × 30
K 100 × 30
L 100 × 20
M 100 × 30

9 The closest estimate of 1178 ÷ 107 is_____.
A 1,100 ÷ 100
B 1,100 ÷ 200
* C 1,200 ÷ 100
D 1,200 ÷ 200

10 Shawana is going skiing with her family and has to buy gloves and socks. The closest estimate of the total cost of the socks and gloves is _____.

Ski mittens $19.99

Ski socks $11.29

J $10
K $20
* L $30
M $40

11 The closest estimate of 789 ÷ 183 is_____.
* A 4
B 5
C 6
D 7

12 The closest estimate of 217 × 885 is_____.
J 200 × 800
* K 200 × 900
L 200 × 800
M 200 × 900

STOP

Answer rows 5 A B ● D 7 A B C ● 9 A B ● D 11 ● B C D
6 ● K L M 8 ● K L M 10 J K ● M 12 J ● L M

47

Review the answers with the students. If any problems caused particular difficulty, work through each of the answer choices. It may be helpful to have volunteers solve each problem at the chalkboard and discuss the rounding and estimation strategies they used.

Have the students indicate completion of the lesson by entering their score for this activity on the progress chart at the beginning of the book.

Lesson 9b Math Estimation

Focus

Mathematics Skill
- estimating and rounding

Test-taking Skills
- eliminating answer choices
- finding the answer without computing
- working methodically

Math Concepts and Estimation

Lesson 9b **Math Estimation**

Directions: Choose the answer that is the best estimate of the exact answer.

Sample A The closest estimate of 19 + 28 is _____.
A 40
* B 50
C 60
D 70

Sample B If one bagel costs 49¢, the closest estimate of the cost of 6 bagels is _____.
* J $3.00
K $4.00
L $5.00
M $6.00

- **Round numbers first and then solve the problem.**

1 A mountain bike costs $367 and a road bike costs $148. Which is the closest estimate of how much more a mountain bike costs than a road bike?
A $100
* B $200
C $300
D $400

2 The closest estimate of 2489 ÷ 6 is between _____.
J 250 and 300
K 300 and 350
L 350 and 400
* M 400 and 450

3 The closest estimate of 612 + 287 + 691 is _____.
A 600 + 200 + 600
B 600 + 200 + 700
C 600 + 300 + 600
* D 600 + 300 + 700

4 One square foot of carpet costs $1.79. Kenny's room is 315 square feet. The closest estimate of how much carpet for the room will cost is _____.
J $60
* K $600
L $6,000
M $60,000

5 The closest estimate of 468 ÷ 93 is _____.
A 4
* B 5
C 6
D 7

6 The closest estimate of 815 ÷ 37 is _____.
* J 20
K 200
L 2,000
M 20,000

48 Answer rows A Ⓐ●ⒸⒹ 1 Ⓐ●ⒸⒹ 3 ⒶⒷⒸ● 5 Ⓐ●ⒸⒹ
B ●ⓀⓁⓂ 2 ⒿⓀⓁ● 4 Ⓙ●ⓁⓂ 6 ●ⓀⓁⓂ

Samples A and B

Distribute scratch paper to the students.

Say **Turn to Lesson 9b on page 48. In this lesson you will solve more problems involving estimation. Read the directions at the top of the page to yourself.**

Allow time for the students to read the directions.

Say **Find Sample A. Read the question to yourselves.** *(pause)* **Think about how to solve the problem. Which answer choice is correct?** *(answer B)* **Yes, answer B is correct. If you round the numbers in the problem and then add, the answer is *50*. Mark answer B for Sample A in the answer rows. Make sure the circle is completely filled in with a dark mark.**

Check to see that the students have filled in the correct answer circle.

Say **Now we'll do Sample B. Read the question to yourself. Remember to round before you solve the problem.** *(pause)* **Which answer is correct?** *(answer J)* **Fill in answer J for Sample B in the answer rows at the bottom of the page. Be sure you fill in the circle with a dark mark.**

Check to see that the students have filled in the correct answer circle. If necessary elaborate on the solutions to the sample items.

TIPS

Say **Now let's look at the tip.**

Have a volunteer read the tip aloud to the group.

Say **The most important thing to remember when you solve estimation problems is to round numbers first. Once you round numbers correctly, it is easy to find the answer.**

Review rounding rules with the students, if necessary.

Practice

Say We are ready for Practice. You are going to do more problems in the same way that we did the samples. Do not write anything except your answer choices in your book. If you think it will help, you may do your work on scratch paper. Remember that you do not have to find an exact answer to the problems. When you have finished working a problem, fill in the circle for your answer in the answer rows at the bottom of the page. Make sure that the circles for your answer choices are completely filled in with dark marks. Completely erase any marks for answers that you change. Work until you come to the STOP sign at the bottom of the page. Do you have any questions? Start working now.

Allow time for the students to fill in their answers.

Say You may stop working now. You have finished Lesson 9b.

Review the answers with the students. If any problems caused particular difficulty, work through each of the answer choices. It may be helpful to have volunteers solve each problem at the chalkboard and discuss the strategy they used.

Have the students indicate completion of the lesson by entering their score for this activity on the progress chart at the beginning of the book.

Math Concepts and Estimation

Lesson 9b **Math Estimation**

Directions: Choose the answer that is the best estimate of the exact answer.

Sample A The closest estimate of 19 + 28 is _____.

A 40
* B 50
C 60
D 70

Sample B If one bagel costs 49¢, the closest estimate of the cost of 6 bagels is _____.

* J $3.00
K $4.00
L $5.00
M $6.00

- **Round numbers first and then solve the problem.**

1 A mountain bike costs $367 and a road bike costs $148. Which is the closest estimate of how much more a mountain bike costs than a road bike?

A $100
* B $200
C $300
D $400

2 The closest estimate of 2489 ÷ 6 is between _____.

J 250 and 300
K 300 and 350
L 350 and 400
* M 400 and 450

3 The closest estimate of 612 + 287 + 691 is _____.

A 600 + 200 + 600
B 600 + 200 + 700
C 600 + 300 + 600
* D 600 + 300 + 700

4 One square foot of carpet costs $1.79. Kenny's room is 315 square feet. The closest estimate of how much carpet for the room will cost is _____.

J $60
* K $600
L $6,000
M $60,000

5 The closest estimate of 468 ÷ 93 is _____.

A 4
* B 5
C 6
D 7

6 The closest estimate of 815 ÷ 37 is _____.

* J 20
K 200
L 2,000
M 20,000

48 Answer rows A Ⓐ ● Ⓒ Ⓓ 1 Ⓐ ● Ⓒ Ⓓ 3 Ⓐ Ⓑ Ⓒ ● 5 Ⓐ ● Ⓒ Ⓓ
B ● Ⓚ Ⓛ Ⓜ 2 Ⓙ Ⓚ Ⓛ ● 4 Ⓙ ● Ⓛ Ⓜ 6 ● Ⓚ Ⓛ Ⓜ

Test Yourself: Math Concepts and Estimation

Focus

Mathematics Skills

- comparing metric and standard units
- estimating and rounding
- understanding place value
- finding perimeter
- sequencing numbers
- recognizing fractional parts
- identifying the best measurement unit
- naming numerals
- understanding average (mean)
- identifying a line of symmetry
- understanding number sentences
- estimating measurement
- finding area
- understanding discounts
- finding volume
- understanding elapsed time
- using a number line
- telling time
- identifying problem solving strategies
- understanding characteristics of related numbers
- identifying parts of a figure
- understanding permutations and combinations

Test-taking Skills

- managing time effectively
- identifying and using key words, numbers, and pictures
- referring to a graphic
- finding the answer without computing
- working methodically
- evaluating answer choices
- rereading a question
- eliminating answer choices

This lesson simulates an actual test-taking experience. Therefore, it is recommended that the directions be read verbatim and that the suggested procedures and time allowances be followed.

Test Yourself: Math Concepts and Estimation

Directions: Read each mathematics problem. Choose the best answer.

Sample A A mile is closest in value to
A a meter.
* B a kilometer.
C a centimeter.
D a millimeter.

Sample B The closest estimate of \$27.48 − \$20.59 is _____.
J \$6
* K \$7
L \$8
M \$9

1 What is the value of the 4 in 13.94?
A 4 tenths
B 4 ones
* C 4 hundredths
D 4 tens

2 What is the value of the 5 in 473.51?
J 5 hundredths
K 5 tens
* L 5 tenths
M 5 thousands

3 A parking lot is in the shape of a square. How many feet of rope are needed to go around the parking lot?
* A 80 ft
B 84 ft
C 100 ft
D 400 ft

20 ft

4 If the 5 in 3,459 is changed to a 1, by how much is the value changed?
J 5
K 10
* L 40
M 50

5 Which number is 100 less than 9,000?
A 8,000
* B 8,900
C 9,100
D 9,900

6 One part of this figure is shaded. Jon wants to shade $\frac{1}{2}$ of the figure. How many more parts of the figure should he shade?
J 2
* K 3
L 4
M 5

GO

Answer rows A Ⓐ ● Ⓒ Ⓓ 1 Ⓐ Ⓑ ● Ⓓ 3 ● Ⓑ Ⓒ Ⓓ 5 Ⓐ ● Ⓒ Ⓓ
B Ⓙ ● Ⓛ Ⓜ 2 Ⓙ Ⓚ ● Ⓜ 4 Ⓙ Ⓚ ● Ⓜ 6 Ⓙ ● Ⓛ Ⓜ

49

Directions

Administration Time: approximately 25 minutes

Distribute scratch paper to the students.

Say Turn to the Test Yourself lesson on page 49.

Point out to the students that this Test Yourself lesson is timed like a real test, but that they will score it themselves to see how well they are doing. Encourage them to read each question carefully, to think about what they are supposed to do, and to work carefully on scratch paper when necessary. They should skip difficult problems and return to them later and take the best guess when they are unsure of the answer.

Say This lesson will check how well you can solve mathematics problems. Remember to make sure that the circles for your answer choices are completely filled in. Press your pencil firmly so that your marks come out dark. Completely erase any marks for answers that you change. Do not write anything except your answer choices in your books.

Look at Sample A. Read the question and the answer choices. Mark the circle for the answer you think is correct.

Allow time for the students to fill in their answers.

Say The circle for answer B should be filled in because a mile is closest to a *kilometer*. If you chose another answer, erase yours and fill in circle B now.

Check to see that the students have filled in the correct answer circle.

Say Now read Sample B and the answer choices. Fill in the circle for the answer you think is correct.

Allow time for the students to fill in their answers.

Say The circle for answer K should be filled in because the right answer is *$7*. If you chose another answer, erase yours and fill in circle K now.

Check to see that the students have filled in the correct answer circle.

Say Now you will do more mathematics problems. You may use the scratch paper I gave you. When you come to a GO sign at the bottom of a page, turn the page and continue working. Work until you come to the STOP sign at the bottom of page 53. Make sure that the circles for your answers are completely filled in with dark marks. Be sure to fill in the circle in the answer row for the problem you are working on. Completely erase any marks for answers that you change. You will have 20 minutes to solve the problems. You may begin.

Allow 20 minutes.

Test Yourself: Math Concepts and Estimation

7 What would be the best choice for measuring the weight of a car?
A Ounces
B Feet
C Grams
* D Pounds

8 Which of these is the same as thirteen thousand ninety-four?
J 1,394
* K 13,094
L 13,940
M 13,000,094

9 Which of these will have a remainder when divided by 8?
A 16
B 24
* C 38
D 56

10 Towanda's height is average for her class. What does this mean?
* J She is about the same height as other students in her class.
K She is taller than most students in her class.
L She is shorter than most students in her class.
M She is the same height as the tallest student in her class.

11 Which number could be divided in half with a line of symmetry?
A 2
C 5
B 4
* D 8

12 What is the missing factor in the number sentence below?

$3 \times \square \times 4 = 6 \times 2$

J 0
* K 1
L 2
M 3

13 A box of juice you would buy at the store holds about
A 2 ounces.
B 5 quarts.
C 10 gallons.
* D 1 pint.

GO

50 Answer rows 7 Ⓐ Ⓑ Ⓒ ● 8 Ⓙ ● Ⓛ Ⓜ 9 Ⓐ Ⓑ ● Ⓓ 10 ● Ⓚ Ⓛ Ⓜ 11 Ⓐ Ⓑ Ⓒ ● 12 Ⓙ ● Ⓛ Ⓜ 13 Ⓐ Ⓑ Ⓒ ●

Test Yourself: Math Concepts and Estimation

14 Which answer has the same area as the figure on the right?

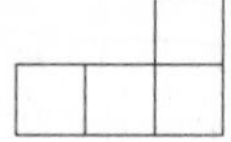

J

K

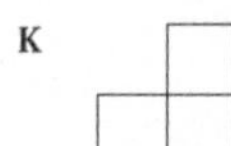

L

* M

15 What should replace the □ in the number sentence below?

23 + 7 < □

A 28
B 29
C 30
* D 31

16 Randy found a mountain bike for $\frac{1}{3}$ off the regular price. Sonya said she found a bike with an even better discount. Which of these discounts did Sonya find?

J $\frac{1}{4}$ off
* K $\frac{1}{2}$ off
L $\frac{1}{5}$ off
M $\frac{1}{8}$ off

17 How many blocks are needed to make the figure below?

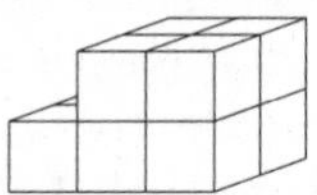

A 9
* B 10
C 12
D 16

18 A train leaves Philadelphia at 11:35 A.M. and arrives in Washington, D.C., at 1:20 P.M. How long does the train ride last?

J 1 hour and 5 minutes
K 1 hour and 15 minutes
* L 1 hour and 45 minutes
M 10 hours and 15 minutes

19 To which number is the arrow pointing on this number line?

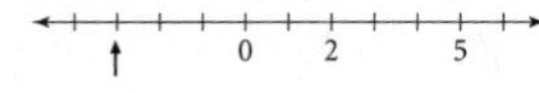

* A −3
B −1
C 2
D 3

GO

Answer rows 14 Ⓙ Ⓚ Ⓛ ● 16 Ⓙ ● Ⓛ Ⓜ 18 Ⓙ Ⓚ ● Ⓜ
15 Ⓐ Ⓑ Ⓒ ● 17 Ⓐ ● Ⓒ Ⓓ 19 ● Ⓑ Ⓒ Ⓓ

51

Test Yourself: Math Concepts and Estimation

20 **Which is the best estimate of the total cost of these office supplies?**

$1.99 $5.19 $3.79 $9.29

* J $2 + $5 + $4 + $9
K $2 + $5 + $3 + $10
L $2 + $5 + $3 + $9
M $2 + $5 + $4 + $10

21 **The closest estimate of 31,945 ÷ 4 is _____.**

A 8
B 80
C 800
* D 8000

22 **A truck delivered 118 pints of milk to a school. The milk comes in boxes that contain 12 pints each. The closest estimate of the number of boxes of milk in the truck is _____.**

118 pints of milk

12 pints

J 9
* K 10
L 12
M 18

23 **Which of these shows the best estimate of 18.14 + 42.59 + 39.03?**

* A 20 + (2 × 40)
B 20 + (2 × 30)
C 20 + 30 + 40
D 3 × 40

24 **Mrs. Nehru works for 7 hours a day. Each hour, she tests an average of 28 electronic parts. The number of electronic parts she tests in a day is _____.**

J between 80 and 140
* K between 140 and 200
L between 200 and 260
M between 260 and 320

25 **386 − 192 is _____.**

A between 100 and 150
B between 50 and 100
* C less than 200
D more than 300

26 **Which best shows how to get the closest estimate of the total number of pets in the school?**

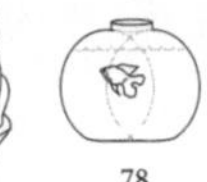

29 51 78 9

J 20 + 50 + 80 + 10
K 30 + 50 + 70 + 10
L 20 + 50 + 70 + 10
* M 30 + 50 + 80 + 10

Answer rows 20 ● K L M 22 J ● L M 24 J ● L M 26 J K L ●
21 A B C ● 23 ● B C D 25 A B ● D

Say **It's time to stop. You have finished the Test Yourself lesson. Check to see that you have completely filled in your answer circles. Make sure that any marks for answers that you changed have been completely erased.**

Go over the lesson with the students. Ask if they had enough time to finish the lesson. Did they work carefully on scratch paper? Which questions required them to guess? What were some of the problems they experienced?

Work through any problems that caused difficulty. Have the students indicate completion of the lesson by entering their score for this activity on the progress chart at the beginning of the book. If necessary, provide additional practice problems similar to the ones in this unit.

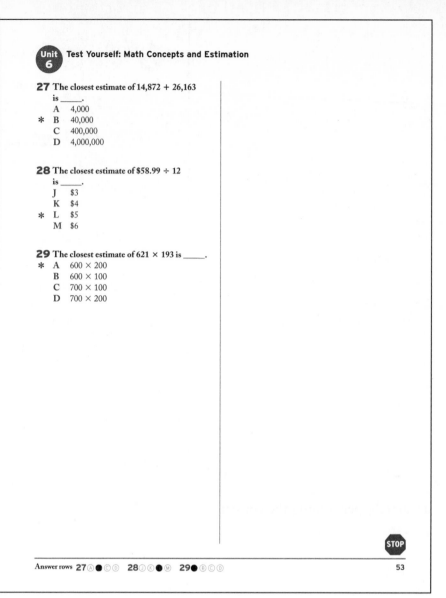

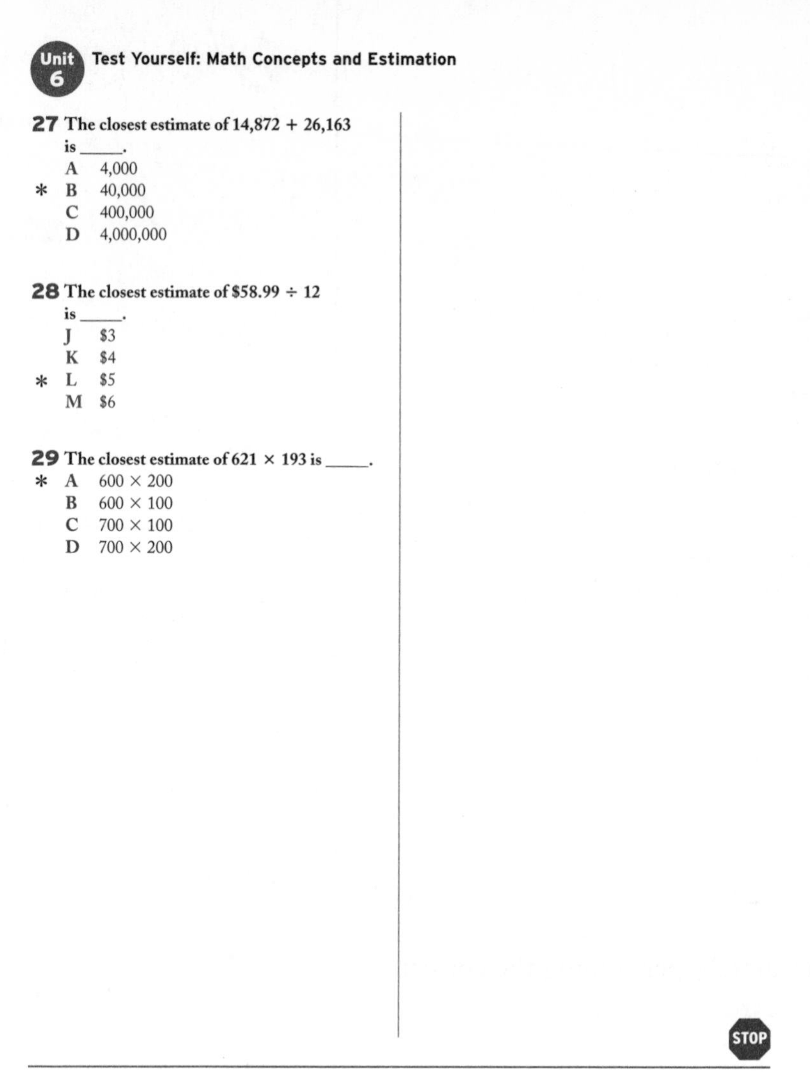
Unit 6 Test Yourself: Math Concepts and Estimation

27 The closest estimate of 14,872 + 26,163 is _____.
A 4,000
* B 40,000
C 400,000
D 4,000,000

28 The closest estimate of $58.99 ÷ 12 is _____.
J $3
K $4
* L $5
M $6

29 The closest estimate of 621 × 193 is _____.
* A 600 × 200
B 600 × 100
C 700 × 100
D 700 × 200

STOP

Answer rows 27 Ⓐ ● Ⓒ Ⓓ 28 Ⓙ Ⓚ ● Ⓜ 29 ● Ⓑ Ⓒ Ⓓ

53

Background

This unit contains five lessons that deal with math problem solving and data interpretation skills.

• **In Lessons 10a and 10b,** students solve word problems. Students indicate that the correct answer is not given. They work methodically and identify and use key words, numbers, and pictures to locate answers. They practice converting items to a workable format and reread questions.

• **In Lessons 11a and 11b,** students solve problems involving data interpretation. Students learn the importance of finding the answer without computing, evaluating answer choices, transferring numbers accurately, performing the correct operation, and computing carefully. They use charts and graphs and work methodically.

• **In the Test Yourself lesson,** the math problem solving, data interpretation, and test-taking skills introduced in Lessons 10a through 11b are reinforced and presented in a format that gives students the experience of taking an achievement test. Techniques for managing time effectively when taking a standardized test are reinforced.

Instructional **Objectives**

Lesson	Objective
Lesson 10a **Math Problem Solving** Lesson 10b **Math Problem Solving**	Given a word problem the student identifies which of four answer choices is correct.
Lesson 11a **Data Interpretation** Lesson 11b **Data Interpretation**	Given a problem involving a chart, diagram or graph, the student identifies which of four answer choices is correct.
Test Yourself	Given questions similar to those in Lessons 10a through 11b, the student utilizes problem solving, data interpretation, and test-taking strategies on achievement test formats.

Lesson 10a Math Problem Solving

Focus

Mathematics Skill
- solving word problems

Test-taking Skills
- indicating that the correct answer is not given
- working methodically
- converting items to a workable format

Math Problem Solving and Data Interpretation

Lesson 10a **Math Problem Solving**

Directions: Read each mathematics problem. Choose the best answer.

Sample A Lyman delivered 54 newspapers on Saturday. He put 37 newspapers in tubes by the road and the rest of the newspapers on the porches of his customers. How many newspapers did he put on porches?
A 7
* B 17
C 18
D 26

Sample B A pilot flew 2,400 miles at a rate of 400 miles an hour. How many hours did she fly?
J 4 hours
K 8 hours
L 9 hours
* M Not given

- **Remember, for some problems, the right answer will not be given. Choose the last answer, Not given.**

Directions: The Rustic Mountain Summer Camp had a scavenger hunt for the campers. The list on the next page gives the items that can be found by the kids and the points they can earn for each item. Use the list to answer questions 1–7.

1 How many more points do you get for an item in category A than in category C?
A 5
* B 25
C 35
D Not given

2 Sally found 3 pine cones. How many points did she get?
J 2.75
* K 5.25
L 6.75
M Not given

3 Molly saw a frog, a rope swing, and a flashlight. How many points did Molly earn?
A 12.5
B 32.5
C 45
* D Not given

GO

54 Answer rows A Ⓐ●ⒸⒹ B ⒿⓀⓁ● 1 Ⓐ●ⒸⒹ 2 Ⓙ●ⓁⓂ 3 ⒶⒷⒸ●

Samples A and B

Distribute scratch paper to the students.

Say **Turn to Lesson 10a on page 54. In this lesson you will solve word problems. Read the directions at the top of the page to yourself.**

Allow time for the students to read the directions.

Say **Find Sample A. Read the question to yourselves.** *(pause)* **Which operation should you use to solve the problem?** *(subtraction)* **Which answer choice is correct? You may use scratch paper to find the answer.** *(answer B)* **Yes, answer B is correct. Lyman put *17* newspapers on customers' porches. Mark answer B for Sample A in the answer rows. Make sure the circle is completely filled in with a dark mark.**

Check to see that the students have filled in the correct answer circle.

Say **Now we'll do Sample B. Read the question to yourself. Choose the answer you think is correct. If the correct solution is not one of the choices, choose answer M, Not given.** *(pause)* **Which answer is correct?** *(answer M)* **The solution to the problem is *6 hours*, but this is not one of the choices. Fill in answer M for Sample B in the answer rows at the bottom of the page. Be sure you fill in the circle with a dark mark.**

Check to see that the students have filled in the correct answer circle. If necessary, elaborate on the solutions to the sample items.

Say **Now let's look at the tip.**

Have a volunteer read the tip aloud to the group.

Say **When you solve word problems, be sure to read them carefully. Use scratch paper, if necessary, and if the answer you find is not one of the choices, choose the last answer, Not given.**

Solve the two sample items on the chalkboard, if appropriate, demonstrating how to set the problems up correctly on scratch paper.

Practice

Say **We are ready for Practice. You are going to do more problems in the same way that we did the samples. Do not write anything except your answer choices in your book. If you think it will help, you may do your work on scratch paper. When you have finished working a problem, fill in the circle for your answer in the answer rows at the bottom of the page. Make sure that the circles for your answer choices are completely filled in with dark marks. Completely erase any marks for answers that you change. When you come to the GO sign at the bottom of the page, continue working. Work until you come to the STOP sign at the bottom of page 55. Do you have any questions? Start working now.**

Allow time for the students to fill in their answers.

Say **You may stop working now. You have finished Lesson 10a.**

Review the answers with the students. If any problems caused particular difficulty, work through each of the answer choices. It may be helpful to have volunteers solve each problem at the chalkboard and discuss the strategy they used.

Have the students indicate completion of the lesson by entering their score for this activity on the progress chart at the beginning of the book.

Lesson 10a **Math Problem Solving**

SCAVENGER HUNT LIST

Category A 30 points	Category B 15 points	Category C 5 points	Category D 2.5 points
Camp flag	Old canoe	Rope swing	Book of songs
Cave	Log cabin	Life vest	Flashlight
Rope bridge	Hollow tree	Sandal	Sleeping bag
		Paddle	
		Plant guide	

2.25 points for a pinecone or 13 points for 5 pinecones
2.5 points for a tent stake or 10 points for 3 tent stakes
5 points for poison oak or lichen
15 points for a frog, a trout, or a squirrel
20 points for a deer, an elk, a rabbit, or a woodpecker
75 points for a four-leaf clover
100 points for a bald eagle

4 **Suzy found 5 items from category C and 1 item from category B. Archie only found 4 items, but he earned exactly as many points as Suzy. From which categories could Archie's items come from?**

J All 4 items were from category C.
K All 4 items were from category B.
* L Two items came from category B and two from category C.
M We cannot tell where Archie's items came from.

5 **Nicolette found 3 tent stakes. How many more points did she get than if she had only found 2 tent stakes?**

* A 5 points
B 2.5 points
C 7.5 points
D 10 points

6 **Don got 60 points for animal sightings and 10 points from category C. What else do you need to know to figure out how many items Don found?**

J He earned 70 points in all.
K He found 2 items from category C.
L He found 2 frogs.
* M All of the animals Don found were woodpeckers.

7 **Philip found 31 pinecones. How can he figure out how many points he earned?**

A Multiply 3 times 13 points; then multiply 16 times 2.25 points and add the results together.
* B Multiply 6 times 13 points and add 2.25 points.
C Multiply 31 times 2.25 points.
D Multiply 31 times 13 points.

Answer rows 4 Ⓙ Ⓚ ● Ⓜ 5 ● Ⓑ Ⓒ Ⓓ  6 Ⓙ Ⓚ Ⓛ ●  7 Ⓐ ● Ⓒ Ⓓ 

55

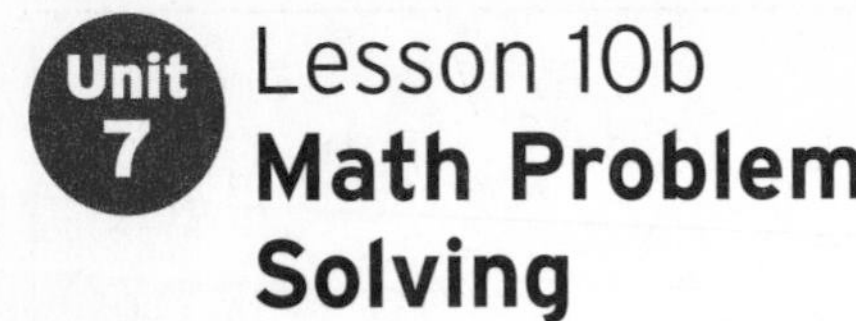

Lesson 10b Math Problem Solving

Focus

Mathematics Skill
- solving word problems

Test-taking Skills
- working methodically
- rereading a question
- identifying and using key words, numbers, and pictures
- indicating that the correct answer is not given

Math Problem Solving and Data Interpretation

Lesson 10b **Math Problem Solving**

Directions: Read each mathematics problem. Choose the best answer.

Sample **A** **Jeremy delivered 61 newspapers on Saturday. He put 43 newspapers in tubes by the road and the rest of the newspapers on the porches of his customers. How many newspapers did he put on porches?**
- A 7
- B 17
- * C 18
- D 26

Sample **B** **A pilot flew 4,500 miles at a rate of 500 miles an hour. How many hours did he fly?**
- J 4 hours
- K 8 hours
- * L 9 hours
- M Not given

- **Read the question, think about it, then read it again. This will help you decide how to solve the problem.**

1 **Victor's mother is driving from Wisconsin to California. She plans on driving 10 hours the first day, 8 hours the second day, and 6 hours the third day. How many hours are left of her 32 hour trip?**
- * A 8
- B 16
- C 18
- D 56

2 **Victor's mother kept track of how many times she had to fill the car up with gas. She filled up 3 times on the first, second, and fourth days, and 2 times on the third day. During the trip how many times did she fill the car up with gas?**
- J 5
- K 8
- L 9
- * M 11

STOP

56 Answer rows A Ⓐ Ⓑ ● Ⓓ B Ⓙ Ⓚ ● Ⓜ 1 ● Ⓑ Ⓒ Ⓓ 2 Ⓙ Ⓚ Ⓛ ●

Samples A and B

Distribute scratch paper to the students.

Say **Turn to Lesson 10b on page 56. In this lesson you will solve more word problems. Read the directions at the top of the page to yourself.**

Allow time for the students to read the directions.

Say **Find Sample A. Read the question to yourselves and find the answer.** *(pause)* **Which answer choice is correct?** *(answer C)* **Yes, answer C is correct. Mark answer C for Sample A in the answer rows. Make sure the circle is completely filled in with a dark mark.**

Check to see that the students have filled in the correct answer circle.

Say **Now do Sample B. Read the problem to yourself. Think about the process you should use before you solve the problem.** *(pause)* **Which answer is correct?** *(answer L)* **Fill in answer L for Sample B in the answer rows at the bottom of the page. Be sure you fill in the circle with a dark mark.**

Check to see that the students have filled in the correct answer circle. If necessary elaborate on the solutions to the sample items.

Say **Now let's look at the tip.**

Have a volunteer read the tip aloud to the group.

Say **You may find it helpful to read a question, think about what the question is asking, and then read it again. This process will help you understand the question better.**

Explain the importance of looking for key words and numbers when they reread a question.

Practice

Say **We are ready for Practice. You are going to do more problems in the same way that we did the samples. Do not write anything except your answer choices in your book. If you think it will help, you may do your work on scratch paper. When you have finished working a problem, fill in the circle for your answer in the answer rows at the bottom of the page. Make sure that the circles for your answer choices are completely filled in with dark marks. Completely erase any marks for answers that you change. Work until you come to the STOP sign at the bottom of the page. Do you have any questions? Start working now.**

Allow time for the students to fill in their answers.

Say **You may stop working now. You have finished Lesson 10b.**

Review the answers with the students. If any problems caused particular difficulty, work through each of the answer choices. It may be helpful to have volunteers solve each problem at the chalkboard and discuss the strategy they used.

Have the students indicate completion of the lesson by entering their score for this activity on the progress chart at the beginning of the book.

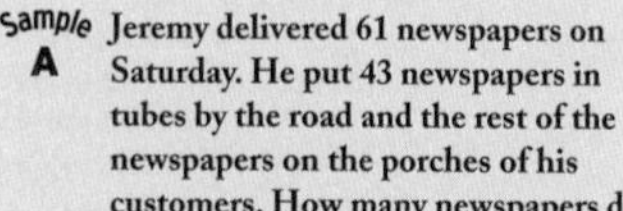

Unit 7 Math Problem Solving and Data Interpretation

Lesson 10b **Math Problem Solving**

Directions: Read each mathematics problem. Choose the best answer.

Sample A Jeremy delivered 61 newspapers on Saturday. He put 43 newspapers in tubes by the road and the rest of the newspapers on the porches of his customers. How many newspapers did he put on porches?

A 7
B 17
* C 18
D 26

Sample B A pilot flew 4,500 miles at a rate of 500 miles an hour. How many hours did he fly?

J 4 hours
K 8 hours
* L 9 hours
M Not given

• **Read the question, think about it, then read it again. This will help you decide how to solve the problem.**

1 Victor's mother is driving from Wisconsin to California. She plans on driving 10 hours the first day, 8 hours the second day, and 6 hours the third day. How many hours are left of her 32 hour trip?

* A 8
B 16
C 18
D 56

2 Victor's mother kept track of how many times she had to fill the car up with gas. She filled up 3 times on the first, second, and fourth days, and 2 times on the third day. During the trip how many times did she fill the car up with gas?

J 5
K 8
L 9
* M 11

STOP

56 Answer rows A Ⓐ Ⓑ ● Ⓓ B Ⓙ Ⓚ ● Ⓜ 1 ● Ⓑ Ⓒ Ⓓ 2 Ⓙ Ⓚ Ⓛ ●

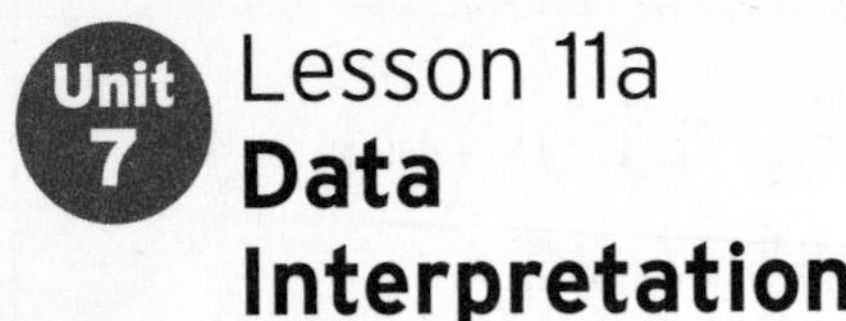

Unit 7 Lesson 11a Data Interpretation

Focus

Mathematics Skill

- interpreting tables and graphs

Test-taking Skills

- finding the answer without computing
- evaluating answer choices
- performing the correct operation
- computing carefully
- using charts and graphs
- transferring numbers accurately

Unit 7 Math Problem Solving and Data Interpretation

Lesson 11a **Data Interpretation**

Directions: Read each mathematics problem. Choose the best answer.

Sample A This table shows the temperature at four different times of the day. What was the difference between the low and high temperatures for the day?

Time	8:00 A.M.	Noon	4:00 P.M.	Midnight
Temperature	57°	67°	73°	54°

A 13°
* B 19°
C 21°
D 29°

TIPS

- **Compare your answer with the information in the chart or graph.**
- **Be sure your answer makes sense.**

Directions: Use the graph below to answer questions 1–4.

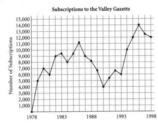

Subscriptions to the Valley Gazette

Number of Subscriptions: 1,000; 2,000; 3,000; 4,000; 5,000; 6,000; 7,000; 8,000; 9,000; 10,000; 11,000; 12,000; 13,000; 14,000; 15,000

Years: 1978, 1983, 1988, 1993, 1998

1 About how many subscriptions to the Valley Gazette were there in 1987?
A 8,000
B 8,500
* C 9,000
D 11,000

2 In which year was the number of subscriptions most nearly the same as the number of subscriptions in 1981?
J 1979
K 1989
L 1992
* M 1993

3 About how many subscriptions to the Valley Gazette are likely to be sold in 1999?
A Between 2,000 and 6,000
B Between 6,000 and 9,000
* C Between 9,000 and 13,000
D Between 13,000 and 15,000

4 Between which years did the number of subscriptions steadily decrease?
* J 1986–1990
K 1990–1993
L 1984–1987
M 1993–1996

GO

Answer rows A Ⓐ●ⒸⒹ 1 ⒶⒷ●Ⓓ 2 ⒿⓀⓁ● 3 ⒶⒷ●Ⓓ 4 ●ⓀⓁⓂ

57

Sample A

Distribute scratch paper to the students.

Say **Turn to Lesson 11a on page 57. In this lesson you will solve problems involving a graph or chart. Read the directions at the top of the page to yourself.**

Allow time for the students to read the directions.

Say **Find Sample A. Look at the table and read the question to yourselves. Use the information in the table to find the answer.** *(pause)* **Which answer choice is correct?** *(answer B)* **Yes, answer B is correct. The difference between the high and low temperatures was** ***19°*****. Mark answer B for Sample A in the answer rows. Make sure the circle is completely filled in with a dark mark.**

Check to see that the students have filled in the correct answer circle.

TIPS

Say **Now let's look at the tips.**

Have a volunteer read the tips aloud to the group.

Say **Be sure to use the chart or graph to find the answer. Sometimes you will have to compute to find the answer, but other times you can find the answer just by looking at the chart or graph. Once you find your answer, check it by comparing the answer to the information in the chart or graph. This will help you decide if your answer makes sense.**

Practice

Say We are ready for Practice. You are going to do more problems in the same way that we did the sample. Be sure to look at the graph or chart when you solve the problems. Do not write anything except your answer choices in your book. If you think it will help, you may do your work on scratch paper. When you have finished working a problem, fill in the circle for your answer in the answer rows at the bottom of the page. Make sure that the circles for your answer choices are completely filled in with dark marks. Completely erase any marks for answers that you change. When you come to the GO sign at the bottom of the page, turn the page and continue working. Work until you come to the STOP sign at the bottom of page 59. Do you have any questions? Start working now.

Allow time for the students to fill in their answers.

Lesson 11a **Data Interpretation**

Directions: John's father is going to buy the family a new car. He compared the weights and gas mileage of different cars. Below is a table showing the weight (wt.) in pounds and the gas mileage (mpg) in miles per gallon for car models in 1995, 1998, and 2000. Use the table to answer questions 5–8.

	1995		1998		2000	
	Wt.	Mpg	Wt.	Mpg	Wt.	Mpg
Express	3,952	20	4,146	18	4,113	17
Jaxx	3,102	20	3,181	19	3,313	19
Jupiter	2,325	34	2,321	34	2,399	35
Champ	3,086	24	2,103	24	3,120	26
Harmony	2,877	28	2,987	28	3,020	27

5 **About how much did the weight of the Jaxx increase from 1995 to 2000?**
A 100 pounds
B 500 pounds
C 300 pounds
* D 200 pounds

6 **What was the weight of the 1995 Champ?**
J 2,400 pounds
K 2,600 pounds
* L 3,086 pounds
M 3,103 pounds

7 **Which of these models had the largest decrease in gas mileage between 1995 and 2000?**
* A Express
B Jaxx
C Jupiter
D Champ

8 **Which best describes the weight of these car models between 1995 and 2000?**
J The weight decreased
* K The weight increased.
L The weight stayed about the same.
M This information cannot be obtained from this graph.

58 Answer rows

Say **You may stop working now. You have finished Lesson 11a.**

Review the answers with the students. If any problems caused particular difficulty, work through each of the answer choices. It may be helpful to have volunteers solve each problem at the chalkboard and discuss the strategy they used. You may also want to review the information in the graph and chart to be sure the students understand how to use them.

Have the students indicate completion of the lesson by entering their score for this activity on the progress chart at the beginning of the book.

Lesson 11a **Data Interpretation**

Directions: Use the graph below to answer questions 9–12.

Animals at Wildlife Refuge in 1997

Moose	○ ○ ○ ○ ○
Bison	○ ○ ○ ○ ○ ○ ○ ◖
Wolf	○ ○ ○
Elk	○ ○ ○ ○ ○ ○ ○ ○
Coyote	○ ○
Bear	○ ○ ○ ○ ◖

Each ○ represents 100 animals

9 **If the wolf population increased by 50% over a 10-year period as a result of a breeding program, how many wolves would there be?**
A 310
B 350
* C 450
D 500

10 **How many bears are there at the refuge?**
J 45
K 350
L 400
* M 450

11 **There are four times as many elk as**
* A coyote.
B wolves.
C bison.
D bears.

12 **How many moose were there at the refuge in 2000?**
J 5
K 500
L 50,000
* M This information cannot be obtained from this graph.

Answer rows 9 Ⓐ Ⓑ ● Ⓓ 10 Ⓙ Ⓚ Ⓛ ● 11 ● Ⓑ Ⓒ Ⓓ 12 Ⓙ Ⓚ Ⓛ ●

59

Lesson 11b Data Interpretation

Focus

Mathematics Skill
- interpreting tables and diagrams

Test-taking Skills
- working methodically
- finding the answer without computing
- using charts and diagrams

Math Problem Solving and Data Interpretation

Lesson 11b **Data Interpretation**

Directions: Read each mathematics problem. Choose the best answer.

Sample A At what time was the temperature the lowest?
A 8:00 A.M.
B Noon
C 4:00 P.M.
* D Midnight

Time	8:00 A.M.	Noon	4:00 P.M.	Midnight
Temperature	57°	67°	73°	54°

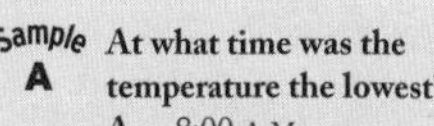

• **Compare your answer with the information in the chart or diagram.**

Directions: Use the diagram of an amusement park below to answer questions 1 and 2. Each line in the diagram is 100 yards.

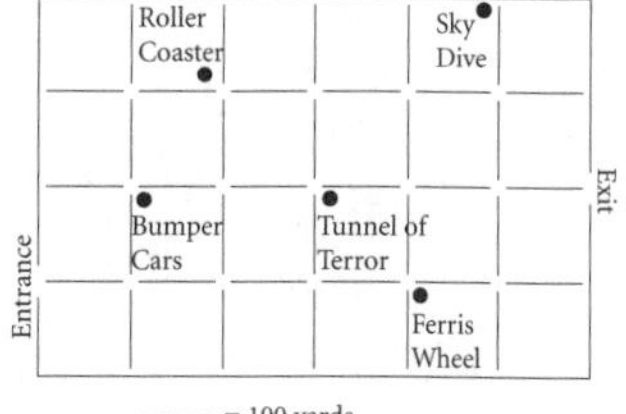

1 **Which ride is farthest from the Bumper Cars?**
A Ferris Wheel
B Tunnel of Terror
C Roller Coaster
* D Sky Dive

2 **If you stay on the grid, about how far is it from the entrance to the Tunnel of Terror?**
J 200 yards
* K 400 yards
L 700 yards
M 800 yards

STOP

60 Answer rows A Ⓐ Ⓑ Ⓒ ● 1 Ⓐ Ⓑ Ⓒ ● 2 Ⓙ ● Ⓛ Ⓜ

Sample A

Say **Turn to Lesson 11b on page 60. In this lesson you will solve more problems involving a diagram. Read the directions at the top of the page to yourself.**

Allow time for the students to read the directions.

Say **Find Sample A. Look at the table; it is the same table we used in the last lesson. Read the question to yourselves. Use the information in the table to find the answer.** *(pause)* **Which answer choice is correct?** *(answer D, midnight)* **The lowest temperature on the chart was at *midnight*. Mark answer D for Sample A in the answer rows. Make sure the circle is completely filled in with a dark mark.**

Check to see that the students have filled in the correct answer circle.

TIPS

Say **Now let's look at the tip.**

Have a volunteer read the tip aloud to the group.

Say **When you solve the problems in this lesson, you should compare each answer to the chart or diagram. It is better to take your time and do this rather than to try to memorize the chart or diagram. Comparing each answer choice to the chart or diagram will help you decide which answer is correct.**

Practice

Say We are ready for Practice. You are going to do more problems in the same way that we did the sample. Be sure to look at the diagram when you solve the problems. Do not write anything except your answer choices in your book. If you think it will help, you may do your work on scratch paper. When you have finished working a problem, fill in the circle for your answer in the answer rows at the bottom of the page. Make sure that the circles for your answer choices are completely filled in with dark marks. Completely erase any marks for answers that you change. Work until you come to the STOP sign at the bottom of the page. Do you have any questions? Start working now.

Allow time for the students to fill in their answers.

Say You may stop working now. You have finished Lesson 11b.

Review the answers with the students. If any problems caused particular difficulty, work through each of the answer choices. It may be helpful to have volunteers solve each problem and discuss the strategy they used.

Have the students indicate completion of the lesson by entering their score for this activity on the progress chart at the beginning of the book.

Math Problem Solving and Data Interpretation

Lesson 11b **Data Interpretation**

Directions: Read each mathematics problem. Choose the best answer.

Sample A At what time was the temperature the lowest?

A 8:00 A.M.
B Noon
C 4:00 P.M.
* D Midnight

Time	8:00 A.M.	Noon	4:00 P.M.	Midnight
Temperature	57°	67°	73°	54°

- **Compare your answer with the information in the chart or diagram.**

Directions: Use the diagram of an amusement park below to answer questions 1 and 2. Each line in the diagram is 100 yards.

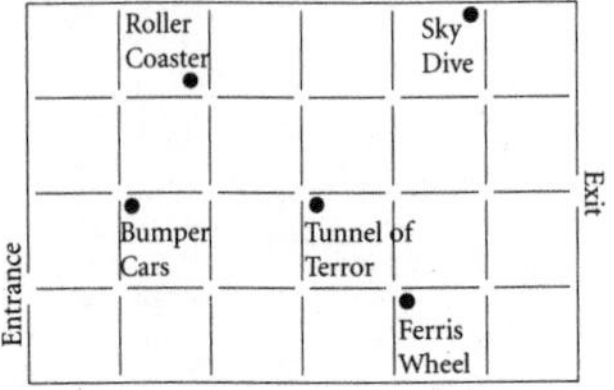

—— = 100 yards

1 **Which ride is farthest from the Bumper Cars?**

A Ferris Wheel
B Tunnel of Terror
C Roller Coaster
* D Sky Dive

2 **If you stay on the grid, about how far is it from the entrance to the Tunnel of Terror?**

J 200 yards
* K 400 yards
L 700 yards
M 800 yards

60 Answer rows A Ⓐ Ⓑ Ⓒ ● 1 Ⓐ Ⓑ Ⓒ ● 2 Ⓙ ● Ⓛ Ⓜ

Test Yourself: **Math Problem Solving and Data Interpretation**

Focus

Mathematics Skills
- solving word problems
- interpreting tables and graphs

Test-taking Skills
- managing time effectively
- indicating that the correct answer is not given
- working methodically
- converting items to a workable format
- rereading a question
- identifying and using key words, numbers, and pictures
- finding the answer without computing
- evaluating answer choices
- performing the correct operation
- computing carefully
- using charts and graphs
- transferring numbers accurately

Test Yourself: Math Problem Solving and Data Interpretation

Directions: Read each mathematics problem. Choose the best answer.

Sample A Ivana and Gregor spend a few hours each Saturday volunteering in a nursing home. Ivana volunteers from 8:00 A.M. to noon, and Gregor volunteers from 9:00 A.M. to 1:00 P.M.

For how many hours are Ivana and Gregor both at the nursing home?
- * A 3 hours
- B 6 hours and 20 minutes
- C 7 hours and 30 minutes
- D Not given

1 **Ramon's mother started her own business. During the first year, she found that she was working about 9 hours a day for 6 days a week. How many hours a week did she work?**
- A 45
- B 48
- C 56
- * D Not given

2 **Ms. Abeyta's first large order was for 50 computers. She bought the computers for $900 each and sold them for $1,500 each. What should Ms. Abeyta do to figure out how much total profit she made on the order?**
- * J Subtract $900 from $1,500 then multiply by 50.
- K Add $900 and $1,500 then multiply by 50.
- L Subtract $900 from $1,500 and then subtract 50 from the difference.
- M Multiply $1,500 by 50 and then subtract $900.

3 **One of Ms. Abeyta's largest expenses is her telephone bill. She spends about $475 each month on phone calls. About how much does Ms. Abeyta spend each year on her telephone bill?**
- A $4,000
- B $5,000
- * C $6,000
- D Not given

4 **Lynette was amazed at the size of a bulldozer. She was almost 5 feet tall, and the seat was 3 feet higher than the top of her head. How high off the ground was the seat of the bulldozer?**
- J 5 feet
- K 6 feet
- * L 8 feet
- M Not given

5 **The bulldozer burned a gallon of fuel every 15 minutes. How many gallons of fuel will the bulldozer use in an hour?**
- A 1 gallon
- B 2 gallons
- C 3 gallons
- * D 4 gallons

GO

Answer rows A ● Ⓑ Ⓒ Ⓓ 1 Ⓐ Ⓑ Ⓒ ● 2 ● Ⓚ Ⓛ Ⓜ 3 Ⓐ Ⓑ ● Ⓓ 4 Ⓙ Ⓚ ● Ⓜ 5 Ⓐ Ⓑ Ⓒ ●

61

This lesson simulates an actual test-taking experience. Therefore, it is recommended that the directions be read verbatim and that the suggested procedures and time allowances be followed.

Directions

Administration Time: approximately 25 minutes

Distribute scratch paper to the students.

Say Turn to the Test Yourself lesson on page 61.

Point out to the students that this Test Yourself lesson is timed like a real test, but that they will score it themselves to see how well they are doing. Encourage them to read each question carefully, to think about what they are supposed to do, and to work carefully on scratch paper when necessary. They should skip difficult problems and return to them later and take the best guess when they are unsure of the answer.

Say This lesson will check how well you can solve mathematics problems like the ones we practiced before. Remember to make sure that the circles for your answer choices are completely filled in. Press your pencil firmly so that your marks come out dark. Completely erase any marks for answers that you change. Do not write anything except your answer choices in your books.

Look at Sample A. Read the story, the question, and the answer choices. Mark the circle for the answer you think is correct.

Allow time for the students to fill in their answers.

Say The circle for answer A should be filled in. The two students are both at the nursing home for *three hours*. If you chose another answer, erase yours and fill in circle A now.

Check to see that the students have filled in the correct answer circle.

Say **Now you will do more mathematics problems. You may use the scratch paper I gave you. When you come to the GO sign at the bottom of a page, turn the page and continue working. Work until you come to the STOP sign at the bottom of page 63. Make sure that the circles for your answer choices are completely filled in with dark marks. Be sure to fill in the circle in the answer row for the problem you are working on. Completely erase any marks for answers that you change. You will have 20 minutes to solve the problems. You may begin.**

Allow 20 minutes.

Unit 7 **Test Yourself: Math Problem Solving and Data Interpretation**

Directions: Use the information below to answer questions 6–9.

Where Parson's Supermarket Buys Grapes

United States	5 grape symbols
Canada	1½ grape symbols
New Zealand	2½ grape symbols
Australia	2 grape symbols

Each [grape] stands for 100 bushels of grapes.

6 How many bushels of grapes did Mr. Parson buy all together?
A 950
B 1,000
C 1,050
* D 1,100

7 How many bushels of grapes were bought from Canada?
J 100
* K 150
L 200
M 250

8 Next year, Mr. Parson expects to buy twice as many grapes from Australia. How many bushels of grapes will he buy from Australia next year?
A 200
B 300
* C 400
D 500

9 How many more bushels of grapes did Mr. Parson buy from the United States than he did from New Zealand?
J 100
K 150
L 200
* M 250

GO

62 Answer rows 6 Ⓐ Ⓑ Ⓒ ● 7 Ⓙ ● Ⓛ Ⓜ 8 Ⓐ Ⓑ ● Ⓓ 9 Ⓙ Ⓚ Ⓛ ●

Say **It's time to stop. You have finished the Test Yourself lesson. Check to see that you have completely filled in your answer circles. Make sure that any marks for answers that you changed have been completely erased.**

Go over the lesson with the students. Ask if they had enough time to finish the lesson. Did they work carefully on scratch paper? Which questions required them to guess? What were some of the problems they experienced? Work through any problems that caused difficulty.

Have the students indicate completion of the lesson by entering their score for this activity on the progress chart at the beginning of the book. If necessary, provide additional practice problems similar to the ones in this unit.

Test Yourself: Math Problem Solving and Data Interpretation

Directions: This is a price list from Driscoll's Hardware Store. Use it to answer questions 10–12.

Item	Price
Nails	$.40 per pound
Large Screws	$1.20 per pound
Nuts	$.04 each
Bolts	$.05 each
Hammer	$9.95
Screwdriver	$4.49
Drill	$29.95
Saw	$40.29

10 **Nadine and her mother are repairing the front porch on their house. They will need 5 pounds of screws. How much will they pay for the screws?**
A $4.80
B $5.00
C $5.20
* D Not given

11 **While they are fixing the porch, Nadine and her mother will repair some chairs. They will need 12 each of nuts and bolts. How much will they pay for the nuts and bolts they need?**
J $1.04
* K $1.08
L $1.09
M $1.19

12 **Nadine's mother is thinking about buying a new drill and saw. How much will she pay for both of them?**
A $60.24
B $69.24
* C $70.24
D Not given

Directions: Use the graph below to do questions 13–15.

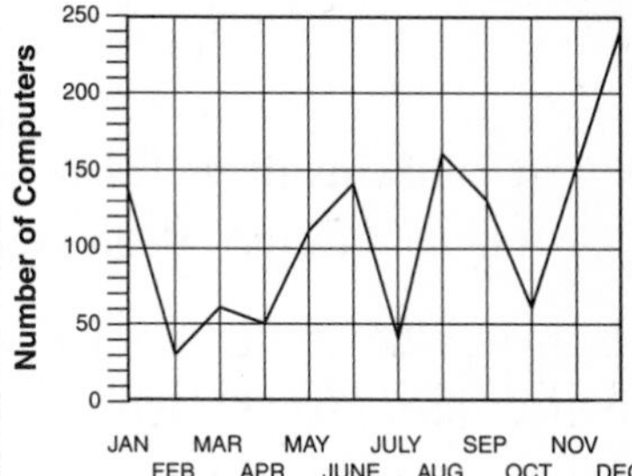

13 **In which two months did MicroWorld sell about the same number of computers?**
* J January and June
K February and June
L June and October
M June and July

14 **How many more computers were sold in December than in April?**
A 98
B 104
* C 190
D 249

15 **In which three month period were most computers sold?**
* J November, December, and January
K February, March, and April
L May, June, and July
M August, September, and October

Answer rows 10 Ⓐ Ⓑ Ⓒ ● 11 Ⓙ ● Ⓛ Ⓜ 12 Ⓐ Ⓑ ● Ⓓ 13 ● Ⓚ Ⓛ Ⓜ 14 Ⓐ Ⓑ ● Ⓓ 15 ● Ⓚ Ⓛ Ⓜ

63

Background

This unit contains three lessons that deal with math computation skills.

• **In Lesson 12a,** students solve problems involving addition, subtraction, multipliction, and division of whole numbers, fractions, and decimals. Students practice performing the correct operation, computing carefully, and transferring numbers accurately. They indicate that the correct answer is not given, convert items to a workable format, and work methodically.

• **In Lesson 12b,** students solve more computation problems. In addition to reviewing the test-taking skills introduced in the previous lesson, students rework problems and take the best guess when unsure of the answer.

• **In the Test Yourself lesson,** the math concepts and estimation skills and test-taking skills introduced in Lessons 12a and 12b are reinforced and presented in a format that gives students the experience of taking an achievement test. Techniques for managing time effectively when taking a standardized test are reinforced.

Instructional **Objectives**

Lesson 12a Lesson 12b	**Computation** **Computation**	Given a problem involving computation, the student identifies which of three answer choices is correct or indicates that the correct answer is not given.
	Test Yourself	Given questions similar to those in Lessons 12a and 12b, the student utilizes math computation, and test-taking strategies on achievement test formats.

Lesson 12a Computation

Focus

Mathematics Skill
- adding, subtracting, multiplying, and dividing whole numbers, fractions, and decimals

Test-taking Skills
- performing the correct operation
- computing carefully
- transferring numbers accurately
- indicating that the correct answer is not given
- converting items to a workable format
- working methodically

Math Computation

Lesson 12a **Computation**

Directions: Solve each problem. Choose the answer you think is correct. If the correct answer is not given, fill in the space for the last answer, N.

Sample A			Sample B		
$613 - 135$		A 251	32×4		J 36
	*	B 478			K 132
		C 611			L 136
		D N		*	M N

- Look at the operation sign before you begin computing.
- Pay close attention to fractions and decimals.

1 $\frac{7}{12} - \frac{5}{12}$
A $\frac{1}{3}$
* B $\frac{1}{6}$
C 1
D N

2 $40 + 20 + 19 + 39$
J 108
* K 118
L 218
M N

3 $19 \times 100 =$
A 190
B 1,090
C 19,000
* D N

4 $836 - 354$
J 325
K 486
* L 482
M N

5 $91 \div 7 =$
A 11
B 11 r3
* C 13
D N

6 205×20
J 225
K 4,010
* L 4,100
M N

7 $8,697 - 81 =$
A 8,516
B 8,661
C 8,778
* D N

8 $44\overline{)2,661}$
* J 60 r21
K 61
L 62 r21
M N

GO

64 Answer rows A Ⓐ●ⒸⒹ 1 Ⓐ●ⒸⒹ 3 ⒶⒷⒸ● 5 ⒶⒷ●Ⓓ 7 ⒶⒷⒸ●
B ⒿⓀⓁ● 2 Ⓙ●ⓁⓂ 4 ⒿⓀ●Ⓜ 6 ⒿⓀ●Ⓜ 8 ●ⓀⓁⓂ

Samples A and B

Distribute scratch paper to the students.

Say **Turn to Lesson 12a on page 64. In this lesson you will solve addition, subtraction, multiplication, and division problems. Read the directions at the top of the page to yourself while I read them out loud.**

Read the directions out loud to the students.

Say **Let's do Sample A. Read the problem and find the answer. You may work on the scratch paper I gave you. If you do work on scratch paper, be sure to transfer numbers accurately and compute carefully.** *(pause)* **Which answer choice is correct?** *(answer B, 478)* **What operation did you use to get this answer?** *(subtraction)* **Mark answer circle B for Sample A in the answer rows at the bottom of the page. Make sure the circle is completely filled in with a dark mark.**

Check to see that the students have filled in the correct answer circle.

Say **Do Sample B yourself. Read the problem and choose the answer you think is correct.** *(pause)* **What is the correct answer?** *(answer M)* **Yes, 32 times 4 is** ***128*****, and** ***128*** **is not one of the answer choices. Fill in circle M for Sample B in the answer rows. Make sure it is completely filled in with a dark mark.**

Check to see that the students have filled in the correct answer circle.

TIPS

Say **Now let's look at the tips.**

Have a volunteer read the tips aloud to the group.

Say **Be sure you read the problem carefully, look at the numbers, and think about the operation you are supposed to perform. Be extra careful if the problem involves fractions or decimals. It's easier to make a mistake with these than with whole numbers.**

Practice

Say **We are ready for Practice. You are going to do more problems in the same way that we did the samples. Do not write anything in your book except your answer choices. If you need to, use scratch paper to work the problems. Transfer numbers accurately to scratch paper and be sure to compute carefully. Pay careful attention to the operation sign for each problem. If you are not sure which answer is correct, be sure to take your best guess. When you come to the GO sign at the bottom of a page, continue working. Work until you come to the STOP sign at the bottom of page 65. Make sure that the circles for your answer choices are completely filled in with dark marks. Erase any marks for answers that you change. You may begin.**

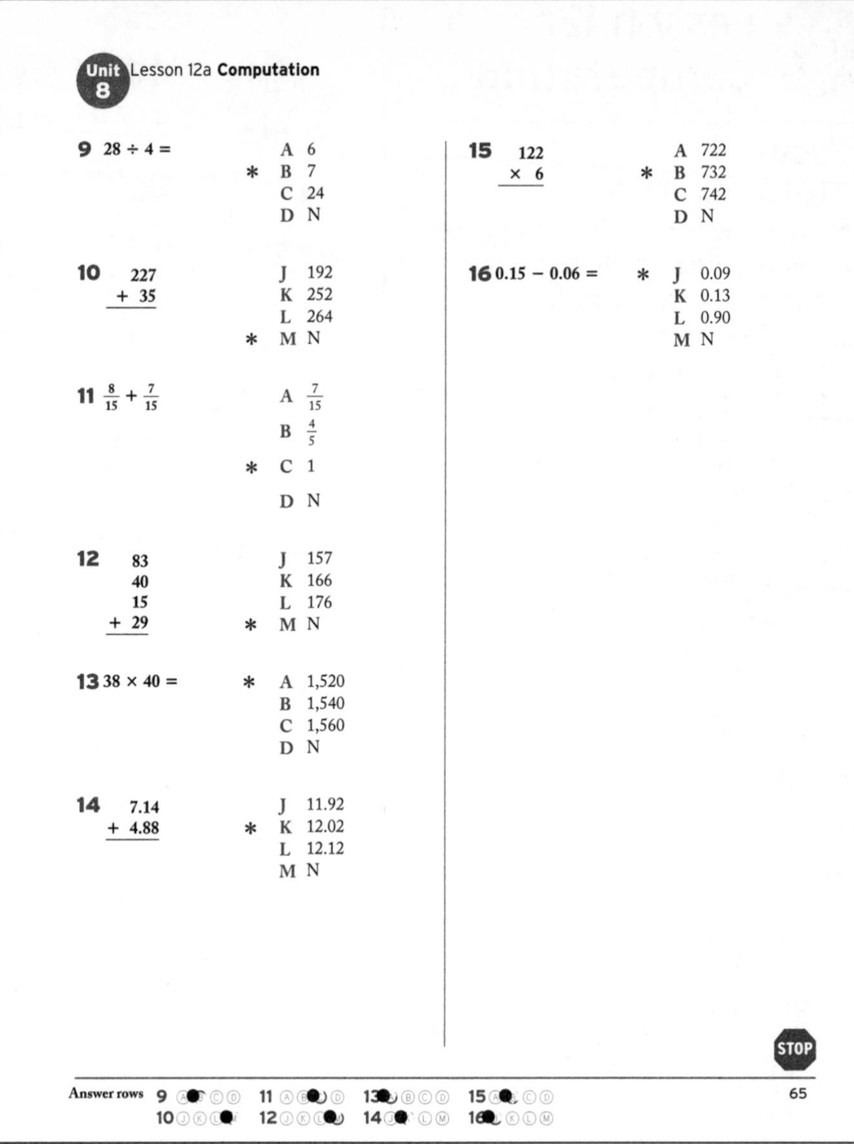

Unit 8 Lesson 12a **Computation**

9 28 ÷ 4 =

A 6
* B 7
C 24
D N

10 227 + 35

J 192
K 252
L 264
* M N

11 $\frac{8}{15} + \frac{7}{15}$

A $\frac{7}{15}$
B $\frac{4}{5}$
* C 1
D N

12 83 + 40 + 15 + 29

J 157
K 166
L 176
* M N

13 38 × 40 =

* A 1,520
B 1,540
C 1,560
D N

14 7.14 + 4.88

J 11.92
* K 12.02
L 12.12
M N

15 122 × 6

A 722
* B 732
C 742
D N

16 0.15 − 0.06 =

* J 0.09
K 0.13
L 0.90
M N

STOP

Answer rows 9 Ⓐ●ⒸⒹ 10 ⒿⓀⓁ● 11 ⒶⒷ●Ⓓ 12 ⒿⓀⓁ● 13 ●ⒷⒸⒹ 14 Ⓙ●ⓁⓂ 15 Ⓐ●ⒸⒹ 16 ●ⓀⓁⓂ

65

Allow time for the students to fill in their answers.

Say **It's time to stop. You have finished Lesson 12a.**

Review the answers with the students. If any problems caused particular difficulty, work through each of the answer choices. Be sure to demonstrate each computation process in detail; processes such as regrouping, multiplying by zero, performing long division, and so on.

Have the students indicate completion of the lesson by entering their score for this activity on the progress chart at the beginning of the book.

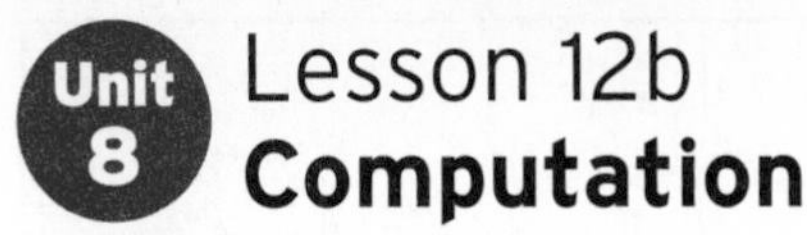

Lesson 12b Computation

Focus

Mathematics Skills
- adding, subtracting, multiplying, and dividing whole numbers, fractions, and decimals

Test-taking Skills
- performing the correct operation
- computing carefully
- transferring numbers accurately
- indicating that the correct answer is not given
- converting items to a workable format
- reworking a problem
- taking the best guess when unsure of the answer

Samples A and B

Distribute scratch paper to the students.

Say Turn to Lesson 12b on page 66. In this lesson you will solve more addition, subtraction, multiplication, and division problems. Read the directions at the top of the page to yourself while I read them out loud.

Read the directions out loud to the students.

Say Let's do Sample A. Read the problem and find the answer. You may work on the scratch paper I gave you. *(pause)* **Which answer choice is correct?** *(answer A, 251)* **Mark answer circle A for Sample A in the answer rows at the bottom of the page. Make sure the circle is completely filled in with a dark mark.**

Check to see that the students have filled in the correct answer circle.

Say Do Sample B yourself. Read the problem and choose the answer you think is correct. *(pause)* **What is the correct answer?** *(answer L)* **Yes, answer L is correct because 7,100 times 5 is** ***35,500.*** **Fill in circle L for Sample B in the answer rows. Make sure it is completely filled in with a dark mark.**

Math Computation

Lesson 12b **Computation**

Directions: Solve each problem. Choose the answer you think is correct. If the correct answer is not given, fill in the space for the last answer, N.

Sample A: 386 − 135
- * A 251
- B 351
- C 611
- D N

Sample B: 7,100 × 5
- J 3,500
- K 35,100
- * L 35,500
- M N

- **Transfer numbers carefully to scratch paper. Work carefully when you compute.**

1 731 + 645
- * A 1,376
- B 1,386
- C 1,476
- D N

2 32 × 4 =
- J 36
- * K 128
- L 136
- M N

3 300 × 54 =
- A 354
- B 1,620
- C 30,054
- * D N

4 84 ÷ 6 =
- * J 14
- K 78
- L 90
- M N

5 4)244
- A 60 r21
- * B 61
- C 62 r21
- D N

6 9 + 224 + 83 =
- J 216
- K 315
- * L 316
- M N

7 15 × 300 =
- A 40,50
- B 40,500
- C 45,500
- * D N

8 7)244
- * J 34 r6
- K 32
- L 130 r2
- M N

GO

66 Answer rows A ● Ⓑ Ⓒ Ⓓ 1 ● Ⓑ Ⓒ Ⓓ 3 Ⓐ Ⓑ Ⓒ ● 5 Ⓐ ● Ⓒ Ⓓ 7 Ⓐ Ⓑ Ⓒ ●
B Ⓙ Ⓚ ● Ⓜ 2 Ⓙ ● Ⓛ Ⓜ 4 ● Ⓚ Ⓛ Ⓜ 6 Ⓙ Ⓚ ● Ⓜ 8 ● Ⓚ Ⓛ Ⓜ

Check to see that the students have filled in the correct answer circle.

★TIPS

Say Now let's look at the tip.

Have a volunteer read the tip aloud to the group.

Say Be sure to transfer the correct numbers to scratch paper and compute carefully. It's easy to make a mistake if you don't take your time and work carefully.

Practice

Say We are ready for Practice. You are going to do more problems in the same way that we did the samples. Do not write anything in your book except your answer choices. If you need to, use scratch paper to work the problems. Pay careful attention to the operation sign for each problem, and rearrange the problem on scratch paper in a way that will help you solve it. If you are not sure which answer is correct, be sure to take your best guess. When you come to the GO sign at the bottom of the page, continue working. Work until you come to the STOP sign at the bottom of page 67. Make sure that the circles for your answer choices are completely filled in with dark marks. Erase any marks for answers that you change. You may begin.

Allow time for the students to fill in their answers.

Say It's time to stop. You have finished Lesson 12b.

Review the answers with the students. If any problems caused particular difficulty, work through each of the answer choices. Demonstrate how to convert problems to a workable format using items 2 through 7.

Have the students indicate completion of the lesson by entering their score for this activity on the progress chart at the beginning of the book.

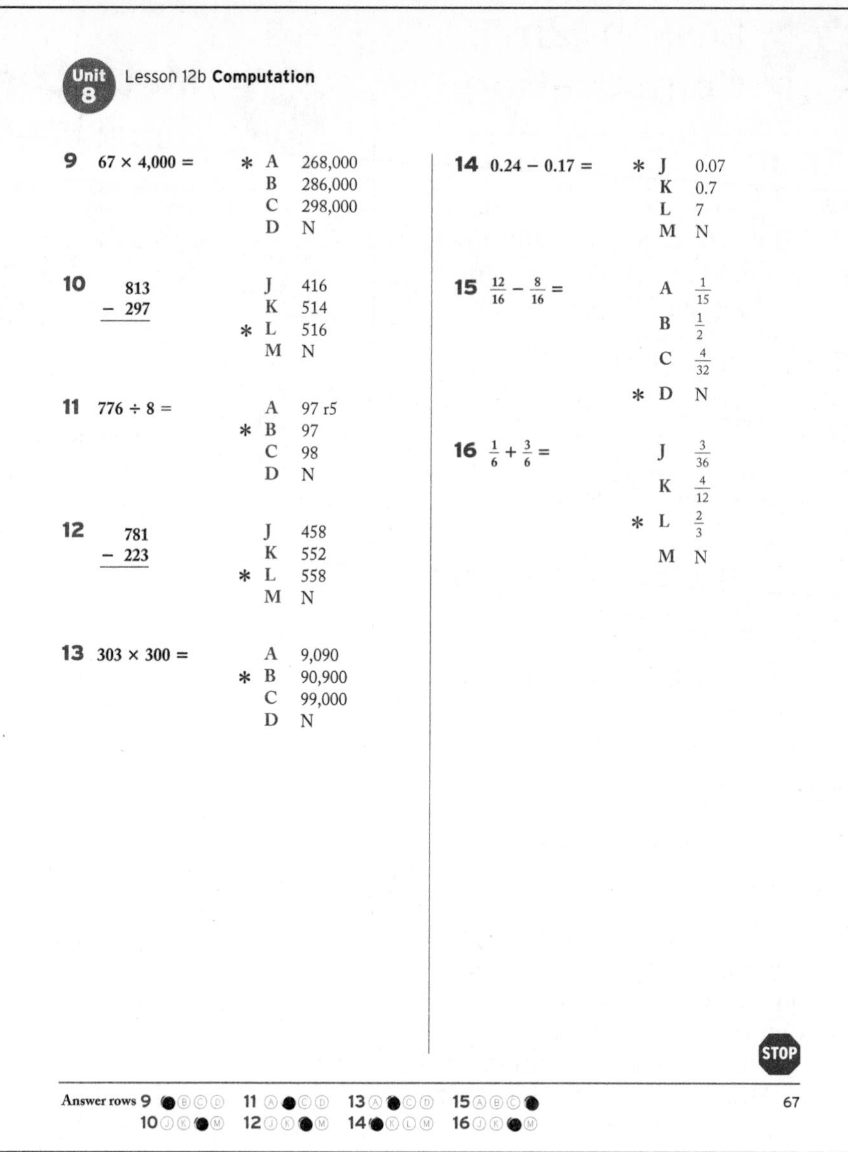

Unit 8 Lesson 12b **Computation**

9 67 × 4,000 =
* ∗ A 268,000
* B 286,000
* C 298,000
* D N

10 813 − 297
* J 416
* K 514
* ∗ L 516
* M N

11 776 ÷ 8 =
* A 97 r5
* ∗ B 97
* C 98
* D N

12 781 − 223
* J 458
* K 552
* ∗ L 558
* M N

13 303 × 300 =
* A 9,090
* ∗ B 90,900
* C 99,000
* D N

14 0.24 − 0.17 =
* ∗ J 0.07
* K 0.7
* L 7
* M N

15 $\frac{12}{16} - \frac{8}{16} =$
* A $\frac{1}{15}$
* B $\frac{1}{2}$
* C $\frac{4}{32}$
* ∗ D N

16 $\frac{1}{6} + \frac{3}{6} =$
* J $\frac{3}{36}$
* K $\frac{4}{12}$
* ∗ L $\frac{2}{3}$
* M N

STOP

Answer rows 9 ● B C D 11 A ● C D 13 A ● C D 15 A B C ●
10 J K ● M 12 J K ● M 14 ● K L M 16 J K ● M

67

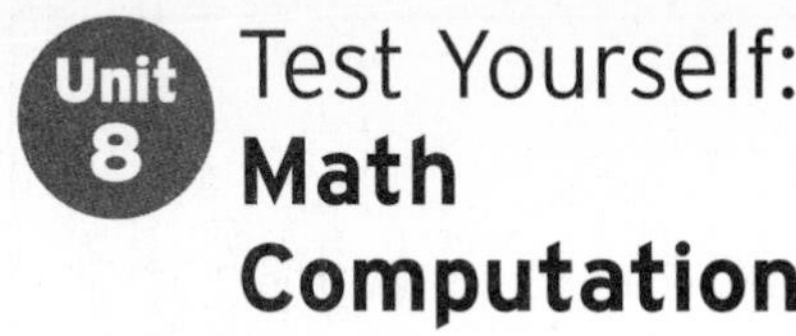

Test Yourself: Math Computation

Focus

Mathematics Skill
- adding, subtracting, multiplying, and dividing whole numbers, fractions, and decimals

Test-taking Skills
- managing time effectively
- performing the correct operation
- computing carefully
- transferring numbers accurately
- indicating that the correct answer is not given
- converting items to a workable format
- working methodically
- reworking a problem
- taking the best guess when unsure of the answer

This lesson simulates an actual test-taking experience. Therefore, it is recommended that the directions be read verbatim and that the suggested procedures and time allowances be followed.

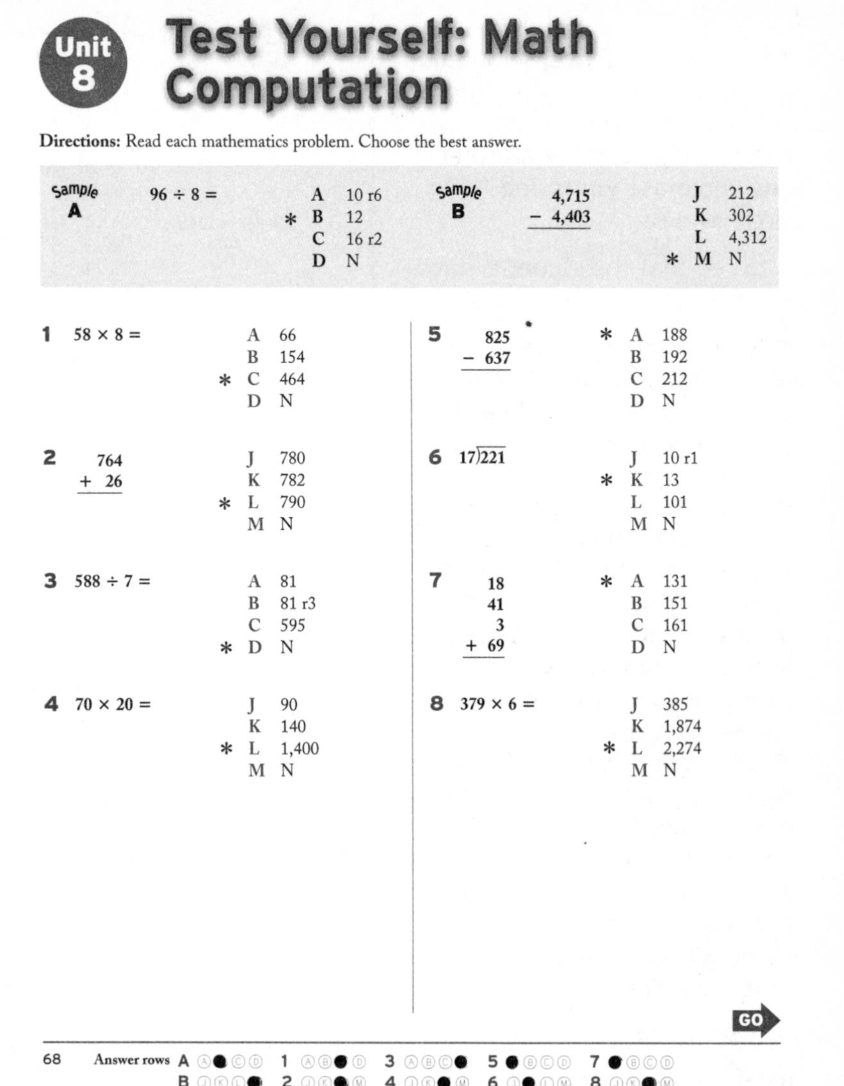

Unit 8 Test Yourself: Math Computation

Directions: Read each mathematics problem. Choose the best answer.

Sample A 96 ÷ 8 =
A 10 r6
* B 12
C 16 r2
D N

Sample B 4,715 − 4,403
J 212
K 302
L 4,312
* M N

1 58 × 8 =
A 66
B 154
* C 464
D N

2 764 + 26
J 780
K 782
* L 790
M N

3 588 ÷ 7 =
A 81
B 81 r3
C 595
* D N

4 70 × 20 =
J 90
K 140
* L 1,400
M N

5 825 − 637
* A 188
B 192
C 212
D N

6 17)221
J 10 r1
* K 13
L 101
M N

7 18 + 41 + 3 + 69
* A 131
B 151
C 161
D N

8 379 × 6 =
J 385
K 1,874
* L 2,274
M N

GO

68 Answer rows A Ⓐ ● Ⓒ Ⓓ 1 Ⓐ Ⓑ ● Ⓓ 3 Ⓐ Ⓑ Ⓒ ● 5 ● Ⓑ Ⓒ Ⓓ 7 ● Ⓑ Ⓒ Ⓓ
B Ⓙ Ⓚ Ⓛ ● 2 Ⓙ Ⓚ ● Ⓜ 4 Ⓙ Ⓚ ● Ⓜ 6 Ⓙ ● Ⓛ Ⓜ 8 Ⓙ Ⓚ ● Ⓜ

Directions

Administration Time: approximately 15 minutes

Distribute scratch paper to the students.

Say **Turn to the Test Yourself lesson on page 68.**

Point out to the students that this Test Yourself lesson is timed like a real test, but that they will score it themselves to see how well they are doing. Encourage them to read each question carefully, to think about what they are supposed to do, and to work carefully on scratch paper when necessary. They should skip difficult problems and return to them later and take the best guess when they are unsure of the answer.

Say **This lesson will check how well you can solve computation problems. Remember to make sure that the circles for your answer choices are completely filled in. Press your pencil firmly so that your marks come out dark. Completely erase any marks for answers that you change. Do not write anything except your answer choices in your books.**

Look at Sample A. Read the question and the answer choices. Mark the circle for the answer you think is correct.

Allow time for the students to fill in their answers.

Say **The circle for answer B should be filled in because 96 divided by 8 is *12*. If you chose another answer, erase yours and fill in circle B now.**

Check to see that the students have filled in the correct answer circle.

Say **Now do Sample B. Solve the problem and fill in the circle for the answer you think is correct.**

Allow time for the students to fill in their answers.

Say The circle for answer M should be filled in because the right answer is not one of the choices. If you chose another answer, erase yours and fill in circle M now.

Check to see that the students have filled in the correct answer circle.

Say Now you will do more mathematics problems. You may use the scratch paper I gave you. Remember, for some items, the correct answer is not given. When this happens, choose the last answer. When you come to the GO sign at the bottom of a page, continue working. Work until you come to the STOP sign at the bottom of page 69. Make sure that the circles for your answer choices are completely filled in with dark marks. Be sure to fill in the circle in the answer row for the problem you are working on. Completely erase any marks for answers that you change. You will have 10 minutes to solve the problems. You may begin.

Allow 10 minutes.

Say It's time to stop. You have finished the Test Yourself lesson. Check to see that you have completely filled in your answer circles. Make sure that any marks for answers that you changed have been completely erased.

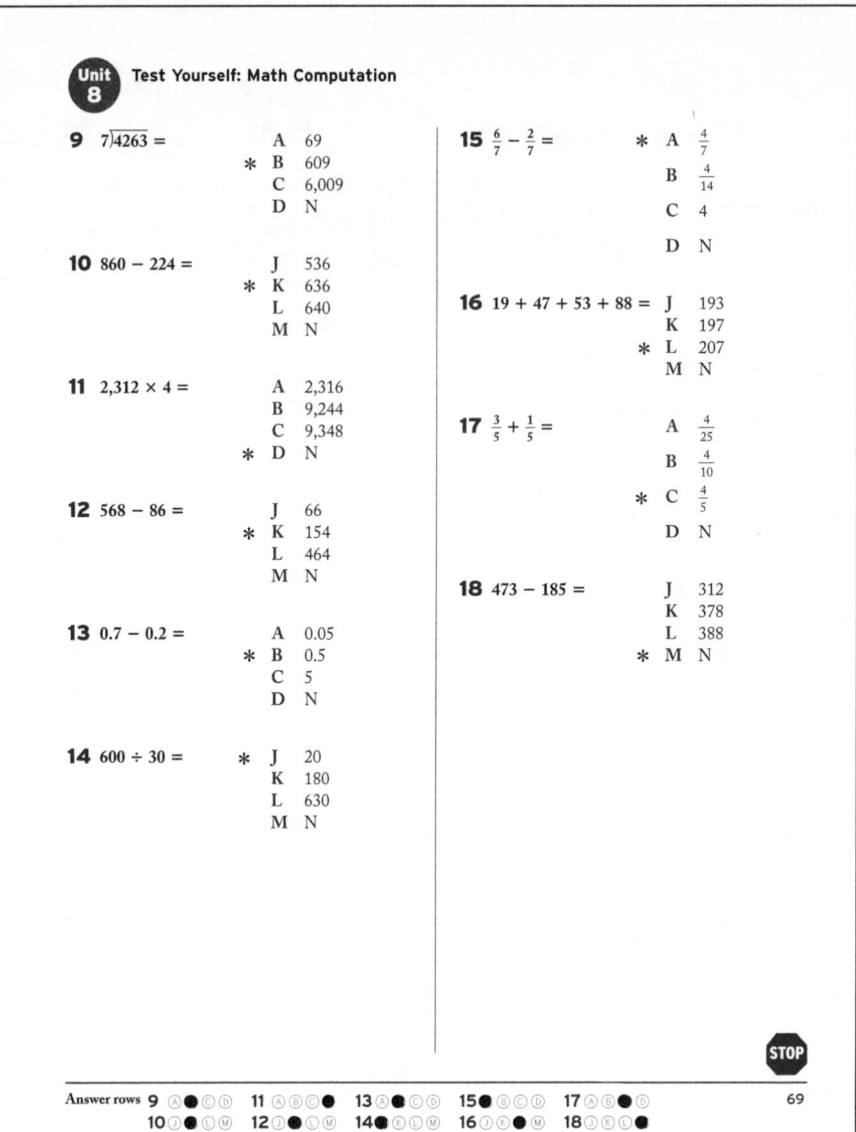

Unit 8 **Test Yourself: Math Computation**

9 $7\overline{)4263}$ =
A 69
* B 609
C 6,009
D N

10 860 − 224 =
J 536
* K 636
L 640
M N

11 2,312 × 4 =
A 2,316
B 9,244
C 9,348
* D N

12 568 − 86 =
J 66
* K 154
L 464
M N

13 0.7 − 0.2 =
A 0.05
* B 0.5
C 5
D N

14 600 ÷ 30 =
* J 20
K 180
L 630
M N

15 $\frac{6}{7} - \frac{2}{7}$ =
* A $\frac{4}{7}$
B $\frac{4}{14}$
C 4
D N

16 19 + 47 + 53 + 88 =
J 193
K 197
* L 207
M N

17 $\frac{3}{5} + \frac{1}{5}$ =
A $\frac{4}{25}$
B $\frac{4}{10}$
* C $\frac{4}{5}$
D N

18 473 − 185 =
J 312
K 378
L 388
* M N

STOP

Answer rows 9 Ⓐ ● Ⓒ Ⓓ 11 Ⓐ Ⓑ Ⓒ ● 13 Ⓐ ● Ⓒ Ⓓ 15 ● Ⓑ Ⓒ Ⓓ 17 Ⓐ Ⓑ ● Ⓓ
10 Ⓙ ● Ⓛ Ⓜ 12 Ⓙ ● Ⓛ Ⓜ 14 ● Ⓚ Ⓛ Ⓜ 16 Ⓙ Ⓚ ● Ⓜ 18 Ⓙ Ⓚ Ⓛ ●

69

Go over the lesson with the students. Ask if they had enough time to finish the lesson. Did they work carefully on scratch paper? Which questions required them to guess? What were some of the problems they experienced? Work through any problems that caused difficulty.

Have the students indicate completion of the lesson by entering their score for this activity on the progress chart at the beginning of the book. If necessary, provide additional practice problems similar to the ones in this unit.

Background

This unit contains seven lessons that deal with study skills.

• **In Lessons 13a and 13b,** students answer questions about a diagram or map. They work methodically, refer to a reference source, and skim a reference source.

• **In Lessons 14a and 14b,** students use a table of contents and alphabetize words. Students learn the importance of working methodically, taking the best guess, and referring to a reference source.

• **In Lesson 15a,** students use an encyclopedia, differentiate among reference sources, and use a catalog card. They review working methodically, skimming a reference source, referring to a reference source, and evaluating answer choices.

• **In Lesson 15b,** students alphabetize words or names, use an encyclopedia, and use a dictionary. They review working methodically, comparing answer choices, skimming a reference source, and referring to a reference source.

• **In the Test Yourself lesson,** the study skills and test-taking skills introduced in Lessons 13a through 15b are reinforced and presented in a format that gives students the experience of taking an achievement test. Techniques for managing time effectively when taking a standardized test are reinforced.

Instructional **Objectives**

Lesson 13a	**Maps and Diagrams**	Given a question about a map or diagram, the student identifies which of four answer choices is correct.
Lesson 13b	**Maps and Diagrams**	
Lesson 14a	**Reference Materials**	Given a question about a reference source, table of contents, dictionary, alphabetical order, or an encyclopedia, the student identifies which of four answer choices is correct.
Lesson 14b	**Reference Materials**	
Lesson 15a	**Reference Materials**	
Lesson 15b	**Reference Materials**	
	Test Yourself	Given questions similar to those in Lessons 13a through 15b, the student utilizes study skills and test-taking strategies on achievement test formats.

Lesson 13a Maps and Diagrams

Focus

Reference Skill
- using a map or diagram

Test-taking Skills
- working methodically
- referring to a reference source

Samples A and B

Say **Turn to Lesson 13a on page 70. In this lesson you will practice using maps. Read the directions at the top of the page to yourself.**

Allow time for the students to read the directions.

Say **Look at the map at the top of the page and read the question for Sample A. What is the correct answer to the question?** *(pause)* **Answer B is correct. Mark circle B for Sample A in the answer rows at the bottom of the page. Make sure the circle is completely filled in. Press your pencil firmly so that your mark comes out dark.**

Check to see that the students have filled in the correct answer circle.

Say **Now do Sample B. Read the question and use the map to find the answer. What is the correct answer to the question?** *(pause)* **Answer M is correct.** ***Benig*** **is farthest from the river. Mark circle M for Sample B in the answer rows at the bottom of the page. Make sure the circle is completely filled in with a dark mark.**

Check to see that the students have filled in the correct answer circle.

TIPS

Say **Now let's look at the tip.**

Have a volunteer read the tip aloud.

Maps, Diagrams, and Reference Materials

Lesson 13a **Maps and Diagrams**

Directions: Read the directions for each section. Choose the best answer.

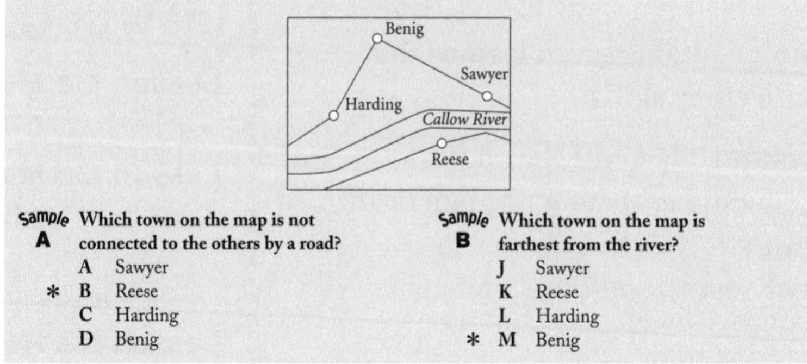

Sample A Which town on the map is not connected to the others by a road?
- A Sawyer
- * B Reese
- C Harding
- D Benig

Sample B Which town on the map is farthest from the river?
- J Sawyer
- K Reese
- L Harding
- * M Benig

- **If a question has a reference source, map, or graphic, be sure you look at it carefully before you choose your answer.**

Directions: The map below shows the first floor of a school. Use the map to answer questions 1–4.

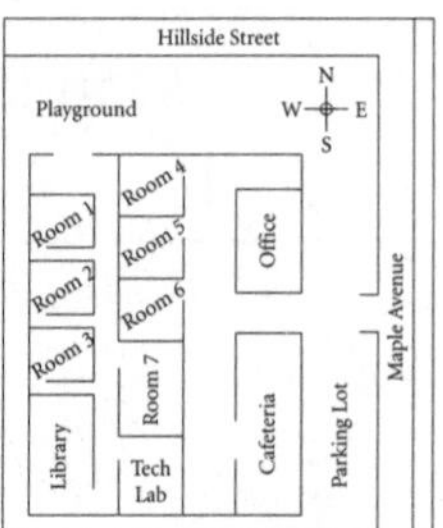

1 On which side of the school is the parking lot?
- A North
- B South
- * C East
- D West

2 Which room is closest to the playground?
- * J Room 4
- K Room 5
- L Room 6
- M Room 7

70 Answer rows A Ⓐ●ⒸⒹ B ⒿⓀⓁ● 1 ⒶⒷ●Ⓓ 2 ●ⓀⓁⓂ

Say **It is important that you use the map or other reference source to answer questions on an achievement test. The answer will always be found in the reference source.**

Practice

Say **Let's do the Practice items now. Read the directions and answer the questions. Think about what the questions are asking and be sure to refer to the map to answer the questions. When you come to the GO sign at the bottom of the page, continue working. Work until you come to the STOP sign at the bottom of page 71. Remember to make sure that your answer circles are completely filled in with dark marks. Completely erase any marks for answers that you change. Any questions? Start working now.**

Allow time for the students to mark their answers.

Say **It's time to stop. You have finished Lesson 13a.**

Review the answers with the students. If any questions caused particular difficulty, work through each of the answer choices.

Have the students indicate completion of the lesson by entering their score for this activity on the progress chart at the beginning of the book.

Lesson 13a **Maps and Diagrams**

3 The main entrance to the school is near the parking lot. When you walk in the main entrance, what is on your left?
A Office
* B Cafeteria
C Library
D Tech Lab

4 What is in the southwest corner of the school?
J Room 3
K Office
L Room 1
* M Library

Directions: The map below shows a shopping mall. Use the map to do questions 5–11.

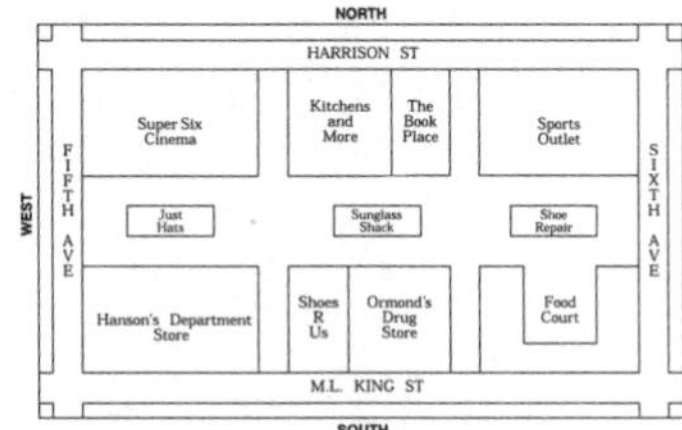

5 Suppose you were walking from the Shoe Repair shop to Just Hats. Which of these would be on your right?
A Ormond's Drug Store
* B The Book Place
C Shoes R Us
D Hanson's Department Store

6 What is on the northwest corner of the shopping mall?
J Hanson's Department Store
K Food Court
L Sports Outlet
* M Super Six Cinema

7 The Food Court is most convenient for workers from
* A Ormond's Drug Store.
B Hanson's Department Store.
C Kitchens and More.
D Shoes R Us.

8 Which of these streets would you probably cross first if you walked east on M. L. King Street beyond Sixth Avenue?
J Fourth Avenue
K Fifth Avenue
* L Seventh Avenue
M Eighth Avenue

9 Which of these is closest to Super Six Cinema?
A Sports Outlet
B Food Court
C Shoes R Us
* D Just Hats

10 Angie lives on the west side of town, about four blocks from the mall. If she walks to the mall, which street will she cross just before reaching the mall?
* J Fifth Avenue
K Sixth Avenue
L Harrison Street
M M. L. King Street

11 The Book Place is having a "compass sale" with another business that is its eastern neighbor. What store is this?
A Hanson's Department Store
B Food Court
* C Sports Outlet
D Super Six Cinema

Answer rows 3 Ⓐ ● Ⓒ Ⓓ 5 Ⓐ ● Ⓒ Ⓓ 7 ● Ⓑ Ⓒ Ⓓ 9 Ⓐ Ⓑ Ⓒ ● 11 Ⓐ Ⓑ ● Ⓓ
4 Ⓙ Ⓚ Ⓛ ● 6 Ⓙ Ⓚ Ⓛ ● 8 Ⓙ Ⓚ ● Ⓜ 10 ● Ⓚ Ⓛ Ⓜ

71

Lesson 13b Maps and Diagrams

Focus

Reference Skill
- using a map or diagram

Test-taking Skills
- skimming a reference source
- working methodically
- referring to a reference source

Samples A and B

Say Turn to Lesson 13b on page 72. In this lesson you will practice reading a map. Read the directions at the top of the page to yourself.

Allow time for the students to read the directions.

Say Look at the highway map below the tip. Read the question for Sample A. What is the correct answer to the question? *(pause)* Answer C is correct. Mark circle C for Sample A in the answer rows at the bottom of the page. Make sure the circle is completely filled in. Press your pencil firmly so that your mark comes out dark.

Maps, Diagrams, and Reference Materials

Lesson 13b **Maps and Diagrams**

Directions: Read the directions for each section. Choose the best answer.

Sample A **Which route goes from Simpson to Homestead?**
A Route 16
* C Route 15
B Route 27
D Route 22

Sample B **Which city has the most services?**
* J Homestead
L Laramie
K Simpson
M Woodside

• **Think about the directions before you choose an answer.**

Directions: The map below shows part of a highway map. Use the map to do questions 1–5.

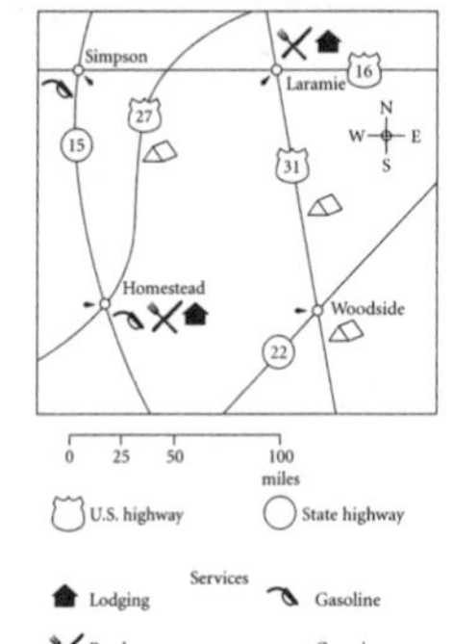

1 **If you went from Laramie to Woodside, what service would be available at about the halfway point?**
A Lodging
B Gasoline
C Food
* D Camping

2 **Which two cities are farthest apart if you travel by road?**
J Simpson and Laramie
* K Woodside and Homestead
L Homestead and Simpson
M Laramie and Woodside

3 **Two roads appear to cross in an area just off the map. Which two roads are they?**
A Routes 27 and 22
B Routes 31 and 16
* C Routes 27 and 31
D Routes 15 and 31

4 **In which direction does Route 16 go?**
J North and South
K Northeast and Southwest
L Northwest and Southeast
* M East and West

5 **About how far is it from Laramie to Woodside?**
A 18 miles
B 51 miles
* C 112 miles
D 310 miles

72 Answer rows A Ⓐ Ⓑ ● Ⓓ 1 Ⓐ Ⓑ Ⓒ ● 3 Ⓐ Ⓑ ● Ⓓ 5 Ⓐ Ⓑ ● Ⓓ
B ● Ⓚ Ⓛ Ⓜ 2 Ⓙ ● Ⓛ Ⓜ 4 Ⓙ Ⓚ Ⓛ ●

Check to see that the students have filled in the correct answer circle.

Say Now do Sample B. Read the question and look at the map again. What is the correct answer to the question? *(pause)* Answer J is correct. Mark circle J for Sample B in the answer rows at the bottom of the page. Make sure the circle is completely filled in with a dark mark.

Check to see that the students have filled in the correct answer circle.

Say When you work with maps or diagrams, the best strategy is to skim the reference source and then look at the questions. Think about what the question is asking and then refer back to the reference source each time you try to answer a question.

TIPS

Say Now let's look at the tip.

Have a volunteer read the tip aloud.

Practice

Say **Let's do the Practice items now. Skim the map or chart and then read the questions. Think about what the questions are asking and be sure to refer to the reference source to answer the questions. When you come to the GO sign at the bottom of the page, continue working. Work until you come to the STOP sign at the bottom of page 73. Remember to make sure that your answer circles are completely filled in with dark marks. Completely erase any marks for answers that you change. Any questions? Start working now.**

Allow time for the students to mark their answers.

Say **It's time to stop. You have finished Lesson 13b.**

Review the answers with the students. If any questions caused particular difficulty, work through each of the answer choices.

Have the students indicate completion of the lesson by entering their score for this activity on the progress chart at the beginning of the book.

Lesson 13b **Maps and Diagrams**

Directions: For a school project, Kara compared some amusement parks in her area. Use the chart she made to answer questions 6–12.

Amusement Park	Entrance Fee	Hours	Number of Rides	Distance from Home (in miles)	Special Shows
Ride On	$10 or less	9:00 A.M.-9:00 P.M.	32	38	Yes
Carousel	$10-$20	8:00 A.M.-10:00 P.M.	29	94	Yes
All's Fair	$10 or less	9:00 A.M.-9:00 P.M.	23	17	No
Great Fun	$20 or more	24 hours	48	12	No
Park USA	$10-$20	9:00 A.M.-5:00 P.M.	36	47	Yes
Four Flags	$10-$20	8:00 A.M.-9:00 P.M.	27	41	No
Rides, Inc.	$20 or more	noon-midnight	53	26	Yes
Super's	$10 or less	24 hours	18	32	No

Note: Entrance fee does NOT include the price of rides. The cost of a ride is from $1 to $5. Discounts are available for multiple-ride tickets.

6 **What is the same about both 24-hour parks?**
J Entrance Fee
K Number of Rides
L Distance from Home
* M No Special Shows

7 **Which park is the least expensive and nearest to home?**
A Ride On
B Carousel
* C All's Fair
D Great Fun

8 **Which park is open the shortest time?**
J Four Flags
* K Park USA
L Rides, Inc.
M All's Fair

9 **Great Fun and Rides, Inc. probably have higher entrance fees than the other parks because**
A they serve free refreshments.
B they are closer to home.
* C they offer more rides.
D they put on better shows.

10 **If Shania wants to go to a park with special shows but her parents are only willing to drive 30 miles, which park will they go to?**
J Park USA
* K Rides, Inc.
L Four Flags
M All's Fair

11 **The Anderson family went to a park after school. They stayed there for five hours and then came home. Which park did they NOT go to?**
A Great Fun
B Rides, Inc.
C Carousel
* D Park USA

12 **Which of these parks might have an entrance fee of $12?**
* J Park USA
K All's Fair
L Super's
M Rides, Inc.

Answer rows 6 Ⓙ Ⓚ Ⓛ ● 7 Ⓐ Ⓑ ● Ⓓ 8 Ⓙ ● Ⓛ Ⓜ 9 Ⓐ Ⓑ ● Ⓓ 10 Ⓙ ● Ⓛ Ⓜ 11 Ⓐ Ⓑ Ⓒ ● 12 ● Ⓚ Ⓛ Ⓜ

Lesson 14a Reference Materials

Focus

Reference Skill
- using a table of contents

Test-taking Skills
- working methodically
- taking the best guess when unsure of the answer
- referring to a reference source

Sample A

Say **Turn to Lesson 14a on page 74. In this lesson you will show how well you can use a table of contents. Read the directions at the top of the page to yourself.**

Allow time for the students to read the directions.

Say **Look at the table of contents for Sample A. Now look at the question. Which answer is correct?** *(pause)* **Yes, answer D is correct because this page is where the chapter about North America begins. Mark circle D for Sample A in the answer rows at the bottom of the page. Make sure the circle is completely filled in. Press your pencil firmly so that your mark comes out dark.**

Check to see that the students have filled in the correct answer circle.

TIPS

Say **Now let's look at the tips.**

Have a volunteer read the tips aloud.

Say **It is important that you read the directions for each part of this lesson. Be sure to refer to the table of contents to answer the questions, and if you are not sure which answer is correct, take your best guess. It is better to guess than to leave an item blank.**

Maps, Diagrams, and Reference Materials

Lesson 14a **Reference Materials**

Directions: Read the directions for each section. Choose the best answer.

Sample A

The Ancient World
Contents

Chapter		Page
1	Africa	1
2	Asia	23
3	Australia	47
4	Europe	65
5	North America	87
6	South America	103

Where should you begin reading to find out about the Cliff Dwellings found in the American Southwest?

A Page 1
B Page 47
C Page 65
* D Page 87

- **Think about the directions before you choose an answer.**
- **Take the best guess when you are unsure of the answer.**

Directions: Use this table of contents to answer questions 1–6.

Roadside Geology
Contents

Chapter		Page
1	The Language of Geology	1
2	Types of Rocks	7
3	Color Clues	11
4	Forces That Shape the Earth	15
5	Timeline of U.S. Geology	23
6	Southeast U.S. Region	29
7	Central U.S. Region	41
8	Northern Rockies U.S. Region	53
9	Far West U.S. Region	65
10	Southwest U.S. Region	71
11	Northeast U.S. Region	85

1 Where should you begin reading to learn about the three major categories into which rocks fall?

* A Page 7
B Page 11
C Page 15
D Page 41

2 Janelle found a rock that was a strange color yellow. Where should she begin reading to learn about this rock?

J Page 1
K Page 7
* L Page 11
M Page 41

GO

74 Answer rows A Ⓐ Ⓑ Ⓒ ● 1 ● Ⓑ Ⓒ Ⓓ 2 Ⓙ Ⓚ ● Ⓜ

Practice

Say Let's do the Practice items now. Read the questions and use the table of contents to find the answer. When you come to the GO sign at the bottom of the page, continue working. Work until you come to the STOP sign at the bottom of page 75. Remember to make sure that your answer circles are completely filled in with dark marks. Completely erase any marks for answers that you change. Any questions? Start working now.

Allow time for the students to mark their answers.

Say It's time to stop. You have finished Lesson 14a.

Review the answers with the students. If any questions caused particular difficulty, work through each of the answer choices.

Have the students indicate completion of the lesson by entering their score for this activity on the progress chart at the beginning of the book.

Lesson 14a **Reference Materials**

3 **Which chapter would tell about the deserts of the Southwest part of the United States?**
A Chapter 6
B Chapter 7
C Chapter 8
* D Chapter 10

4 **Which chapter should you use to look up the term *tectonic*?**
* J Chapter 1
K Chapter 2
L Chapter 3
M Chapter 4

5 **What would chapter 4 tell you most about?**
A Where the oldest mountains are
B Why prairies have few trees
* C How erosion creates canyons
D Which state has the longest coastline

6 **What chapter would tell you when the Sierra Nevada mountains were formed?**
J Chapter 7
* K Chapter 5
L Chapter 9
M Chapter 11

Answer rows 3 Ⓐ Ⓑ Ⓒ ● 4 ● Ⓚ Ⓛ Ⓜ 5 Ⓐ Ⓑ ● Ⓓ 6 Ⓙ ● Ⓛ Ⓜ 75

Lesson 14b Reference Materials

Focus

Reference Skill
- alphabetizing words

Test-taking Skills
- working methodically
- skimming a reference source
- referring to a reference source

Maps, Diagrams, and Reference Materials

Lesson 14b **Reference Materials**

Directions: Choose the word or name that would appear first if the four words or names were arranged in alphabetical order.

Sample A
A register
B regular
C region
* D regain

Sample B
J monster
* K monkey
L monthly
M monsoon

- **Don't forget; alphabetical order involves more than just the first letter.**

1
* A Landis, Abbey
B Landis, Arthur
C Landis, Abraham
D Landis, Adona

2
J standard
K star
* L stain
M standing

3
A hatching
* B hatchback
C hatches
D hatched

4
J Fayetteville, New York
K Fayetteville, North Carolina
* L Fayetteville, Arkansas
M Fayetteville, Pennsylvania

STOP

76 Answer rows A Ⓐ Ⓑ Ⓒ ● 1 ● Ⓑ Ⓒ Ⓓ 3 Ⓐ ● Ⓒ Ⓓ
B Ⓙ ● Ⓛ Ⓜ 2 Ⓙ Ⓚ ● Ⓜ 4 Ⓙ Ⓚ ● Ⓜ

Sample A

Say **Turn to Lesson 14b on page 76. In this lesson you will show how well you can alphabetize words. Read the directions at the top of the page to yourself.**

Allow time for the students to read the directions.

Say **Look at the four words for Sample A. If you put the words in alphabetical order, which one would come first?** *(pause)* **Yes, answer D, *regain*, would come first in alphabetical order. Mark circle D for Sample A in the answer rows at the bottom of the page. Make sure the circle is completely filled in. Press your pencil firmly so that your mark comes out dark.**

Check to see that the students have filled in the correct answer circle.

Say **Now do Sample B. If you put the words in alphabetical order, which one would come first?** *(pause)* **Yes, answer K, *monkey*, would come first in alphabetical order. Mark circle K for Sample B in the answer rows at the bottom of the page. Make sure the circle is completely filled in. Press your pencil firmly so that your mark comes out dark.**

Check to see that the students have filled in the correct answer circle.

Say **Now let's look at the tip.**

Have a volunteer read the tip aloud.

Say **Alphabetical order involves more than just the first letter. When the answers all begin with the same first letter, look at the second letter, then the third, and so on. For names, you should alphabetize by last name and then by first name.**

Practice

Say **Let's do the Practice items now. They all involve alphabetizing. Work until you come to the STOP sign at the bottom of the page. Remember to make sure that your answer circles are completely filled in with dark marks. Completely erase any marks for answers that you change. Any questions? Start working now.**

Allow time for the students to mark their answers.

Say **It's time to stop. You have finished Lesson 14b.**

Review the answers with the students. If any questions caused particular difficulty, work through each of the answer choices.

Have the students indicate completion of the lesson by entering their score for this activity on the progress chart at the beginning of the book.

Maps, Diagrams, and Reference Materials

Lesson 14b **Reference Materials**

Directions: Choose the word or name that would appear first if the four words or names were arranged in alphabetical order.

Sample A
- A register
- B regular
- C region
- * D regain

Sample B
- J monster
- * K monkey
- L monthly
- M monsoon

- **Don't forget; alphabetical order involves more than just the first letter.**

1
- * A Landis, Abbey
- B Landis, Arthur
- C Landis, Abraham
- D Landis, Adona

2
- J standard
- K star
- * L stain
- M standing

3
- A hatching
- * B hatchback
- C hatches
- D hatched

4
- J Fayetteville, New York
- K Fayetteville, North Carolina
- * L Fayetteville, Arkansas
- M Fayetteville, Pennsylvania

STOP

76 Answer rows A Ⓐ Ⓑ Ⓒ ● 1 ● Ⓑ Ⓒ Ⓓ 3 Ⓐ ● Ⓒ Ⓓ
B Ⓙ ● Ⓛ Ⓜ 2 Ⓙ Ⓚ ● Ⓜ 4 Ⓙ Ⓚ ● Ⓜ

Lesson 15a Reference Materials

Focus

Reference Skills
- using an encyclopedia
- using a catalog card
- differentiating among reference sources

Test-taking Skills
- working methodically
- skimming a reference source
- referring to a reference source
- evaluating answer choices

Maps, Diagrams, and Reference Materials

Lesson 15a **Reference Materials**

Directions: Read the directions for each section. Choose the best answer.

Sample A Which volume would tell you most about how fish breathe, how they swim, and what they eat?
- A Volume 1
- B Volume 2
- * C Volume 3
- D Volume 8

Sample B Which of these would you find in a library's periodicals section?
- * J Magazines
- K Almanacs
- L Biographies
- M Dictionaries

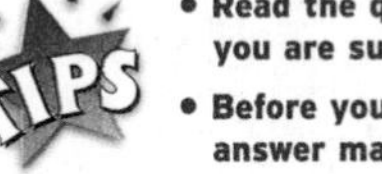

- Read the question carefully. Be sure you understand what you are supposed to do.
- Before you mark your answer, ask yourself: "Does this answer make sense?"

Directions: Use this encyclopedia set to do questions 1–3.

1 Which volume would tell you most about the deserts, jungles, and mountain ranges in Africa?
- * A Volume 1
- B Volume 2
- C Volume 3
- D Volume 4

2 Which volume would tell you most about the late president of Egypt, Anwar Sadat?
- J Volume 3
- K Volume 5
- L Volume 7
- * M Volume 8

3 Which volume would tell you most about the sixteenth century Spanish writer Miguel de Cervantes?
- A Volume 1
- * B Volume 2
- C Volume 5
- D Volume 8

4 Which of these would you find in the glossary of a biology book?
- J The page numbers for each chapter.
- K A list of books about plants and animals
- * L A definition of the word *protozoa*
- M A list of pages that tell about leaves

GO

Answer rows A Ⓐ Ⓑ ● Ⓓ 1 ● Ⓑ Ⓒ Ⓓ 3 Ⓐ ● Ⓒ Ⓓ
B ● Ⓚ Ⓛ Ⓜ 2 Ⓙ Ⓚ Ⓛ ● 4 Ⓙ Ⓚ ● Ⓜ

77

Samples A and B

Say **Turn to Lesson 15a on page 77. In this lesson you will show how well you understand how to use different reference sources. Read the directions at the top of the page to yourself.**

Allow time for the students to read the directions.

Say **Look at the encyclopedia set below the tips. Now read the question for Sample A. Which answer is correct?** *(pause)* **Answer C is correct because information about *fish* would be found in Volume 3. Mark circle C for Sample A in the answer rows at the bottom of the page. Make sure the circle is completely filled in. Press your pencil firmly so that your mark comes out dark.**

Check to see that the students have filled in the correct answer circle. Discuss why "fish" is the correct topic and Volume 3 is the right answer.

Say **Now do Sample B. Read the question and decide which answer is correct.** *(pause)* **Answer J is correct because a *magazine* is a periodical. Mark circle J for Sample B in the answer rows at the bottom of the page. Make sure the circle is completely filled in. Press your pencil firmly so that your mark comes out dark.**

Check to see that the students have filled in the correct answer circle. Explain what a periodical is and why the other answer choices are wrong.

Say **Now let's look at the tips.**

Have a volunteer read the tips aloud.

Say **Be sure you understand what a question is asking before you choose an answer. If you hurry when you read a question, you may misunderstand it, and this will cause you to choose the wrong answer. You should also evaluate your answer to be sure it makes sense when compared with the reference source.**

Practice

Say **Let's do the Practice items now. There are different kinds of items in this lesson, so be sure to read the directions for each section. Think about what the questions are asking, and if there is a reference source, be sure to refer back to it to find the answers. When you come to a GO sign at the bottom of a page, turn the page and continue working. Work until you come to the STOP sign at the bottom of page 80. Remember to make sure that your answer circles are completely filled in with dark marks. Completely erase any marks for answers that you change. Any questions? Start working now.**

Allow time for the students to mark their answers.

Directions: Use this information from a library catalog system to answer questions 5–8.

Thomas, Robin
570.3 The greatest inventor of all time: the
T784 biography of Leonardo da Vinci / by
Robin Thomas; illustrated by Rich Geary.
–New York: Jackson-Fife, 1978.
72 p.: ill.; 26 cm.
1. Inventors. 2. Biography. 3. da Vinci.
I. Geary, Richard M.
II. Title

5 **If you wanted to find other books on this topic at the library, which of these should you use?**
A "The Greatest Inventor" as a topic
B "Jackson-Fife" as an author
C "Thomas, Robin" as an author.
* D "da Vinci, Leonardo" as a topic

6 **What kind of catalog entry is this?**
J A subject listing
* K An author listing
L A publisher listing
M A title listing

7 **Into which category would this book fall?**
* A Biography
B Reference
C Fiction
D Periodicals

8 **What is the importance of 1978 in this card catalog?**
J It is the year da Vinci was born.
K It is the year Robin Thomas began the book.
* L It is the year the book was published.
M It is the number of pages in the book.

 Answer rows 5 Ⓐ Ⓑ Ⓒ ● 6 Ⓙ ● Ⓛ Ⓜ 7 ● Ⓑ Ⓒ Ⓓ 8 Ⓙ Ⓚ ● Ⓜ

Lesson 15a **Reference Materials**

Directions: Questions 9–14 are about using library materials. Choose the best answer to each question.

9 Which of these would you find in the table of contents of a book about weather?

A A list of other helpful or related books about weather.
B A list of weather-related words and their definitions.
* C A list of chapters about weather and their page numbers.
D A list of the people who worked together on the weather book.

10 Which of these would contain information about when to expect the next full moon?

* J An almanac
K An atlas
L A dictionary
M An encyclopedia

11 Which of these would tell you the meaning of the word arboretum?

A A language book
* B A dictionary
C An encyclopedia
D An almanac

12 Which of these would tell you when a plant called "kudzu" was introduced to America?

J A dictionary
K An almanac
L An atlas
* M An encyclopedia

13 Which of these would tell you which states have cities that are named "Anderson"?

A An encyclopedia
* B An atlas
C A dictionary
D A language book

14 Which of these magazines would most likely have a story about an expedition to an undeveloped island?

J *U.S. News Today*
K *Fantasy and Science Fiction*
* L *Geographic Traveler*
M *Funny Times*

Answer rows 

Say It's time to stop. You have finished Lesson 15a.

Review the answers with the students. If any questions caused particular difficulty, work through each of the answer choices.

Have the students indicate completion of the lesson by entering their score for this activity on the progress chart at the beginning of the book.

Lesson 15a **Reference Materials**

Directions: Use this information from a library catalog system to answer questions 15–18.

Birds, North American

526 Henderson, Don
H285 A Guide to North American Birds
/ by Don Henderson;
photos by Maryann Barr.
–Chicago, IL: Natural Things Press, 1994
512 p.: photos; 19 cm.

1. Birds, North American.
2. Birds.
3. Wildlife. I. Barr, Maryann II. Title.

15 What is the title of this book?
* A A Guide to North American Birds
B Birds, North American
C Natural Things
D North American Birds

16 Who is Don Henderson?
J The publisher of the book
K The photographer of the book
* L The author of the book
M The editor of the book

17 In which section of the card catalog would you find this card?
A Author
B Title
* C Subject
D Reference

18 Which of these should you use to find other books in the library on this topic?
J "A Guide" as a title
K "Maryann Barr" as an author
L "Natural Things Press" as a publisher
* M "North American Birds" as a subject

Directions: Question 19–22 are about using library materials. Choose the best answer to each question.

19 Which of these would most likely be discussed in a history book?
A The reasons why plants need sunlight and water
* B The purchase of the Louisiana Territories from France in 1803
C How to register to vote in different states
D Restoring a house that was built during the Civil War

20 Which of these would tell you how to pronounce the word abeyance?
J A thesaurus
K An atlas
L An encyclopedia
* M A dictionary

21 Which of these magazines would be most likely to have a story about deserts in Asia?
A *Business Week*
B *Readers Digest*
* C *National Geographic*
D *Seventeen*

22 In which section of the library would you find a horror story?
* J Fiction
K Nonfiction
L Periodicals
M Reference

80 Answer rows 15● Ⓑ Ⓒ Ⓓ 17 Ⓐ Ⓑ ● Ⓓ 19 Ⓐ ● Ⓒ Ⓓ 21 Ⓐ Ⓑ ● Ⓓ
16 Ⓙ Ⓚ ● Ⓜ 18 Ⓙ Ⓚ Ⓛ ● 20 Ⓙ Ⓚ Ⓛ ● 22● Ⓚ Ⓛ Ⓜ

Lesson 15b Reference Materials

Focus

Reference Skill
- using a dictionary

Test-taking Skills
- working methodically
- comparing answer choices
- skimming a reference source
- referring to a reference source

Maps, Diagrams, and Reference Materials

Lesson 15b **Reference Materials**

Directions: Read the directions for each section. Choose the best answer.

Sample A **Choose the word that would appear first if the four words were arranged in alphabetical order.**

A bench
* B bask
C breathe
D board

Sample B **Which of these would tell you about the history of Colorado?**

J A dictionary
K An almanac
L An atlas
* M An encyclopedia

- **If you aren't sure which answer is correct, take your best guess.**
- **Skip difficult items and come back to them later.**

Directions: For questions 1–5, choose the word or name that would appear first if the four words or names were arranged in alphabetical order.

1 A acquire
B active
* C acid
D actress

2 J dismal
K dissolve
L display
* M disk

3 A brood
* B broil
C brow
D brown

4 J Carbo, Georgia
K Carter, Illinois
* L Camhi, Ohio
M Cardin, California

5 A Rush, Brenda
B Rush, Bob
C Rush, Bill
* D Rush, Beth

GO

Answer rows A Ⓐ●ⒸⒹ 1 ⒶⒷ●Ⓓ 3 Ⓐ●ⒸⒹ 5 ⒶⒷⒸ●
B ⒿⓀⓁ● 2 ⒿⓀⓁ● 4 ⒿⓀ●Ⓜ

81

Samples A and B

Say **Turn to Lesson 15b on page 81. In this lesson you will practice more reference skills. Read the directions at the top of the page to yourself.**

Allow time for the students to read the directions.

Say **Look at the four words for Sample A. If you put the words in alphabetical order, which one would come first?** *(pause)* **Yes, answer B, *bask*, would come first in alphabetical order. Mark circle B for Sample A in the answer rows at the bottom of the page. Make sure the circle is completely filled in. Press your pencil firmly so that your mark comes out dark.**

Check to see that the students have filled in the correct answer circle.

Say **Now do Sample B. Read the question and decide which answer is correct.** *(pause)* **Answer M is correct because an *encyclopedia* would tell you most about the history of Colorado. Mark circle M for Sample B in the answer rows at the bottom of the page. Make sure the circle is completely filled in. Press your pencil firmly so that your mark comes out dark.**

Check to see that the students have filled in the correct answer circle. If necessary, discuss the kind of information each of the answer choices would contain.

TIPS

Say **Now let's look at the tips.**

Have a volunteer read the tips aloud.

Say **Don't be afraid to guess if you are not sure which answer is correct. And if a question seems difficult, skip it and come back to the question later. This will give you a chance to try all of the questions.**

Remind the students how important it is to try all the questions. If they spend too much time on a difficult question, they won't have time to do other questions that might be easier.

Practice

Say Let's do the Practice items now. Read the questions and answer choices carefully, and be sure to use the reference source to find the answers. When you come to the GO sign at the bottom of the page, turn the page and continue working. Work until you come to the STOP sign at the bottom of page 83. Remember to make sure that your answer circles are completely filled in with dark marks. Completely erase any marks for answers that you change. Any questions? Start working now.

Allow time for the students to mark their answers.

Directions: Use this encyclopedia set to answer questions 6–10.

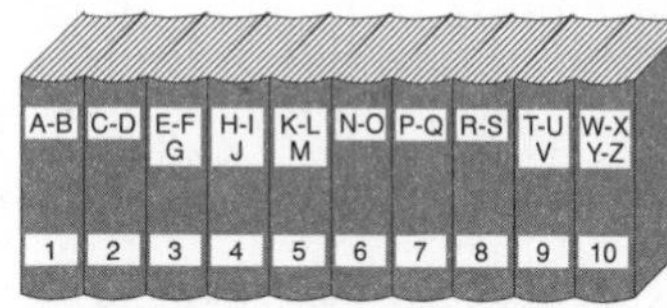

6 Which volume would tell you if zebra are found on any continents other than Africa?
J Volume 1
K Volume 2
L Volume 6
* M Volume 10

7 Which volume would tell you what language is spoken in Zimbabwe, a country in the southern part of Africa?
A Volume 1
B Volume 2
C Volume 8
* D Volume 10

8 Which volume would tell you most about John James Audubon, the famous naturalist who lived more than a century ago?
* J Volume 1
K Volume 2
L Volume 3
M Volume 5

9 Which volume would tell you most about Marie Curie, a woman scientist who won the Nobel Prize twice?
* A Volume 2
B Volume 5
C Volume 8
D Volume 10

10 Which volume would tell you most about the grackle, an American bird that is related to crows and blackbirds?
J Volume 1
K Volume 2
* L Volume 3
M Volume 10

GO

82 Answer rows 6 Ⓙ Ⓚ Ⓛ ● 7 Ⓐ Ⓑ Ⓒ ● 8 ● Ⓚ Ⓛ Ⓜ 9 ● Ⓑ Ⓒ Ⓓ 10 Ⓙ Ⓚ ● Ⓜ

Say **It's time to stop. You have finished Lesson 15b.**

Review the answers with the students. If any questions caused particular difficulty, work through each of the answer choices.

Have the students indicate completion of the lesson by entering their score for this activity on the progress chart at the beginning of the book.

Lesson 15b **Reference Materials**

Directions: Use this dictionary page to answer questions 11–16.

dormant • dote

dor•mant (**dôr**′ ment) *adj.* 1. lying asleep 2. inactive

dor•mer (**dôr**′ mer) *n.* a vertical window built from a sloping roof

dor•mitory (**dôr**′ mĭ tōr′ ē) *n., pl.* –ries. 1. residence hall, as at a college 2. room containing a number of beds and serving as community sleeping quarters

dor•mouse (**dôr**′ mous′) *n., pl.* –mice. small, furry-tailed rodent resembling a small squirrel

dor•sal (**dôr**′ sel) *adj.* pertaining to the back

dor•y (**dōr**′ ē) *n., pl.* –ries. 1. boat with a high bow and a narrow, flat bottom 2. fish in the family Zeidae

dos•si er (**dŏs**′ ē ā′) *n.* group of papers or documents on the same subject

dot (dŏt) *n.* small spot or speck. –*v.* to make a small mark

dote (dōt) *v.* to give excessive love or affection

1. Pronunciation Guide:

ă sat	ŏ lot	ə represents
ā day	ō so	a in alone
ä calm	ŏŏ look	e in open
â pare	ōō root	i in easily
ĕ let	ôr or	o in gallop
ē me	ŭ cut	u in circus
ĭ sit	û purr	
ī lie		

2. Abbreviations: *n.*, noun; *v.*, verb; *adj.*, adjective; *pl.*, plural

11 **What is the plural of the word *dory*?**
A dorys
B doryes
C doreys
* D dories

12 **How many syllables are in the word *dossier*?**
J One
K Two
* L Three
M Four

13 **The "o" in *dote* sounds most like the "o" in**
* A so.
B lot.
C look.
D root.

14 **Which word fits best in the sentence "The volcano on the island has been ________ for more than a century."**
J dormer
* K dormant
L dossier
M dorsal

15 **A dorsal fin would be found on a fish's**
A head.
* B back.
C side.
D tail.

16 **To make a dormer, you would probably need a**
J plumber.
K electrician.
* L carpenter.
M chef.

Answer rows 11 Ⓐ Ⓑ Ⓒ ● 13 ● Ⓑ Ⓒ Ⓓ 15 Ⓐ ● Ⓒ Ⓓ
12 Ⓙ Ⓚ ● Ⓜ 14 Ⓙ ● Ⓛ Ⓜ 16 Ⓙ Ⓚ ● Ⓜ

83

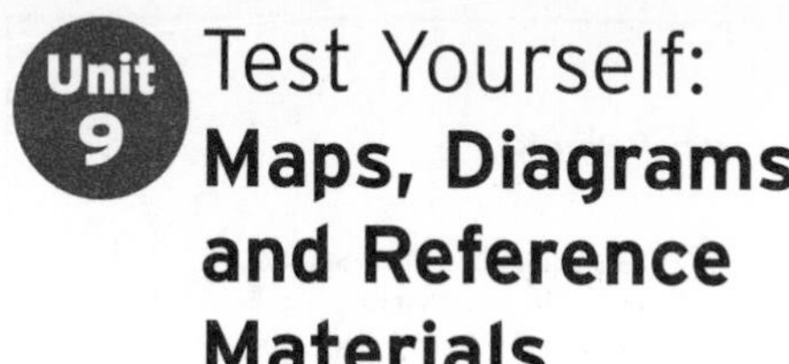

Test Yourself: Maps, Diagrams and Reference Materials

Focus

Reference Skills
- alphabetizing words or names
- differentiating among reference sources
- using a chart
- using a map or diagram
- using an encyclopedia
- using a dictionary
- using a catalog card

Test-taking Skills
- managing time effectively
- working methodically
- referring to a reference source
- skimming a reference source
- taking the best guess when unsure of the answer
- evaluating answer choices
- comparing answer choices

Test Yourself: Maps, Diagrams, and Reference Materials

Directions: Read the directions for each section. Choose the best answer.

Sample A
A
* B beach
C stand
D lose

A curry

Sample B Which of these would tell you the principal highways in Nebraska?
J A dictionary
K An almanac
L An encyclopedia
* M An atlas

Directions: Lynn made this chart to compare activities at some different swimming pools. Use the chart to answer questions 1–7.

	Adult Laps	Lifeguard Classes	Open Swimming	Pool Party	Preschool Paddle	Swim Lessons	Swim Team	Water Aerobics
Alameda	X	X		X		X		X
Dishman	X		X	X		X		X
Fulton	X	X	X	X				X
Hillside		X	X	X	X	X	X	
Hosford	X		X	X	X	X	X	X
Jackson	X	X		X	X	X		X
Laurelhurst	X		X	X	X			X
Montavilla		X	X	X	X		X	X
Oliver		X		X	X	X		X

GO

84 Answer rows A Ⓐ ● Ⓒ Ⓓ B Ⓙ Ⓚ Ⓛ ●

This lesson simulates an actual test-taking experience. Therefore it is recommended that the directions be read verbatim and that the suggested procedures and time allowances be followed.

Directions

Administration Time: approximately 35 minutes

Say **Turn to the Test Yourself lesson on page 84.**

Point out to the students that this Test Yourself lesson is timed like a real test, but that they will score it themselves to see how well they are doing. Remind the students to work quickly and not to spend too much time on any one item. Encourage them to compare their answers with the reference material and to take the best guess when they are unsure of the answer.

Say **This lesson will check how well you learned the reference skills you practiced in other lessons. Remember to make sure that the circles for your answer choices are completely filled in. Press your pencil firmly so that your marks come out dark. Completely erase any answers that you change. Do not write anything except your answer choices in your books.**

Look at the words for Sample A. If you put the words in alphabetical order, which one would come first? Mark the circle for your answer.

Allow time for the students to mark their answers.

Say **The circle for answer B should have been filled in. If you chose another answer, erase yours and fill in circle B now.**

Check to see that the students have marked the correct answer circle.

Say **Now do Sample B. Read the question and decide which answer is correct.**

Allow time for the students to mark their answers.

Say **The circle for answer M should have been filled in. If you chose another answer, erase yours and fill in circle M now.**

Check to see that the students have marked the correct answer circle.

Say **Now you will do more items. Do not spend too much time on any one question and pay attention to the directions for each section of the lesson. If you are not sure of an answer, take your best guess and mark the circle for the answer you think might be right. When you come to the GO sign at the bottom of a page, turn the page and continue working. Work until you come to the STOP sign at the bottom of page 90. When you have finished, you can check over your answers to this lesson. Then wait for the rest of the group to finish. Do you have any questions? You will have 30 minutes. Begin working now.**

Allow 30 minutes.

Test Yourself: Maps, Diagrams, and Reference Materials

1 **At which pool might you learn about water safety?**
A Dishman
B Hosford
C Laurelhurst
* D Hillside

2 **Which pool offers programs most similar to Dishman's programs?**
J Fulton
K Hillside
* L Hosford
M Oliver

3 **If you wanted to go to a pool that had programs for both teenagers and preschoolers, to which of these would you go?**
A Alameda
B Dishman
C Fulton
* D Hillside

4 **At which pool could you go just to cool off and have fun?**
J Oliver
* K Dishman
L Jackson
M Alameda

5 **Which of these could people do at Montavilla Pool that they could not do at Oliver Pool?**
A Do water aerobics
B Take a swimming lesson
* C Join a swim team
D Lifeguard classes

6 **Which of these pools offers a program that would probably let you compete with people at other pools?**
J Alameda
K Oliver
* L Hillside
M Jackson

7 **Which program is offered at the greatest number of pools?**
A Swim team
B Swim lessons
C Lifeguard classes
* D Pool Party

Answer rows 1 Ⓐ Ⓑ Ⓒ ● 3 Ⓐ Ⓑ Ⓒ ● 5 Ⓐ Ⓑ ● Ⓓ 7 Ⓐ Ⓑ Ⓒ ●
2 Ⓙ Ⓚ ● Ⓜ 4 Ⓙ ● Ⓛ Ⓜ 6 Ⓙ Ⓚ ● Ⓜ

Test Yourself: Maps, Diagrams, and Reference Materials

Directions: The map below shows part of a make-believe town. Use the map to do questions 8–14.

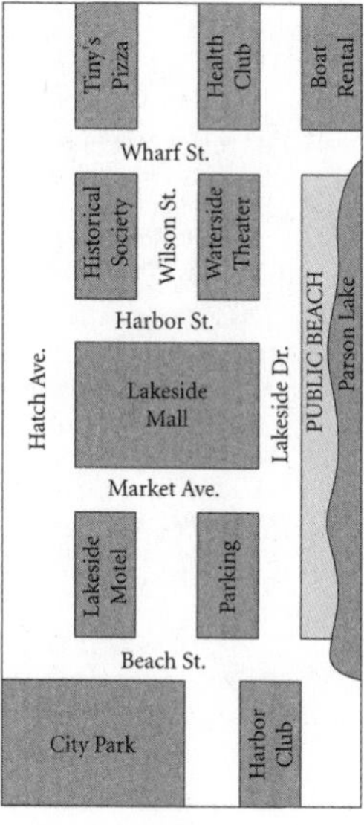

8 The main entrance to the Historical Society is on the east side of the building. What street is it on?

* J Wilson Street
K Harbor Street
L Hatch Avenue
M Wharf Street

9 Allen was at the Lakeside Motel. He walked two blocks east and three blocks north. Where was he going?

A Lakeside Mall
B Harbor Club
C City Park
* D Boat Rental

10 Which of these is farthest from City Park?

* J Tiny's Pizza
K Waterside Theater
L Lakeside Mall
M Parking

11 Ms. Pardy is at the Hatch Ave. entrance to the mall. Which directions best explain how she should walk to the Health Club?

A South for two blocks, east for one block
* B North for one block, east for two blocks.
C South for one block, west for two blocks
D West for two blocks, north for three blocks

GO

86 Answer rows 8 ● Ⓚ Ⓛ Ⓜ 9 Ⓐ Ⓑ Ⓒ ● 10 ● Ⓚ Ⓛ Ⓜ 11 Ⓐ ● Ⓒ Ⓓ

Unit 9 Test Yourself: Maps, Diagrams, and Reference Materials

12 **About how many blocks long is the public beach?**
- J One
- * K Three
- L Five
- M Six

13 **What is in the southeast corner of the map?**
- A City Park
- * B Harbor Club
- C Boat Rental
- D Tiny's Pizza

14 **If you were at the Lakeside Mall, which direction would the City Park be?**
- J North
- * K South
- L East
- M West

Directions: For questions 15–19, choose the word or name that comes first in alphabetical order.

15
- A dense
- B desk
- * C deer
- D dew

16
- J capital
- K capon
- * L capable
- M captain

17
- A Towson, John
- * B Towson, Joanne
- C Towson, José
- D Towson, Jonathan

18
- J street
- K stretch
- L stress
- * M streak

19
- * A Madison, Georgia
- B Madison, Pennsylvania
- C Madison, Kansas
- D Madison, New Hampshire

Answer rows 12  14 16 18
13 15 17 19

87

Test Yourself: Maps, Diagrams, and Reference Materials

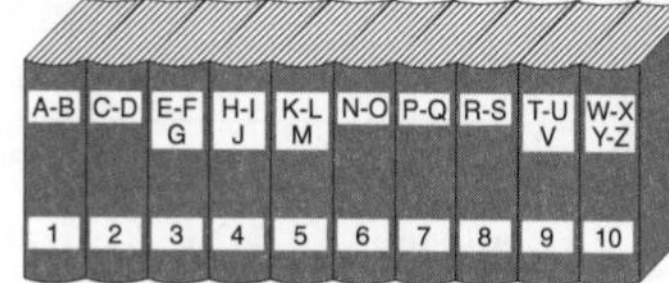

Directions: Use this encyclopedia set to do questions 20–24.

20 **Which volume would tell you where weasels are found in the wild and their living habits?**

J Volume 1
K Volume 4
L Volume 5
* M Volume 10

21 **Which volume would tell you about Queen Elizabeth I, the daughter of Henry VIII?**

A Volume 2
* B Volume 3
C Volume 4
D Volume 7

22 **Which volume would tell you most about Jupiter, the largest planet in our solar system?**

J Volume 2
* K Volume 4
L Volume 7
M Volume 8

23 **Which volume would tell you most about dynamite, the explosive which was invented by Alfred Nobel?**

* A Volume 2
B Volume 3
C Volume 6
D Volume 10

24 **Which volume would tell you most about passenger pigeons, which became extinct in the early part of the twentieth century?**

J Volume 2
K Volume 3
* L Volume 7
M Volume 9

GO

 Answer rows 20 Ⓙ Ⓚ Ⓛ ● 21 Ⓐ ● Ⓒ Ⓓ 22 Ⓙ ● Ⓛ Ⓜ 23 ● Ⓑ Ⓒ Ⓓ 24 Ⓙ Ⓚ ● Ⓜ

Unit 9 Test Yourself: Maps, Diagrams, and Reference Materials

Directions: Use this dictionary page to answer questions 25–30.

accolade • atmosphere

ac•co•lade (ăc′ ə lād′) *n.* 1. any award, honor, or notice 2. the ceremony of becoming a knight

af•fa•ble (ăf′ ə bəl) *adj.* easy to talk to

a•gil•i•ty (ə jĭl′ ĭ tē) *n.* the power of moving quickly and easily

ag•i•ta•tor (aj′ ĭ tā′ tər) *n.* a person who stirs up trouble

ail•ment (āl′ mənt) *n.* a physical disorder or illness

an•noy•ance (ə noi′ əns) *n.* a person or thing that annoys: Unwanted guests are an annoyance.

ap•a•thet•ic (ăp′ ə thĕt′ ĭk) *adj.* 1. having or showing little or no emotion 2. uninterested

ap•pli•cant (ăp′ lĭ kənt) *n.* a person who applies for something, like a job

ap•ti•tude (ăp′ tĭ to͞od′) *n.* the capability or ability to do something; talent

ar•id (ăr′ ĭd) *adj.* being without moisture; extremely dry

ar•ti•fice (är′ tə fĭs) *n.* a clever trick or craftiness

at•mos•phere (ăt′ mə sfîr′) *n.* 1. the gaseous envelope surrounding Earth 2. the mood or tone of an environment

25 Which of these is most likely to describe a person with a good sense of humor?
- A artificial
- * B affable
- C apathetic
- D arid

26 What word best completes the sentence "Doctors are pleased to have found a cure for the ________."
- J annoyance
- K accolade
- * L ailment
- M aptitude

27 In which sentence is the second meaning of the word *apathetic* used correctly?
- * A The clown tried his best, but the apathetic crowd took little notice.
- B Sally showed her brother she was apathetic by giving him a hug.
- C Yancy enjoyed apathetic games, like pretending to be someone else.
- D When the two-year-old child began to sob, it was an apathetic sight.

28 Which word would best describe what you receive when you accomplish something important?
- J aptitude
- K artifice
- L agility
- * M accolade

29 Which word would best describe a place in which very little rain falls?
- A accolade
- B agility
- * C arid
- D artifice

30 Which of these might be described with the word *atmosphere*?
- J An old pair of shoes
- K A new coat
- L An expensive car
- * M A nice restaurant

GO

Answer rows 25 Ⓐ ● Ⓒ Ⓓ 27 ● Ⓑ Ⓒ Ⓓ 29 Ⓐ Ⓑ ● Ⓓ
26 Ⓙ Ⓚ ● Ⓜ 28 Ⓙ Ⓚ Ⓛ ● 30 Ⓙ Ⓚ Ⓛ ●

89

Say **It's time to stop. You have finished the Test Yourself lesson. Check to see that you have completely filled in your answer circles with dark marks. Make sure that any marks for answers that you changed have been completely erased.**

Go over the lesson with the students. Ask them if they had enough time to finish the lesson. Did they remember to take their best guess when unsure of an answer? Did they refer to the reference sources to answer the questions?

Work through any questions that caused difficulty. If necessary, provide additional practice questions similar to the ones in this unit.

Have the students indicate completion of the lesson by entering their score for this activity on the progress chart at the beginning of the book.

Test Yourself: Maps, Diagrams, and Reference Materials

Directions: Use this information from a library catalog system to answer questions 31–34.

> Meyer, Carolyn
>
> 874.6 People Who Make Things: How
> ME42p American Craftspeople Live and Work / by Carolyn Meyer; illustrated by Annie Halfacre. –New York: McClelland & Stewart, 1975.
> 200 p.: ill.; 25 cm.
>
> 1. Handcraft. 2. Artisans.
> 3. Occupations. I Halfacre, Annabelle P. II. Title.

31 What kind of catalog entry is this?
A A subject listing
* B An author listing
C A title listing
D A publisher listing

32 Who are McClelland and Stewart?
J The people who wrote the book
K The artist who drew the pictures for the book
* L The company that published the book
M The people the book is about

33 What is the title of this book?
* A People Who Make Things: How American Craftspeople Live and Work
B People Who Make Things
C How American Craftspeople Live and Work
D American Craftspeople

34 Which of these should you use to find other books in the library on this topic?
J "People Who Make Things" as a title
K "McClelland" as an author
L "Meyer, Carolyn" as an author
* M "Craftspeople, American" as a subject

35 In which section of the library would you find a book about building a dog house?
A Biography
B Fiction
* C Nonfiction
D Periodicals

36 Which of these magazines would be most likely to have a story about the discovery of a new galaxy in space?
J *Reader's Digest*
K *Sports Illustrated*
L *Business Week*
* M *Scientific American*

37 In which section of the library would you find today's newspaper?
* A Periodicals
B Reference
C Fiction
D Nonfiction

38 Which of these would tell you the most important events that happened in the past year?
J An atlas
* K An almanac
L A dictionary
M A social studies book

90 Answer rows 31 Ⓐ ● Ⓒ Ⓓ 33 ● Ⓑ Ⓒ Ⓓ 35 Ⓐ Ⓑ ● Ⓓ 37 ● Ⓑ Ⓒ Ⓓ
32 Ⓙ Ⓚ ● Ⓜ 34 Ⓙ Ⓚ Ⓛ ● 36 Ⓙ Ⓚ Ⓛ ● 38 Ⓙ ● Ⓛ Ⓜ

Background

This unit contains three lessons that deal with science skills.

• **In Lessons 16a and 16b,** students answer questions about science. They refer to a passage, skim items, and skip items and return to them later. Students work methodically, compare questions and answer choices, and identify and use key words, numbers, and pictures.

• **In the Test Yourself lesson,** the science skills and test-taking skills introduced in Lessons 16a and 16b are reinforced and presented in a format that gives students the experience of taking an achievement test. Techniques for managing time effectively when taking a standardized test are reinforced.

Instructional **Objectives**

Lesson 16a **Science Skills** Lesson 16b **Science Skills**		Given a question about science, the student identifies which of four answer choices is correct.
	Test Yourself	Given questions similar to those in Lessons 16a and 16b, the student utilizes science skills and test-taking strategies on achievement test formats.

Lesson 16a Science Skills

Focus

Science Skills

- understanding the history and language of science
- understanding scientific instruments, measurement, and processes
- understanding plant and animal behaviors and characteristics
- differentiating the source of natural and manufactured products
- recognizing states, properties, and composition of matter
- identifying the best unit of measurement
- recalling characteristics of Earth and bodies in space
- recalling characteristics and functions of the human body
- using illustrations, charts, and graphs
- understanding gravity, inertia, and friction
- understanding sound

Test-taking Skills

- referring to a passage to answer a question
- skimming items
- skipping items and returning to them later

Science

Lesson 16a **Science Skills**

Directions: Read each question and the answer choices. Choose the best answer.

Sample A **An example of migration is**
A rabbits burrowing in loose soil.
B deer growing more fur in fall.
* C birds flying south in winter.
D fish swimming under the ice.

Sample B **Which of these is about a meter long?**
* J A large dog
K A small bird
L An insect
M An elephant

- **When a passage is part of a science test, be sure to read it before trying to answer the items.**
- **Don't be bothered if a page has many items. Skim the items on the page and do the ones you know first. Then go back and try the other items.**

1 **Most animals have developed features that help them survive. Which of the following would not be an adaptation for survival?**
A A giraffe's long neck
B A skunk's odor
C A turtle's shell
* D A horse's brown eyes

2 **All of these processes help form topsoil except**
J the decaying of trees.
* K the movement of oceans.
L the erosion of hills.
M the weathering of rocks.

GO

Answer rows A Ⓐ Ⓑ ● Ⓓ 1 Ⓐ Ⓑ Ⓒ ● B ● Ⓚ Ⓛ Ⓜ 2 Ⓙ ● Ⓛ Ⓜ

91

Samples A and B

Say **Turn to Lesson 16a on page 91. In this lesson you will answer questions about science. Read the directions at the top of the page to yourself.**

Allow time for the students to read the directions.

Say **Look at Sample A and read the question. Which answer is an example of migration?** *(pause)* **Answer C is correct because *birds flying south in winter* is an example of migration. Mark circle C for Sample A in the answer rows at the bottom of the page. Make sure the circle is completely filled in. Press your pencil firmly so that your mark comes out dark.**

Check to see that the students have filled in the correct answer circle.

Say **Move over to Sample B. Read the question and answer choices. What is the correct answer to the question?** *(pause)* **Answer J is correct because *a large dog* is about a meter long. Mark circle J for Sample B in the answer rows at the bottom of the page. Make sure the circle is completely filled in. Press your pencil firmly so that your mark comes out dark.**

Check to see that the students have filled in the correct answer circle. Review the answers to the sample items, if necessary.

★TIPS

Say Now let's look at the tips.

Have a volunteer read the tips aloud.

Say **Sometimes a short passage appears on a science test. One or more items ask about information in the passage. It is important that you read the passage before trying to answer the questions that are about it. And remember, you don't have to answer the items on a page in the order they appear. If there are many items on a page, skim them and answer the easiest ones first. You can go back later and try the other items.**

Lesson 16a **Science Skills**

3 Water is made of
* A hydrogen and oxygen.
B oxygen and carbon dioxide.
C hydrogen and carbon.
D carbon and oxygen.

4 When does an endangered animal become extinct?
J When there are only a few of the animals left
K When the only remaining animals are in captivity
* L When no more of the animals are alive
M When the animal lives only in a limited habitat

5 Adam weighed his cat and measured from her nose to the tip of her tail. Which of these would probably be his measurements?
* A 8 pounds, 2 feet
B 9 liters, 12 inches
C 8 kilograms, 2 meters
D 1 ton, 1 yard

6 When Earth is seen from outer space, it appears mostly blue. This is because much of Earth's surface is covered with
J polar ice caps.
K forests.
L grassy plains.
* M oceans.

7 The skeleton does all of the following except
A form the frame of the human body.
* B circulate nutrients around the body.
C give the body shape and support.
D protect the organs.

GO

92 **Answer rows** 3 ● B C D 4 J K ● M 5 ● B C D 6 J K L ● 7 A ● C D

Practice

Say **Let's do the Practice items now. Skim the items on a page and do the easiest ones first. Be sure to read the passage that relates to some items. When you come to the GO sign at the bottom of a page, turn the page and continue working. Work until you come to the STOP sign at the bottom of page 96. Remember to make sure that your answer circles are completely filled in with dark marks. Completely erase any marks for answers that you change. Any questions? Start working now.**

Allow time for the students to mark their answers.

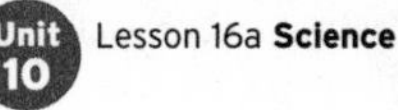

Lesson 16a **Science Skills**

Directions: Use the information below to answer questions 8–10.

Roberto laid out three cards with the numbers 1, 2, and 3 on them. He asked fifteen people to choose a card. While they chose, he played the song "You are Number One" in the background. Eight people selected number 1, three chose number 2, and four chose number 3.

8 What was Roberto trying to find out?

J What numbers are the most popular
K If older or younger people prefer number 1
* L If song lyrics influence a person's number choice
M How people decide on their favorite song or number

9 Which of these conclusions is most reasonable based on Roberto's results?

A A song about numbers can control a person's mind.
* B Song lyrics may influence a person's behavior.
C People are most likely to choose the number 1.
D Most people who like music like the number 1.

10 If Roberto tries this experiment again, how can he confirm his results?

J Use lots of different numbers.
K Play the music softly, so people aren't distracted when they are choosing.
L Limit the ages of the people who are choosing numbers.
* M Try the experiment with and without music to see if the results are different.

Answer rows 8 Ⓙ Ⓚ ● Ⓜ 9 Ⓐ ● Ⓒ Ⓓ 10 Ⓙ Ⓚ Ⓛ ●

Lesson 16a **Science Skills**

11 Which of these is a plant?

A Mushrooms
B Molds
C Yeasts
* D Conifers

12 All if these statements about Pluto are true except?

* J Pluto can be seen without a telescope.
K Pluto is much colder than Earth
L Pluto's surface is very cold.
M Pluto is usually farthest from the sun.

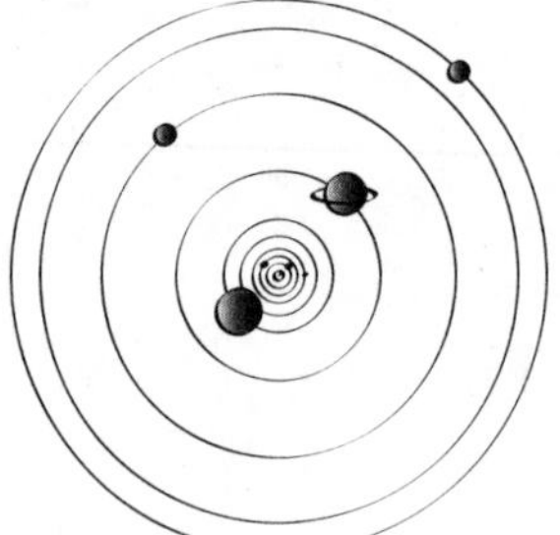

13 Animals protect themselves in many ways. Which of these is not a form of animal defense?

A Camouflage
B Armor
* C Extinction
D Poison

14 Which of Earth's layers is the thinnest?

J Inner core
K Mantle
L Outer core
* M Crust

15 When solids reach their melting points, they become

* A liquids.
B gases.
C water.
D crystals.

GO

94 Answer rows 11 Ⓐ Ⓑ Ⓒ ● 12 ● Ⓚ Ⓛ Ⓜ 13 Ⓐ Ⓑ ● Ⓓ 14 Ⓙ Ⓚ Ⓛ ● 15 ● Ⓑ Ⓒ Ⓓ

 Lesson 16a **Science Skills**

Directions: Use the information below to answer questions 16–18.

Ari spread a pile of metal shavings in a circle on a sheet of white paper. He held a magnet different distances from the paper and recorded the amount of metal shavings the magnet attracted.

Distance from Paper	Amount of Shavings Picked Up
1/4 inch	all the shavings were picked up
1 inch	most of the shavings were picked up, less than 1/4 left on paper
2 inches	shavings nearest magnet were picked up, 1/2 the pile left on paper
3 inches	no shavings were picked up

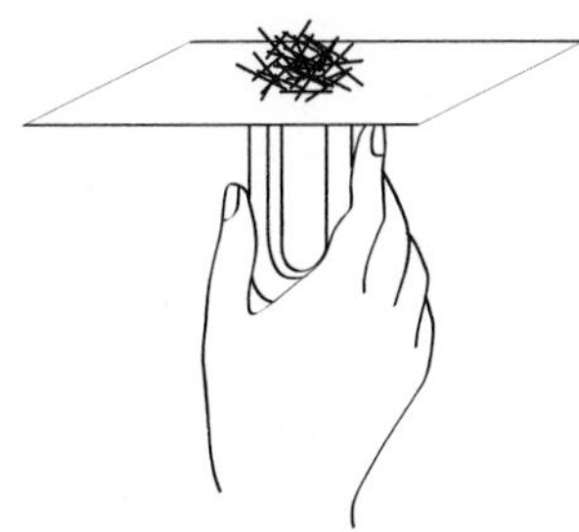

16 At what distance was Ari able to pick up the most shavings?

* J 1/4 inch
K 1 inch
L 2 inches
M 3 inches

17 Why did the magnet pick up no shavings on one of the tries?

A The magnet was backwards so the polarization was wrong.
B Ari did not allow enough time for the magnet to work.
* C The magnet was not strong enough.
D There were no more filings to pick up.

18 What did Ari's experiment show?

* J The force of a magnet's attraction increases as distance between it and the object decreases.
K The force of a magnet's attraction varies depending on how fast objects are picked up.
L The force of a magnet's attraction increases as distance between it and the object increases.
M The force of a magnet's attraction varies depending on how many objects a magnet picks up.

Answer rows 16 ● Ⓚ Ⓛ Ⓜ 17 Ⓐ Ⓑ ● Ⓓ 18 ● Ⓚ Ⓛ Ⓜ

Say **It's time to stop. You have finished Lesson 16a.**

Review the answers with the students. If any questions caused particular difficulty, work through each of the answer choices. If necessary, review the science principles associated with each item.

Have the students indicate completion of the lesson by entering their score for this activity on the progress chart at the beginning of the book.

 Lesson 16a **Science Skills**

19 All the stars you can see without a telescope are part of
* A the Milky Way galaxy.
B a meteor shower.
C the Andromeda galaxy.
D the Big dipper.

20 Which of these would not be a good insulator for the walls of a house?
J Plastic
* K Copper
L Fiberglass
M Air

21 In a deciduous forest, trees
A rarely produce seeds.
* B lose their leaves in autumn.
C stay green all year round.
D are often choked out by vines.

22 A car skids less on a dry road than on a wet one. This is true because
J the force of gravity is greater on a dry road.
K the absorption of a tire is greater on a dry road.
* L there is more friction between tires and a dry road.
M a dry road has stronger magnetic attraction to a tire.

23 Ahn sees lightning and hears thunder ten seconds afterwards. The next time he hears thunder five seconds after he see lightning. What can Ahn tell about the storm?
A It is moving farther away.
B Its intensity is lessening.
* C It is moving closer.
D It is almost over.

96 Answer rows 19  Ⓑ Ⓒ Ⓓ 20 Ⓙ ● Ⓛ Ⓜ 21 Ⓐ ● Ⓒ Ⓓ 22 Ⓙ Ⓚ ● Ⓜ 23 Ⓐ Ⓑ ● Ⓓ

Lesson 16b Science Skills

Focus

Science Skills

- recognizing forms, sources, and principles of energy
- recalling characteristics of Earth and bodies in space
- differentiating living and nonliving things
- understanding gravity, inertia, and friction
- understanding scientific instruments, measurement, and processes
- understanding plant and animal behaviors and characteristics
- understanding fossilization
- understanding life cycles and reproduction
- recognizing states, properties, and composition of matter
- using illustrations, charts, and graphs
- understanding weather, climate, and seasons

Test-taking Skills

- working methodically
- comparing questions and answer choices
- identifying and using key words, numbers, and pictures

Science

Lesson 16b **Science Skills**

Directions: Read each question and the answer choices. Choose the best answer.

Sample A **On a cold day, the wind makes a person feel colder because**

* A the wind blows heat from a person's body.
B cold air is moved more easily by the wind.
C people feel uncomfortable when the wind is blowing.
D moisture is attracted to the person by the wind.

Sample B **The force of gravity on a person would be less on the moon because**

J the moon's magnetic force is much less than Earth's.
K Earth's gravity would repel a person on the moon just a little.
* L the mass of the moon is less than the mass of Earth.
M the moon's atmosphere is denser than Earth's.

- **After choosing your answer, don't mark the space until you compare it with the question to be sure it is correct.**
- **Look for words such as <u>least</u>, <u>most</u>, and <u>not</u>. If you miss one of these small words, you will misunderstand the question.**

1 **Which of the following is <u>not</u> a characteristic of living things?**

A Reproduction
B Growth
C Digestion
* D Invisibility

2 **Waterfalls flow downward because**

J of strong water pressure.
K streams push them that direction.
* L gravity pulls the water toward Earth.
M they are usually near magnetic centers.

GO

Answer rows A ● B C D 1 A B C ●
B J K ● M 2 J K ● M

97

Samples A and B

Say **Turn to Lesson 16b on page 97. In this lesson you will answer more questions about science. Read the directions at the top of the page to yourself.**

Allow time for the students to read the directions.

Say **Look at Sample A at the top of the page and read the question. Why does the wind sometimes make you feel colder?** *(pause)* **Answer A is correct.** ***The wind blows heat from a person's body.*** **Mark circle A for Sample A in the answer rows at the bottom of the page. Make sure the circle is completely filled in. Press your pencil firmly so that your mark comes out dark.**

Check to see that the students have filled in the correct answer circle.

Say **Move over to Sample B. Read the question and answer choices. What is the correct answer to the question?** *(pause)* **Answer L is correct. The gravity would be less because** ***the mass of the moon is less than the mass of Earth.*** **Mark circle L for Sample B in the answer rows at the bottom of the page. Make sure the circle is completely filled in. Press your pencil firmly so that your mark comes out dark.**

Check to see that the students have filled in the correct answer circle. Review the answers to the sample items, if necessary.

★TIPS

Say **Now let's look at the tips.**

Have a volunteer read the tip aloud.

Say **Once you decide which answer is correct, compare it with the other choices before you mark your answer. Doing this makes it more likely you will choose the right answer. You should also be sure to read the question and answer choices carefully. Look at every word, especially important words that might cause you to misunderstand a question.**

Practice

Say **Let's do the Practice items now. Read each question carefully, and be sure to look at each word. Skipping a word may cause you to answer a question wrong. Compare the answer you think is right with the other choices before you mark your answer.**

When you come to the GO sign at the bottom of the page, turn the page and continue working. Work until you come to the STOP sign at the bottom of page 102. Remember to make sure that your answer circles are completely filled in with dark marks. Completely erase any marks for answers that you change. Any questions? Start working now.

Allow time for the students to mark their answers.

Unit 10 Lesson 16b **Science Skills**

Directions: Use the information below to answer questions 3–6.

Lily wondered if age affects people's sense of smell. She placed food in empty tin cans, covered them with foil, and poked several small holes in the top. She asked eight of her friends to identify what they smelled in each can. After school, she took the cans to her great-grandmother's nursing home and asked eight residents there to smell them. The chart below shows the number of people who answered correctly.

	Cinnamon	Onions	Chocolate	Dried Fish	Orange
Fifth Graders	5	6	7	7	6
Nursing Home Residents	5	6	4	6	5

3 **What smell did most people find the easiest to identify?**
- A Cinnamon
- * B Dried fish
- C Chocolate
- D Onions

4 **What smell was the hardest for seniors to identify?**
- J Oranges
- K Onions
- * L Chocolate
- M Cinnamon

5 **What did Lily's results show?**
- A The nursing home residents recognized more smells than fifth graders.
- * B Slightly more fifth graders correctly identified smells than did seniors.
- C Both groups correctly identified very few smells.
- D Smelling chocolate prevented people from smelling orange.

6 **What might have had the greatest effect on Lily's results?**
- * J The cans had been exposed to air longer when Lily went to the nursing home.
- K The type of container Lily used could have affected the smells of different foods.
- L The foods Lily chose were too difficult for most people to identify by smell.
- M The time of day might have affected how well people could smell foods.

98 Answer rows 3 Ⓐ●ⒸⒹ 4 ⒿⓀ●Ⓜ 5 Ⓐ●ⒸⒹ 6 ●ⓀⓁⓂ

7 **A cactus can live without water for weeks. This adaptation helps it survive in a climate that is**

A cold.
* B dry.
C windy.
D mild.

8 **A fossilized skeleton can tell scientists all of these except**

J how the animal moved.
K how the animal's bones fit together.
L how large the animal was.
* M how the animal cared for its young.

9 **Sunspots appear to be darker than the rest of the sun's surface because they are**

A mountain ranges on the sun's surface.
B on the shadowed side of the sun's surface.
* C cooler than the rest of the sun's surface.
D deep crevices in the sun's surface.

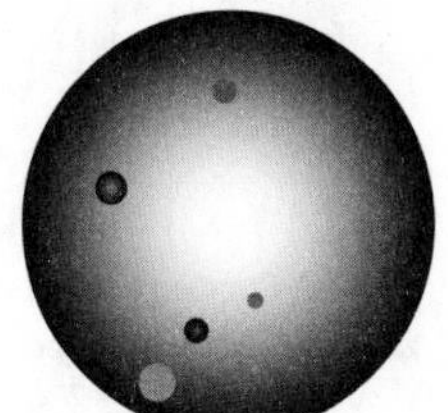

10 **The process by which a tadpole turns into a frog is called**

J germination.
* K metamorphosis.
L fertilization.
M duplication.

11 **What happens to water when it cools?**

* A It expands.
B It contracts.
C It stays the same size.
D It changes magnetism.

GO

Answer rows 7  8  9  10 Ⓙ●ⓁⓂ 11 ●ⒷⒸⒹ

 Lesson 16b **Science Skills**

Directions: Use the information below to answer questions 12–15.

D. J. wondered if cats could see as well in the dark as in the daylight. He put his cat in an upstairs bedroom and asked his brother to open the door when he called the cat for her breakfast. He timed how long it took for her to reach her bowl. Then he waited until after dark, closed all the blinds, and turned off the lights before repeating the experiment with her dinner. His results are on the chart below.

	In Daylight	At Night
Day 1	5.5 seconds	5.6 seconds
Day 2	5.9 seconds	5.3 seconds

12 When did the cat respond the fastest?

J In daylight on day 1
K At night on day 1
L In daylight on day 2
* M At night on day 2

13 What can D.J. conclude about his results?

A The cat moved faster in daylight than at night.
B The cat moved faster in the dark.
C The cat was hungrier in the morning.
* D No conclusion can be reached because the times were so close.

14 Which of these factors most likely did <u>not</u> influence D. J.'s results?

J The cat's familiarity with the route to the food bowl
K How hungry the cat was when it was called
* L The breed and age of the cat
M How far the cat was from the bedroom door when D. J. called

15 Which of these would be <u>least</u> helpful if D. J. wants to repeat the experiment to confirm his results?

A Use a toy rather than food to be sure the cat is guided by sight rather than smell.
* B Try the experiment at a different time of year.
C Conduct the experiment in a place that is unfamiliar to the cat.
D Repeat the experiment with many different cats.

 Answer rows 12 Ⓙ Ⓚ Ⓛ ● 13 Ⓐ Ⓑ Ⓒ ● 14 Ⓙ Ⓚ ● Ⓜ 15 Ⓐ ● Ⓒ Ⓓ

16 Which of these is not an instinctive behavior?
J Birds building a nest
K Groundhogs hibernating
* L Horses pulling a plow
M Moles burrowing underground

17 Where is erosion by wind likely to be the greatest?
A On snow-covered mountains
B In forested areas
C In meadows and grasslands
* D In areas that get little rain

18 Which of these is positively charged?
J Neutron
K Electron
* L Proton
M Nucleus

19 Which of these describes an animal that is least likely to become extinct?
A An animal that eats only one kind of food
B An animal that has just one baby every few years
C An animal that nests in a very specialized area
* D An animal that adapts quickly to different conditions

20 What is the name for the amount of space that matter takes up?
* J Volume
K Surface
L Weight
M Mass

Answer rows 16 Ⓙ Ⓚ ● Ⓜ 17 Ⓐ Ⓑ Ⓒ ● 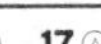 18 Ⓙ Ⓚ ● Ⓜ 19 Ⓐ Ⓑ Ⓒ ● 20 ● Ⓚ Ⓛ Ⓜ

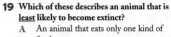

Say **It's time to stop. You have finished Lesson 16b.**

Review the answers with the students. If any questions caused particular difficulty, work through each of the answer choices. Pay extra attention to the items that are based on science concepts with which some students may be unfamiliar.

Have the students indicate completion of the lesson by entering their score for this activity on the progress chart at the beginning of the book.

Lesson 16b **Science Skills**

Directions: Use the information below to answer questions 21–23.

Erin put one ice cube in each of three bowls. Then she covered each bowl with a different colored cloth and set the bowls on a windowsill. She used a clock to see how long it took the ice cubes to melt. Her results are below.

Black Cloth	Red Cloth	White Cloth
1 hour	1 hour, 4 minutes	1 hour, 10 minutes

21 What was Erin trying to find out?

A How fast ice cubes melt when covered by cloth

* B Which color cloth absorbs the most heat

C Whether or not ice cubes will melt under cloth

D If sunlight causes ice to melt more rapidly

22 What did Erin's results reveal?

J Putting cloth over the ice made it melt faster than without cloth.

K White cloth caused the water to evaporate after the ice melted.

L The color of the cloth had little effect on how fast the ice melted.

* M The lighter the color of the cloth, the slower the ice will melt.

23 What else beside the color of the cloth might have influenced the results?

A How long the bowls were left in the sunlight

* B How much sunlight each bowl received

C The temperature of the ice cubes when they were placed in the bowl

D The size of the bowls in relation to the ice cubes

 Answer rows 21 Ⓐ ● Ⓒ Ⓓ 22 Ⓙ Ⓚ Ⓛ ● 23 Ⓐ ● Ⓒ Ⓓ

Unit 10 Test Yourself: Science

Focus

Science Skills

- recalling characteristics of Earth and bodies in space
- recognizing characteristics of a habitat
- recognizing states, properties, and composition of matter
- understanding plant and animal behaviors and characteristics
- recalling characteristics and functions of the human body
- understanding scientific instruments, measurement, and processes
- understanding life cycles and reproduction
- understanding gravity, inertia, and friction
- understanding weather, climate, and seasons
- understanding fossilization
- recognizing forms, sources, and principles of energy
- recognizing chemical changes
- using illustrations, charts, and graphs
- understanding the history and language of science
- identifying the best unit of measurement

Test-taking Skills

- managing time effectively
- referring to a passage to answer a question
- skimming items
- skipping items and returning to them later
- working methodically
- comparing questions and answer choices
- identifying and using key words, numbers, and pictures

Test Yourself: Science

Directions: Read each question and the answer choices. Choose the best answer.

Sample A **When the sand on a beach erodes in a storm, what happens to the sand?**
A It rises to the surface and blows away.
B It becomes rocks on the bottom of the ocean.
C It is changed into another substance.
* D It is moved somewhere else.

Sample B **Grazing animals like bison or zebra are usually found**
J in rainforests.
* K on grassy plains.
L in desert areas.
M on mountain ranges.

1 **What happens when the plates that form Earth's surface collide?**
A Sinkholes are formed.
B The plates crack in half.
* C Mountains are formed.
D The plates are attached together.

2 **Substances that don't conduct heat or electricity are called**
J conductors.
K absorbers.
L inductors.
* M insulators.

3 **Which of these is true about plants?**
* A Plants use carbon dioxide and release oxygen.
B Plants use oxygen and give off water vapor.
C Plants use energy from the sun to make carbon dioxide.
D Plants use oxygen and release carbon dioxide.

4 **Which of these is true about the planet Saturn?**
J It's surface is hotter than Earth's.
* K It has rings.
L It is made mostly of frozen water.
M It is the most distant planet.

Answer rows A Ⓐ Ⓑ Ⓒ ● 1 Ⓐ Ⓑ ● Ⓓ 3 ● Ⓑ Ⓒ Ⓓ
B Ⓙ ● Ⓛ Ⓜ 2 Ⓙ Ⓚ Ⓛ ● 4 Ⓙ ● Ⓛ Ⓜ

103

This lesson simulates an actual test-taking experience. Therefore it is recommended that the directions be read verbatim and that the suggested procedures and time allowances be followed.

Directions

Administration Time: approximately 50 minutes

Say Turn to the Test Yourself lesson on page 103.

Point out to the students that this Test Yourself lesson is timed like a real test, but that they will score it themselves to see how well they are doing. Remind the students to work quickly and not to spend too much time on any one item.

Say This lesson will check how well you learned the science skills you practiced in other lessons. Remember to make sure that the circles for your answer choices are completely filled in. Press your pencil firmly so that your marks come out dark. Completely erase any answers that you change. Do not write anything except your answer choices in your books.

Look at Sample A. Read the question and answer choices. Mark the circle for the answer you think is correct.

Allow time for the students to mark their answers.

Say The circle for answer D should have been marked. If you chose another answer, erase yours and fill in circle D now.

Check to see that the students have marked the correct answer circle.

Say Move over to Sample B. Read the question and answer choices. Mark the circle for the answer you think is correct.

Allow time for the students to mark their answers.

Say The circle for answer K should have been marked. If you chose another answer, erase yours and fill in circle K now.

Check to see that the students have marked the correct answer circle.

Say Now you will do more items. Do not spend too much time on any one question and pay attention to the directions. If you are not sure of an answer, take your best guess. Mark the circle for the answer you think might be right. When you come to the GO sign at the bottom of a page, turn the page and continue working. Work until you come to the STOP sign at the bottom of page 112. When you have finished, you can check over your answers to this lesson. Then wait for the rest of the group to finish. Do you have any questions? You will have 45 minutes. Begin working now.

Allow 45 minutes.

Test Yourself: Science

5 The spines on a cactus are most similar to
- * A the shell of a turtle.
- B the tail of a squirrel.
- C the neck of a giraffe.
- D the mane of a lion.

6 Which of these is not true about Earth's surface?
- J The continents were once grouped closer together.
- K Earth's surface is made up of separate plates.
- L The plates under Earth's surface are in constant motion.
- * M The continents have now stopped moving.

7 All of these are true about gases except
- A gases take the shape of the container they are in.
- B gases become liquids when they condense.
- * C gases change into solids when they are cooled.
- D the atoms in gases are spread out more than in solids.

8 The patterns that stars seem to form in the sky are called
- * J constellations.
- K meteor showers.
- L black holes.
- M solar systems.

9 The expansion of a person's chest causes
- A the heart to beat.
- * B the lungs fill with air.
- C the stomach to digest food.
- D the eyes to blink.

104 Answer rows 5 ● B C D 6 J K L ● 7 A B ● D 8 ● K L M 9 A ● C D

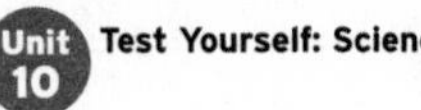

Test Yourself: Science

Directions: Use the information below to answer questions 10–12.

Kyla poured one cup of vinegar and one cup of olive oil into a glass jar and shook it until they were mixed. Later she noticed that the oil had separated again and was floating on top of the vinegar.

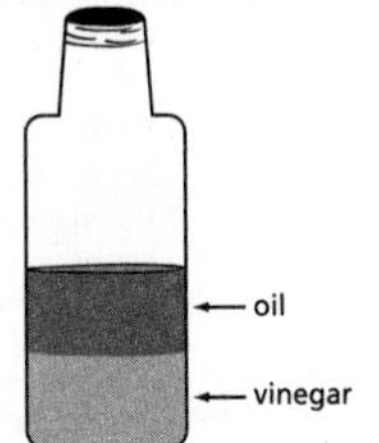

10 What will happen if Kyla shakes the jar a second time?

* J Both ingredients will mix and separate again.
K The ingredients will form several layers.
L The vinegar will rise to the top.
M Both ingredients will be changed into a new compound.

11 What can Kyla conclude about the densities of oil and vinegar?

A Oil is more dense because it sank.
B Vinegar and oil have the same density.
C Vinegar is less dense because it sank.
* D Oil is less dense because it rose to the top.

12 Suppose Kyla makes salad dressing using one quarter cup of vinegar and one cup of oil, what will happen?

J The vinegar will rise to the top because there is less of it.
K The oil will dissolve the vinegar because there is more of it.
* L The oil will still rise to the top.
M The vinegar will change to the color of the oil.

GO

Answer rows 10 ● K L M 11 A B C ● 12 J K ● M

Test Yourself: Science

13 What will happen to a plant if all its flowers are picked?

A It will be unable to absorb sunlight.
B It will be unable to grow taller.
* C It will be unable to produce seeds.
D It will be unable to produce its own food.

14 Which of these is the result of friction?

J Water increases its volume when it freezes.
K Rocks pick up speed when they roll down a mountain.
L Warm air rises and cold air falls.
* M Your skin gets warm when you rub it quickly.

15 Which of these is least useful when predicting weather?

A Air pressure
* B Pollen count
C Wind direction
D Temperature

16 Green plants are most important to herbivores because plants

J prevent erosion and give off nitrogen.
K absorb moisture and nutrients from the soil.
* L provide food and give off oxygen.
M consume oxygen and excess water vapor.

17 Scientists discover how plants and animals have changed and developed throughout history mostly by studying

A climate.
* B fossils.
C rock formations.
D endangered species.

Answer rows 13 Ⓐ Ⓑ ● Ⓓ 14 Ⓙ Ⓚ Ⓛ ● 15 Ⓐ ● Ⓒ Ⓓ 16 Ⓙ Ⓚ ● Ⓜ 17 Ⓐ ● Ⓒ Ⓓ 

Test Yourself: Science

18 The heat from the sun gets to Earth by

J conduction.
* K radiation.
L precipitation.
M condensation.

19 All of these are stages in the life cycle of a plant except

A germination.
B seedling.
* C pupa.
D pollination.

20 Which of these is an example of a chemical change?

J Sand mixing with water
* K Silver tarnishing
L Water condensing
M Clay mixing with topsoil

21 Which of the following is not associated with reproduction?

* A Scales
B Spores
C Eggs
D Seeds

22 If a grape and an orange are dropped at the same time from the same height,

J the grape will hit the ground first because it's lighter.
K the orange will hit the ground first because it's heavier.
* L they will both hit the ground at the same time.
M they will fall at different rates depending on temperature.

Answer rows 18 Ⓙ ● Ⓛ Ⓜ 19 Ⓐ Ⓑ ● Ⓓ 20 Ⓙ ● Ⓛ Ⓜ 21 ● Ⓑ Ⓒ Ⓓ 22 Ⓙ Ⓚ ● Ⓜ

Test Yourself: Science

Directions: Use the information below to answer questions 23–26.

A store manager believes that there are too many kinds of cereal on her store's shelves. She thinks the number of boxes on the shelves makes it harder for customers to decide what they want to buy, so they buy nothing. The manager designed the following study to test her belief.

The manager kept close track of cereal sales for a week and used this as her baseline. She then had a stocker choose ten percent of the cereal brands and pull them from the shelves for one week. The following week, the stocker did it again with different randomly selected kinds of cereal. For the next two weeks, the stocker repeated the process, but this time twenty percent of the cereal brands were removed from the shelves for each week. In all cases, the same kind of cereal was not removed more than once. The table below shows the results of the study.

Week	Amount of Cereal on Shelf	Total Sales
1	100%	$21,882
2	90%	$19,376
3	90%	$18,294
4	80%	$14,115
5	80%	$12,392

23 What did the store manager vary on purpose so she could determine its effect?

A The price of the cereal on the shelves
B The kind of cereal that was removed from the shelves
C The total sales for the week
* D The amount of cereal on the shelves

24 Which of these was most important in order for the store manager to make sense of the study?

* J To be sure that nothing else was affecting the total sales of cereal
K To be sure that the same stocker removed the cereal each time
L To be sure that the temperature in the store was the same
M To be sure that no customers saw the cereal being removed from the shelves

25 Why was it so important to measure total sales during week 1?

A So the stocker would know which cereals to remove each week.
B So the customers would have a chance to stock up on their regular brands of cereal.
* C So the manager would know the amount of cereal sold during a normal week.
D So there would be enough money to buy more cereal the following weeks.

26 Which of these conclusions about the study is correct?

J The average price for a box of cereal decreased from week 1 to week 5.
* K The less cereal that is on the shelves, the less cereal people buy.
L The number of customers in the store decreased because there was less cereal.
M The stocker must have removed the most popular cereal from the shelves.

108 Answer rows 23  24  25  26 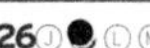

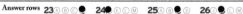

27 What is it called when the characteristics of an animal species change over time in such a way that its members are better able to survive?

A Migration
B Metamorphosis
* C Adaptation
D Imitation

28 The renewable source of energy that comes directly from the sun is called

J nuclear power.
* K solar power.
L hydro power.
M thermal power.

29 Neutrons and protons make up the

A flow of an electric current.
B spores of a fungus.
C seed of a flowering plant.
* D nucleus of an atom.

30 Which of these increases the chances that an animal will become extinct?

J Breeding the animal in captivity
K Increasing the size of the animal's natural habitat
L Reducing the number of predators and poachers
* M Decreasing the amount of the animal's food supply

31 In six minutes, Amah ran 1 mile, Santhi ran 1 kilometer, and Jordan ran 1200 yards. Who was the fastest runner?

* A Amah
B Santhi
C Jordan
D Jordan and Santhi tied

Test Yourself: Science

Directions: Use the information below to answer questions 32–34.

When Lia's parents made tea, she noticed that they left the teabags in for different lengths of time. Her mother left it in longer, and her tea was darker.

Lia wondered if the color of the tea could be changed by filtering it. She lined a funnel with a paper coffee filter and filled it halfway with some of the crushed charcoal her dad had bought for his fish tank filter. She poured tea through the funnel into a glass and noticed that the tea got lighter.

32 Why did the tea change color?

* J The filters took some of the solids out of the tea.
K The tea mixed with charcoal on its way through the funnel.
L The charcoal added moisture that diluted the tea.
M The glass reflected light so the tea appeared lighter.

33 What will probably happen if Lia pours the lighter colored tea through the filter again?

A It will get darker.
* B It will get lighter.
C It will stay about the same.
D It will clear up completely.

34 What removed the solids from the tea?

J The funnel
K Only the charcoal
L Only the paper filter
* M The charcoal and the paper filter

Test Yourself: Science

35 Nathan made a list of the characteristics of metals. His teacher said one of the characteristics was wrong. Which of these characteristics of metals is wrong?

A They shine brightly when polished.
* B They are poor conductors of electricity and heat.
C They are solid at room temperature.
D They are opaque, except when they are in very thin sheets.

36 Which of these is a decomposer, breaking down matter from dead plants and animals?

J A cactus
* K A mushroom
L A conifer
M A cattail

37 What is a galaxy?

A A small group of planets
B A gigantic cloud of dark-colored dust
C A large shower of meteors
* D A large group of stars and planets

38 Which of these is the main function of a plant's roots?

J Manufacturing food
K Making seeds
* L Absorbing nutrients
M Storing chlorophyll

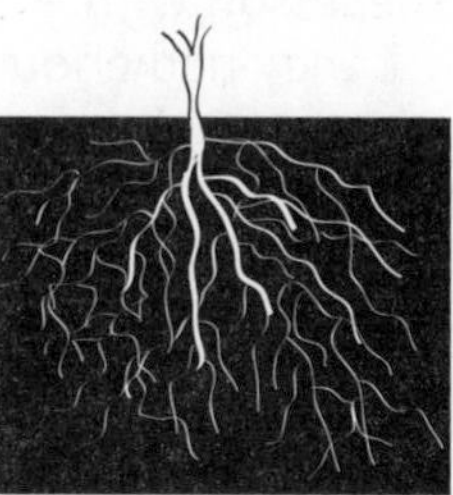

39 Which of these is not a type of rock?

A Igneous
B Metamorphic
C Sedimentary
* D Pulmonary

GO

Answer rows 35 Ⓐ ● Ⓒ Ⓓ 36 Ⓙ ● Ⓛ Ⓜ 37 Ⓐ Ⓑ Ⓒ ● 38 Ⓙ Ⓚ ● Ⓜ 39 Ⓐ Ⓑ Ⓒ ●

Say It's time to stop. You have finished the Test Yourself lesson. Check to see that you have completely filled in your answer circles with dark marks. Make sure that any marks for answers that you changed have been completely erased.

Go over the lesson with the students. Ask them if they had enough time to finish the lesson. Did they read the questions and answer choices carefully? Did they compare their answer with the other choices to be sure it was correct?

Work through any questions that caused difficulty. If necessary, provide additional practice questions similar to the ones in this unit.

Have the students indicate completion of the lesson by entering their score for this activity on the progress chart at the beginning of the book.

Unit 10 Test Yourself: Science

Directions: Use the information below to answer questions 40–42.

Raj covered the bottom of an aquarium with a thick layer of sand. Then he covered the sand with water to a depth of two inches. He put a board in the water and moved it back and forth in a regular motion. The board made waves that traveled to the opposite side of the aquarium. Raj observed that the waves caused sand to build up against the opposite wall.

40 What did Raj probably want to find out?

J If sand scratches aquarium glass
* K If waves cause sand to build up
L If the board would attract sand
M If sand and water mix

41 What did Raj discover?

A Sand stops wave action.
B Sand and water combine chemically.
* C Sand is moved by wave action.
D Sand is not affected by wave action.

42 What action in nature did Raj's experiment most closely resemble?

J The formation of sand dunes by wind
K The building of mountains by tectonic movement
* L The depositing of sand on beaches by waves
M The formation of a tsunami by an earthquake

112 Answer rows 40 Ⓙ ● Ⓛ Ⓜ 41 Ⓐ Ⓑ ● Ⓓ 42 Ⓙ Ⓚ ● Ⓜ

Test Practice

To the Teacher:

The Test Practice unit provides the students with an opportunity to apply the reading, spelling, language arts, mathematics, science, study skills, and test-taking skills practiced in the lessons of this book. It is also a final practice activity to be used prior to administering the Iowa Tests of Basic Skills®. By following the step-by-step instructions on the subsequent pages, you will be able to simulate the structured atmosphere in which achievement tests are given. Take time to become familiar with the administrative procedures before the students take the tests.

Scheduling the Tests

Allow 10–15 minutes for the students to complete the identifying data on the Name and Answer Sheet before beginning Test 1.

Each test may be administered in a separate session, or you may follow the schedule below that indicates the recommended testing sessions.

Two sessions may be scheduled for the same day if a sufficient break in time is provided between sessions.

Recommended Session	Test	Administration Time (minutes)
1	1 Vocabulary	20
	2 Reading Comprehension	35
2	3 Spelling	25
	4 Capitalization	20
	5 Punctuation	20
3	6 Part 1 Usage	25
	6 Part 2 Expression	20
4	7 Part 1 Math Concepts	20
	7 Part 2 Math Estimation	20
5	8 Part 1 Math Problem Solving	15
	8 Part 2 Data Interpretation	15
	9 Math Computation	20
6	10 Maps and Diagrams	25
	11 Reference Materials	25
7	12 Science	45

Preparing for the Tests

1. **Remove the Name and Answer Sheet from each student's book.**
2. **Put a "Testing—Do Not Disturb" sign on the classroom door to eliminate unnecessary interruptions.**
3. **Make sure the students are seated at comfortable distances from each other and that their desks are clear.**
4. **Provide each student sharpened pencils with erasers. Have an extra supply of pencils available. For the mathematics items, provide each student with scratch paper.**
5. **Distribute the students' books and answer sheets.**
6. **Instruct the students in filling out the identifying data on their Name and Answer Sheets. Instructions are given on the next page of this Teacher's Edition.**
7. **Encourage the students with a "pep talk."**

Administering the Tests

1. **Follow the time limit provided for each test by using a clock or a watch with a second hand to ensure accuracy.**
2. **Read the "Say" copy verbatim to the students and follow all the instructions given.**
3. **Make sure the students understand the directions for each test before proceeding.**
4. **Move about the classroom during testing to see that the directions are being followed. Make sure the students are working on the correct page and are marking their answers properly.**
5. **Without distracting the students, provide test-taking tips at your discretion. If you notice a student is unable to answer a question, encourage him or her to skip the question and go on to the next one. If students finish the test before time is called, suggest they go back to any skipped questions within that part of the test. However, do not provide help with the content of any question.**

Name and Answer Sheet

To the Student:

Now that you have completed the lessons in this book, you are on your way to scoring high! The tests in this part of your *Scoring High on the ITBS* will give you a chance to put the tips you have learned to work.

A few reminders...

- Be sure you understand all the directions before you begin each test. You may ask the teacher questions about the directions if you do not understand them.
- Work as quickly as you can during each test.
- When you change an answer, be sure to erase your first mark completely.
- You can guess at an answer or skip difficult items and go back to them later.
- Use the tips you have learned whenever you can.
- It is okay to be a little nervous.

LAST	FIRST	MI	SCHOOL
			TEACHER
			FEMALE ○ MALE ○

BIRTH DATE

MONTH	DAY	YEAR
JAN ○ FEB ○ MAR ○ APR ○ MAY ○ JUN ○ JUL ○ AUG ○ SEP ○ OCT ○ NOV ○ DEC ○	⓪①②③ / ⓪①②③④⑤⑥⑦⑧⑨	⓪⑦⑧⑨ / ⓪①②③④⑤⑥⑦⑧⑨

④ ⑤ ⑥

113

Preparing the Name and Answer Sheet

Proper marking of the grids on a machine-scorable answer sheet is necessary for the correct listing of students' test results. Use the directions below to give the students practice in completing the identifying data on an answer sheet.

Say **You have to fill in some information on your Name and Answer Sheet before you begin the Test Practice section. I am going to tell you how to do this.**

Make sure your Name and Answer Sheet is facing up and the heading STUDENT'S NAME is above the boxes with circles. In the boxes under the word LAST, print your last name. Start at the left and put one letter in each box. Print as many letters of your last name as will fit before the heavy rule. In the boxes under the word FIRST, print your first name. Put one letter in each box and print only as many letters of your first name as will fit before the heavy rule. If you have a middle name, print your middle initial in the box under MI.

Allow time for the students to print their names.

Say **Look at the columns of letters under the boxes. In each column, fill in the space for the letter you printed in the box. Fill in only one space in each column. Fill in the empty space at the top of a column if there is no letter in the box.**

Allow time for the students to fill in the spaces. Give help to individual students as it is needed.

Say Print the name of your school after the word SCHOOL.

Print your teacher's last name after the word TEACHER.

Fill in the space after the word FEMALE if you are a girl. Fill in the space after the word MALE if you are a boy.

Look at the heading BIRTH DATE. In the box under the word MONTH, print the first three letters of the month in which you were born. In the column of months under the box, fill in the space for the month you printed in the box.

In the box under the word DAY, print the one or two numerals of your birth date. In the columns of numerals under the box, fill in the spaces for the numerals you printed in the box. If your birth date has just one numeral, fill in the space with a zero in it in the column on the left.

In the box under the word YEAR, print the last two numerals of your year of birth. In the columns of numerals under the box, fill in the spaces for the numerals you printed in the box.

Look at the heading GRADE. Fill in the space for the numeral that stands for your grade.

Check to see that the students have filled in all the identifying data correctly. Then have them identify the part of the Answer Sheet that corresponds to each part of the Test Practice section.

TEST 1 VOCABULARY

TEST 2 READING COMPREHENSION

TEST 3 SPELLING

TEST 4 CAPITALIZATION

TEST 5 PUNCTUATION

TEST 6 USAGE AND EXPRESSION

Part 1 Usage

Part 2 Expression

114

TEST 7 MATH CONCEPTS AND ESTIMATION

Part 1 Math Concepts

A Ⓐ ● Ⓒ Ⓓ
B ● Ⓚ Ⓛ Ⓜ
1 Ⓐ ● Ⓒ Ⓓ
2 Ⓙ ● Ⓛ Ⓜ
3 ● Ⓑ Ⓒ Ⓓ
4 Ⓙ Ⓚ Ⓛ ●
5 Ⓐ ● Ⓒ Ⓓ
6 Ⓙ Ⓚ Ⓛ ●
7 ● Ⓑ Ⓒ Ⓓ
8 Ⓙ ● Ⓛ Ⓜ
9 Ⓐ Ⓑ Ⓒ ●
10 Ⓙ Ⓚ ● Ⓜ
11 ● Ⓑ Ⓒ Ⓓ
12 Ⓙ Ⓚ Ⓛ ●
13 Ⓐ Ⓑ Ⓒ ●

Part 2 Math Estimation

A Ⓐ Ⓑ ● Ⓓ
B Ⓙ Ⓚ Ⓛ ●
1 Ⓐ ● Ⓒ Ⓓ
2 Ⓙ Ⓚ Ⓛ ●
3 Ⓐ ● Ⓒ Ⓓ
4 Ⓙ Ⓚ Ⓛ ●
5 Ⓐ Ⓑ Ⓒ ●
6 Ⓙ Ⓚ ● Ⓜ
7 Ⓐ ● Ⓒ Ⓓ
8 Ⓙ Ⓚ ● Ⓜ
9 ● Ⓑ Ⓒ Ⓓ
10 Ⓙ Ⓚ ● Ⓜ

TEST 8 MATH PROBLEM SOLVING AND DATA INTERPRETATION

Part 1 Math Problem Solving

A Ⓐ Ⓑ ● Ⓓ
1 Ⓐ Ⓑ ● Ⓓ
2 Ⓙ ● Ⓛ Ⓜ
3 Ⓐ Ⓑ Ⓒ ●
4 Ⓙ Ⓚ Ⓛ ●

Part 2 Data Interpretation

1 ● Ⓑ Ⓒ Ⓓ
2 Ⓙ ● Ⓛ Ⓜ
3 Ⓐ Ⓑ ● Ⓓ
4 Ⓙ ● Ⓛ Ⓜ

TEST 9 MATH COMPUTATION

A Ⓐ ● Ⓒ Ⓓ
B Ⓙ Ⓚ Ⓛ ●
1 Ⓐ Ⓑ ● Ⓓ
2 Ⓙ ● Ⓛ Ⓜ
3 ● Ⓑ Ⓒ Ⓓ
4 Ⓙ ● Ⓛ Ⓜ
5 ● Ⓑ Ⓒ Ⓓ
6 ● Ⓚ Ⓛ Ⓜ
7 Ⓐ Ⓑ ● Ⓓ
8 Ⓙ Ⓚ ● Ⓜ
9 Ⓐ ● Ⓒ Ⓓ

TEST 10 MAPS AND DIAGRAMS

A Ⓐ ● Ⓒ Ⓓ
B Ⓙ Ⓚ Ⓛ ●
1 Ⓐ ● Ⓒ Ⓓ
2 ● Ⓚ Ⓛ Ⓜ
3 Ⓐ Ⓑ ● Ⓓ
4 ● Ⓚ Ⓛ Ⓜ
5 Ⓐ Ⓑ Ⓒ ●
6 Ⓙ Ⓚ Ⓛ ●
7 ● Ⓑ Ⓒ Ⓓ
8 Ⓙ Ⓚ Ⓛ ●
9 ● Ⓑ Ⓒ Ⓓ
10 Ⓙ ● Ⓛ Ⓜ
11 Ⓐ Ⓑ ● Ⓓ

TEST 11 REFERENCE MATERIALS

A Ⓐ Ⓑ ● Ⓓ
B Ⓙ Ⓚ Ⓛ ●
1 Ⓐ Ⓑ Ⓒ ●
2 ● Ⓚ Ⓛ Ⓜ
3 Ⓐ ● Ⓒ Ⓓ
4 ● Ⓚ Ⓛ Ⓜ
5 Ⓐ Ⓑ ● Ⓓ
6 Ⓙ Ⓚ Ⓛ ●
7 Ⓐ ● Ⓒ Ⓓ
8 Ⓙ Ⓚ ● Ⓜ
9 Ⓐ Ⓑ Ⓒ ●
10 ● Ⓚ Ⓛ Ⓜ
11 ● Ⓑ Ⓒ Ⓓ
12 Ⓙ Ⓚ ● Ⓜ
13 Ⓐ Ⓑ ● Ⓓ
14 Ⓙ Ⓚ Ⓛ ●
15 Ⓐ Ⓑ ● Ⓓ
16 ● Ⓚ Ⓛ Ⓜ

115

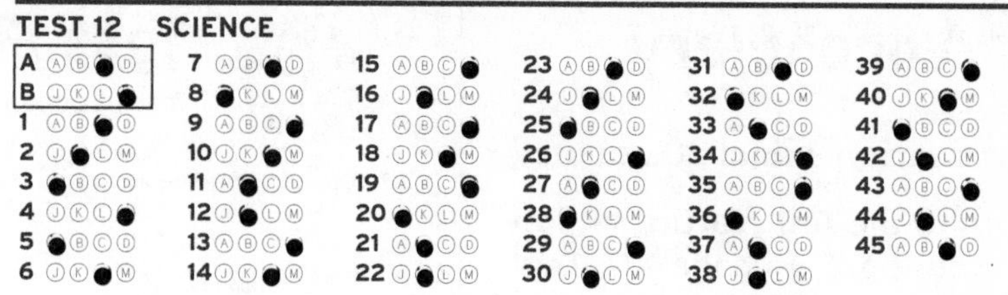

116

Unit 11 Test 1 Vocabulary

Administration Time: 20 minutes

Say Turn to the Test Practice section of your book on page 117. This is Test 1, Vocabulary.

Check to see that the students have found page 117.

Say Look at your answer sheet. Find the part of the answer sheet called Test 1, Vocabulary. All your answers for this test should be marked on your answer sheet, not in your book.

Check to see that the students have found the correct part of the answer sheet.

Say This test will check how well you know vocabulary words. Remember to make sure that the circles for your answer choices are completely filled in. Press your pencil firmly so that your marks come out dark. Completely erase any marks for answers that you change.

Look at Sample A. Read the phrase and fill in the circle for the answer that means the same as the underlined word. Mark your answer in the row for Sample A on the answer sheet.

Test Practice

Test 1 **Vocabulary**

Directions: Read the phrase and the answer choices. Choose the answer that means the same as the underlined word.

Sample A Load a <u>barge</u>
A car
* B boat
C plane
D cart

Sample B <u>Refine</u> oil
J burn
K drill for
L explore for
* M purify

1 To <u>shuffle</u> papers
A fold
B pile neatly
C dye
* D move around

2 A <u>noble</u> family
J large
K kind
* L royal
M close

3 A huge <u>ostrich</u>
A kind of fish
* B flightless bird
C hairless dog
D stinging insect

4 Feel the <u>breeze</u>
J wooden peg
K cold water
* L small wind
M shaking ground

5 To <u>alter</u> a plan
* A change
B make
C like
D explain

6 To <u>whoop</u> at the game
J sit in rows
* K yell loudly
L eat and drink
M be with friends

7 Their decision was <u>hasty.</u>
A strange
B foolish
C correct
* D fast

8 A beautiful <u>gown</u>
J couch
K party
L room
* M dress

GO

117

Allow time for the students to read the item and mark their answers.

Say You should have filled in answer circle B because a *barge* is a kind of *boat*. If you did not fill in answer B, erase your answer and fill in answer B now.

Check to see that the students have filled in the correct answer circle.

Say Do Sample B now. Read the phrase and fill in the circle for the answer that means the same as the underlined word. Mark your answer in the row for Sample B on the answer sheet.

Allow time for the students to read the item and mark their answers.

Say You should have filled in answer circle M because *refine* means about the same as *purify*. If you did not fill in answer M, erase your answer and fill in answer M now.

Check to see that the students have filled in the correct answer circle.

Say **Now you will answer more questions. Read each item. Fill in the space for your answers on the answer sheet. Be sure the number of the answer row matches the item you are doing. Work by yourself. When you come to the GO sign at the bottom of the page, turn to the next page and continue working. Work until you come to the STOP sign at the bottom of page 118. When you have finished, you can check over your answers to this test. Then wait for the rest of the group to finish. Do you have any questions?**

Answer any questions that the students have.

Say **Start working now. You have 15 minutes.**

Allow 15 minutes.

Say **It's time to stop. You have completed Test 1. Check to see that you have completely filled in your answer circles with dark marks. Make sure that any marks for answers that you changed have been completely erased. Now you may close your books.**

Review the items with the students. Have them indicate completion of the lesson by entering their score for this activity on the progress chart at the beginning of the book. Then collect the students' books and answer sheets if this is the end of the testing session.

Test 1 **Vocabulary**

9 We climbed a dune.
* * A hill of sand
* B icy cliff
* C rocky trail
* D wooden ladder

10 To irrigate a field
* J plow
* * K water
* L harvest
* M plant

11 A dense fog
* A pleasant
* B mysterious
* C cold
* * D thick

12 A heavy boulder
* J concrete bench
* K iron bar
* L log
* * M rock

13 Whirl around the room
* * A spin
* B walk
* C slide
* D pace

14 The size of a walrus
* J hunting bird
* * K sea animal
* L farm horse
* M large car

15 Stopped instantly
* * A immediately
* B carefully
* C foolishly
* D exactly

16 A tiring voyage
* J sport
* * K trip
* L parade
* M movie

17 The violet flower
* A white
* B red
* * C purple
* D orange

18 Fold the trousers
* * J pants
* K shirts
* L socks
* M sweaters

19 A coiled rope
* A used for climbing
* B strong
* * C wound into loops
* D short

20 The dew on the grass
* J piece of cloth
* K dust
* * L moisture
* M kind of bird

STOP

118

Unit 11 Test 2 Reading Comprehension

Administration Time: 35 minutes

Say Turn to the Test Practice section of your book on page 119. This is Test 2, Reading Comprehension.

Check to see that the students have found page 119.

Say Look at your answer sheet. Find the part called Test 2, Reading Comprehension. All your answers for this test should be marked on your answer sheet, not in your book.

Check to see that the students have found the correct part of the answer sheet.

Say This test will check your reading comprehension. Remember to make sure that the circles for your answer choices are completely filled in. Press your pencil firmly so that your marks come out dark. Completely erase any marks for answers that you change.

Look at Sample A. Read the passage to yourself. Then read the question beside the passage. On your answer sheet, find the answer circles for Sample A. Mark the circle for the answer you think is right.

Allow time for the students to read the item and mark their answers.

Say You should have filled in answer circle C. You can figure out from the passage that *father* hung the flower box outside the window. If you did not fill in answer C, erase your answer and fill in answer C now.

Check to see that the students have filled in the correct answer circle.

Unit 11 Test Practice

Test 2 **Reading Comprehension**

Directions: Read the passage and questions. Choose the best answer.

Sample A Jeff and Patty made something for their mother's birthday. Grandfather helped them. It was a window box. The children filled it with flowers. Their father hung it outside the window. They couldn't wait for Mother to come home from work.

Who hung the flower box outside the window?

A Jeff
B Grandfather
* C Father
D Patty

Did you know you can learn to cook a wonderful meal by watching television? Today, cooking shows crowd the airwaves, but this wasn't always the case. The first cooking show aired in 1963 and starred a woman named Julia Child.

Julia was born in Pasadena, California, in 1912. She was an active, mischievous girl who preferred the outdoors to the kitchen. The closest she came to cooking was throwing mud pies.

When World War II broke out, Julia took a job at the Office of Strategic Services—the early C.I.A. She was thrilled to work around spies, and she jumped at the chance for an overseas assignment in Ceylon. Unfortunately, her own work as a research assistant was far from thrilling. The papers she processed were top-secret but very dull.

Julia never regretted her work for the O.S.S., though. In Ceylon, she met Paul Child. Julia and Paul fell in love and got married. Paul was a lover of fine food, especially French cooking. Paul's interest in food was the driving force behind Julia's desire to learn to cook.

After the war, Julia set sail on a new career. She enrolled at the world-famous Cordon Bleu cooking school in Paris, where she was the only female student. Julia's teacher thought she lacked natural ability but found her energy and commitment remarkable. Before long, Julia and two friends opened a French cooking school of their own. It was designed especially for Americans living in Paris. Ten years later, Julia and her partners published a book called *Mastering the Art of French Cooking*. This in turn led to her greatest success, a television show called *The French Chef*.

Julia's television show changed the way Americans cook and eat. Julia was completely at ease in front of the camera. She puttered around the kitchen, calmly showing her audience how to deal with spilled sauces and burnt roasts. At the same time, she showed Americans the importance of fresh ingredients and good kitchen equipment. By teaching Americans how to prepare French foods, she changed the appetite of the entire country.

119

Say **Now you will answer more questions. Read the passages and the questions that follow them. Fill in the space for your answers on the answer sheet. Be sure the number of the answer row matches the item you are doing. Work by yourself. When you come to the GO sign at the bottom of a page, turn to the next page and continue working. Work until you come to the STOP sign at the bottom of page 123. When you have finished, you can check over your answers to this test. Then wait for the rest of the group to finish. Do you have any questions?**

Answer any questions that the students have.

Say **Start working now. You have 30 minutes.**

Allow 30 minutes.

Unit 11 Test 2: **Reading Comprehension**

1 In the fifth paragraph, what is the meaning of the phrase "set sail on"?

* A Began
B Learned
C Became bored with
D Left the country

2 What does the phrase "she changed the appetite of the entire country" mean?

J Julia encouraged people to eat more.
K Through Julia's work, the laws about food quality were written.
L Julia educated an entire generation of American chefs.
* M Because of Julia's show, Americans learned to enjoy new foods.

3 In what way was Paul Child the "driving force" behind Julia's cooking career?

A Paul made Julia stop working at the O.S.S.
B Paul got Julia her job as a television chef.
C Paul demanded that Julia become a better cook.
* D Paul's love of food made Julia want to learn to cook.

4 The author presents Julia as

J a natural chef.
* K a determined woman.
L someone with a sense of humor.
M a person who enjoys being famous.

5 What is this passage mainly about?

A Julia Child's childhood and college education
* B How Julia Child became a famous chef
C The importance of fresh ingredients
D The influence of French cooking on professional chefs

6 Why was Julia unhappy about her work for the O.S.S.?

J She was lonely.
K Her co-workers were rude.
* L Her work was boring.
M She did not like Ceylon.

7 How does Julia act when she is filming a cooking show?

A Excited about showing off her abilities
B Concerned that everything go smoothly
* C Relaxed and unconcerned about her mistakes
D Interested in catching her audience's attention

GO

The waters of the mighty Mississippi flow south with amazing force. But in the winter of 1811–1812, the Mississippi River appeared to flow backward. What power could cause such a strange event? It was a series of earthquakes on the New Madrid fault.

The New Madrid fault runs through parts of Illinois, Missouri, Arkansas, Kentucky, and Tennessee. It is an area where two huge plates of land meet and slowly grind against each other. When the plates push against one another, tension builds until the plates snap into new positions. This movement causes an earthquake. Earthquakes can be so small that only the most delicate instruments can detect them or so large that they topple cities. The New Madrid fault earthquakes of 1811–1812 were enormous.

On December 16, 1811, the New Madrid fault erupted into action. In the middle of the night, settlers awoke to a roaring like distant thunder, followed by violent shaking. The shock was felt a thousand miles away in Boston. On January 23 and February 7, 1812, two more severe earthquakes struck. In between the major quakes, and for more than a year afterwards, small earthquakes and aftershocks shook the ground. One settler recorded almost two thousand quakes.

When the earthquakes hit, bluffs fell, the course of the Mississippi was changed, islands disappeared, and large cracks opened in the ground. In the Mississippi, waves caused by the earthquakes sometimes moved against the current, making the river appear to flow backwards. The landscape was permanently changed.

Most large earthquakes today hurt thousands of people and damage many buildings. The 1811–1812 New Madrid fault earthquakes did not do this. At that time, few people lived in the area where the quakes hit. Their homes were simple structures, mostly log cabins that withstood the shaking very well. Instead of people and buildings, these earthquakes mostly affected the landscape.

If the New Madrid fault erupted into an earthquake today, the effects would be more severe. The closest major city to the fault, Memphis, sits on a high bluff overlooking the Mississippi. The builders of the city did not know the history of the fault, so many of the buildings of downtown Memphis are not earthquake-safe. Even though the New Madrid fault has been quiet for many decades, government officials are prepared to act if the ground starts shaking again.

GO

8 According to the passage, in 1811–1812, the New Madrid fault area was

J unknown to settlers.
K beyond the U.S. boundaries.
L heavily settled, especially in Memphis.
* M lightly populated.

9 Why did people think the Mississippi was flowing backwards in 1811–1812?

A The frequent earthquakes confused people in the area.
B Bluffs dropped into the river and island disappeared.
C The force of the earthquakes changed the river's course.
* D Earthquake shocks made waves that flowed north.

10 How has the author developed the fifth paragraph?

J By describing the area where the New Madrid fault is located
K By listing the events leading up to the worst New Madrid fault earthquake
* L By explaining why there wasn't much damage to people or buildings
M By comparing the effects of the 1811–1812 earthquakes with more recent earthquakes

11 Which of these best summarizes the author's view of the New Madrid fault today?

* A The fault has not been active for many years.
B The fault damaged Memphis just a few years ago.
C The fault will not damage many buildings.
D The fault has gradually moved backward.

12 According to the passage, what causes earthquakes?

* J Plates of land grinding together and then jolting free
K Areas of land sliding smoothly past one another
L Rivers flowing backwards in their banks
M Cities being built on high areas near rivers

13 Which of these was the first sign of the December 16 earthquake?

A A shock felt a thousand miles away
B Several small aftershocks
* C A noise like thunder
D Waves flowing against the Mississippi's current

GO

Say **It's time to stop. You have completed Test 2. Check to see that you have completely filled in your answer circles with dark marks. Make sure that any marks for answers that you changed have been completely erased. Now you may close your books.**

Review the items with the students. Have them indicate completion of the lesson by entering their score for this activity on the progress chart at the beginning of the book. Then collect the students' books and answer sheets if this is the end of the testing session.

Test 2 **Reading Comprehension**

"I can't wait to get back to school." Lyle spoke to his sister as he carried a trash can out to the curb.

Beatrice looked at her brother and shook her head. She struggled with the other trash can that was loaded with stuff they were cleaning out of the garage.

"How can anyone want to go back to school? Seven hours a day, five days a week, thirty-six weeks a year. It's a prison. The only things I like about school are lunch, gym, and going home."

"This year I have Mrs. Miller. Everyone knows she's the best teacher in the school. The kids in her class spend most of the day working on computers. I don't know what she does, but Jerrod says he liked to take tests when he was in her class. Sounds like my kind of teacher."

As they walked back to the house, Bea put her arm around her brother's shoulder. "Little brother, you are a wacky guy. Every year you have another reason for looking forward to going back to school. Last year it was the new library. The year before, you were excited about the media center. Face it, Lyle, you like school."

When they reached the porch, Beatrice grabbed a basketball and headed toward the driveway. Lyle went into the house and turned the television on. He flicked through the channels until he reached the special on the history of medicine. Bea was right. He loved school, and he really wanted to be a doctor.

He heard Bea in the driveway practicing her three-point shot. He thought Bea was amazing. She was a super-jock who loved every sport, but she still did well in school. In fact, she was a straight-A student, and he couldn't understand how she did it. Lyle had to study hours every night, but Bea seemed to learn effortlessly.

During the special about medicine, Lyle took lots of notes. He knew Mrs. Miller had her students write research reports, and he wanted to write one about medicine. If he started now, it would be easy to write the report later.

14 **What kind of girl is Bea?**
- J Concerned
- * K Talented
- L Silly
- M Powerful

15 **How does Lyle feel about Beatrice?**
- * A He admires her.
- B He is envious of her.
- C He wants to be like her.
- D He feels sorry for her.

16 **What is the meaning of the word "effortlessly" in the next to last paragraph?**
- J With other people around
- K With a lot of hard work
- * L Without difficulty
- M Without talking

17 **If Lyle had a test in school, he would probably**
- A wait to study for the test until the last minute.
- * B start studying for the test long before it was given.
- C not worry about it because he learns so quickly.
- D watch television or play basketball with his sister.

18 **The description of the walk back to the house in the fifth paragraph helps the reader to see**
- J why Bea likes basketball.
- K where the children live.
- L how different the children are.
- * M that Bea really loves her brother.

123

Test 3 Spelling

Administration Time: 25 minutes

Say Turn to Test 3 on page 124.

Check to see that the students have found page 124.

Say Look at your answer sheet. Find the part called Test 3, Spelling. All your answers for this test should be marked on your answer sheet, not in your book.

Check to see that the students have found the correct part of the answer sheet.

Say This test will check how well you can find misspelled words. Remember to make sure that the circles for your answer choices are completely filled in. Press your pencil firmly so that your marks come out dark. Completely erase any marks for answers that you change.

Look at the words for Sample A. Find the word that has a spelling mistake. If none of the words has a mistake, choose the last answer, No mistakes. Mark the circle for your answer.

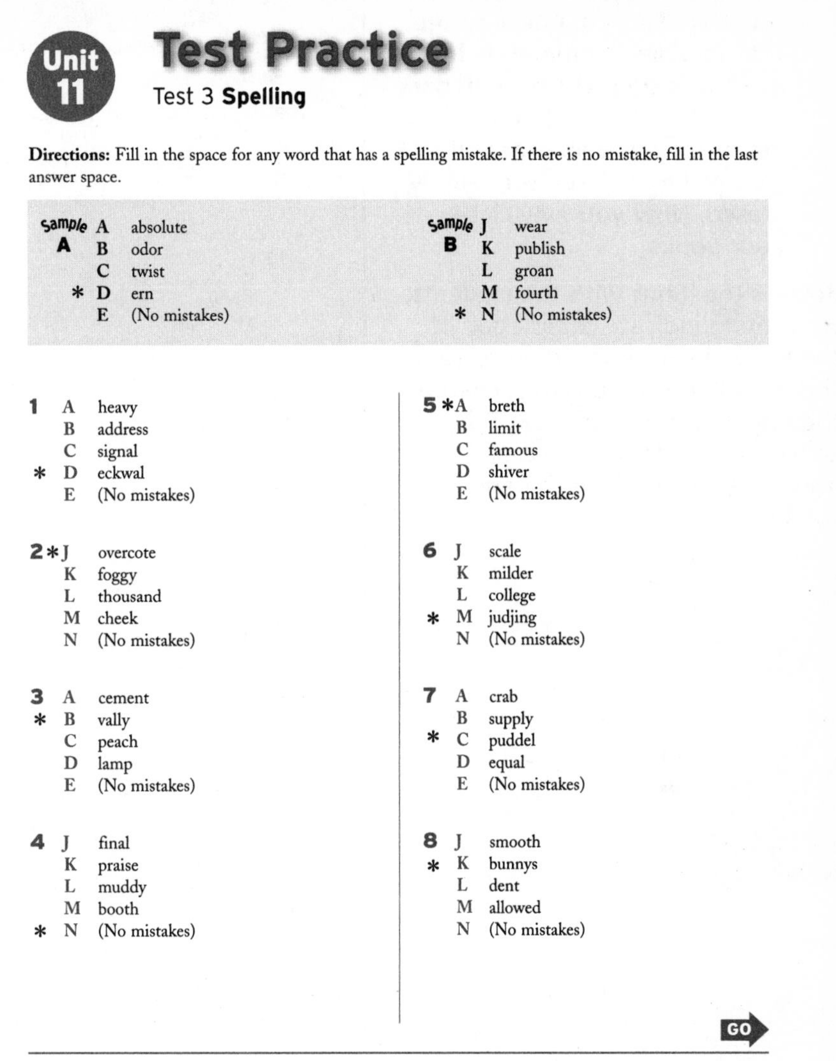

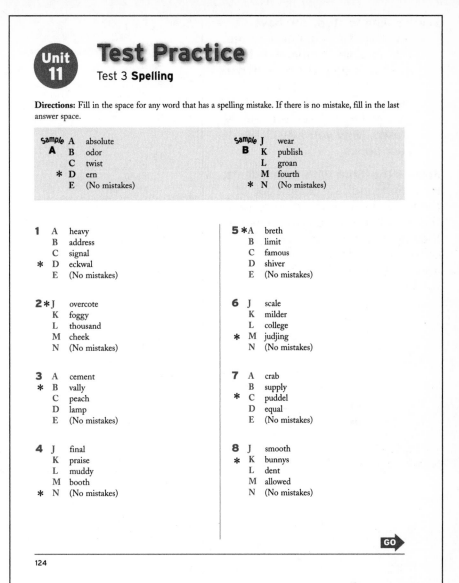

Unit 11 **Test Practice**

Test 3 **Spelling**

Directions: Fill in the space for any word that has a spelling mistake. If there is no mistake, fill in the last answer space.

Sample A
A absolute
B odor
C twist
* D ern
E (No mistakes)

Sample B
J wear
K publish
L groan
M fourth
* N (No mistakes)

1 A heavy
B address
C signal
* D eckwal
E (No mistakes)

2 * J overcote
K foggy
L thousand
M cheek
N (No mistakes)

3 A cement
* B vally
C peach
D lamp
E (No mistakes)

4 J final
K praise
L muddy
M booth
* N (No mistakes)

5 * A breth
B limit
C famous
D shiver
E (No mistakes)

6 J scale
K milder
L college
* M judjing
N (No mistakes)

7 A crab
B supply
* C puddel
D equal
E (No mistakes)

8 J smooth
* K bunnys
L dent
M allowed
N (No mistakes)

GO

124

Allow time for the students to mark their answers.

Say Answer circle D, *e-r-n*, should have been marked because it is a misspelling of *e-a-r-n*. If you chose another answer, erase yours and fill in answer circle D now.

Check to see that the students have filled in the correct answer circle.

Say Look at Sample B. Find the word that has a spelling mistake. If none of the words has a mistake, choose the last answer, No mistakes. Mark the circle for your answer.

Allow time for the students to mark their answers.

Say Answer circle N should have been marked because all the words are spelled correctly. If you chose another answer, erase yours and fill in answer circle N now.

Check to see that the students have filled in the correct answer circle.

Say Now you will do more spelling items. Look for a word that has a spelling mistake. If none of the words has a mistake, choose the last answer. Work by yourself. When you come to the GO sign at the bottom of the page, turn to the next page and continue working. Work until you come to the STOP sign at the bottom of page 125. When you have finished, you can check over your answers to this test. Then wait for the rest of the group to finish. Any questions?

Answer any questions that the students have.

Say Start working now. You will have 20 minutes.

Allow 20 minutes.

Say **It's time to stop. You have completed Test 3. Check to see that you have completely filled in your answer circles with dark marks. Make sure that any marks for answers that you changed have been completely erased. Now you may close your books.**

Review the items with the students. Have them indicate completion of the lesson by entering their score for this activity on the progress chart at the beginning of the book. Then collect the students' books and answer sheets if this is the end of the testing session.

Test 3 **Spelling**

9
A discovery
B aim
C trouble
* D rownd
E (No mistakes)

10
J chalk
* K sises
L pair
M obtain
N (No mistakes)

11
A winter
B airline
* C pervent
D broom
E (No mistakes)

12
J lane
* K peper
L deliver
M helmet
N (No mistakes)

13
A beard
* B generious
C prevent
D broom
E (No mistakes)

14
J lawn
K balance
L motor
M twig
* N (No mistakes)

15
* A decizion
B arrive
C owner
D stitch
E (No mistakes)

16
J parent
K connect
* L warryer
M army
N (No mistakes)

17
* A sollid
B high
C mirror
D ferry
E (No mistakes)

18
J package
K expect
* L shugar
M arrow
N (No mistakes)

19
A risky
* B mistre
C invite
D bath
E (No mistakes)

20
J waste
K battery
L hotel
* M exet
N (No mistakes)

125

Unit 11 Test 4 Capitalization

Administration Time: 20 minutes

Say **Turn to Test 4 on page 105.**

Check to see that the students have found page 126.

Say **Look at your answer sheet. Find the part called Test 4, Capitalization. All your answers for this test should be marked on your answer sheet, not in your book.**

Check to see that the students have found the correct part of the answer sheet.

Say **This test will check how well you can find capitalization mistakes. Remember to make sure that the circles for your answer choices are completely filled in. Press your pencil firmly so that your marks come out dark. Completely erase any marks for answers that you change.**

Look at Sample A. Read the answer choices. Find the answer that has a capitalization mistake. If there is no mistake, choose the last answer. Mark the circle for your answer on the answer sheet.

Test Practice

Test 4 **Capitalization**

Directions: Fill in the space for the answer that has a capitalization mistake. Fill in the last answer space if there is no mistake.

Sample A
A After the flood last year,
*B the red cross helped us
C find a place to live.
D (No mistakes)

Sample B
J This can't be right. I was
K sure we paid this bill
L in either March or April.
* M (No mistakes)

1
A My sister wanted to go to
* B dental school after hearing mr.
C Smith talk about what dentists do.
D (No mistakes)

2
*J Jesse eats at new york deli
K every other Tuesday. He usually
L orders the same sandwich each time.
M (No mistakes)

3
A Sometimes my uncle watches me
B play soccer on Saturdays. When he
* C comes, i say hello to him at half time.
D (No mistakes)

4
*J The jefferson memorial is at
K the edge of the Tidal Basin. This
L setting is beautiful in the spring.
M (No mistakes)

5
A How many times did we go
B to the park last week? I remember
* C going thursday and friday.
D (No mistakes)

6
J Nancy moved across town at
K the end of the summer. Her new
* L address is 12334 Freemont street.
M (No mistakes)

7
A Lewis and Clark explored
* B Idaho in 1805. the state's first
C settlement was a trading post.
D (No mistakes)

8
*J The people of iceland elected
K the first woman president
L in history in 1980.
M (No mistakes)

9
A Kurt watched as the parade
B passed by. When he saw his
* C sister, he yelled, "good job!"
D (No mistakes)

10
J Our dog, Bullet, loves to chase
K cars as they pass by. He barks
L until the cars are out of sight.
* M (No mistakes)

126

Allow time for the students to mark their answers.

Say **Answer circle B should have been marked because *Red Cross* should be capitalized. If you chose another answer, erase yours and fill in answer circle B now.**

Check to see that the students have filled in the correct answer circle.

Say **Look at Sample B. Find the answer that has a capitalization mistake. If there is no mistake, choose the last answer. Mark the circle for your answer.**

Allow time for the students to mark their answers.

Say **Answer circle M should have been marked because none of the answer choices has a capitalization mistake. If you chose another answer, erase yours and fill in answer circle M now.**

Check to see that the students have filled in the correct answer circle.

Say **Now you will do more items. Look for an answer that has a capitalization mistake. If none of the answers has a mistake, choose the last answer. Work by yourself until you come to the STOP sign at the bottom of the page. When you have finished, you can check over your answers to this test. Then wait for the rest of the group to finish. Any questions?**

Answer any questions that the students have.

Say **Start working now. You will have 15 minutes.**

Allow 15 minutes.

Say **It's time to stop. You have completed Test 4. Check to see that you have completely filled in your answer circles with dark marks. Make sure that any marks for answers that you changed have been completely erased. Now you may close your books.**

Review the items with the students. Have them indicate completion of the lesson by entering their score for this activity on the progress chart at the beginning of the book. Then collect the students' books and answer sheets if this is the end of the testing session.

Test Practice

Test 4 **Capitalization**

Directions: Fill in the space for the answer that has a capitalization mistake. Fill in the last answer space if there is no mistake.

Sample A
A After the flood last year,
*B the red cross helped us
C find a place to live.
D (No mistakes)

Sample B
J This can't be right. I was
K sure we paid this bill
L in either March or April.
* M (No mistakes)

1
A My sister wanted to go to
* B dental school after hearing mr.
C Smith talk about what dentists do.
D (No mistakes)

2
*J Jesse eats at new york deli
K every other Tuesday. He usually
L orders the same sandwich each time.
M (No mistakes)

3
A Sometimes my uncle watches me
B play soccer on Saturdays. When he
* C comes, i say hello to him at half time.
D (No mistakes)

4
*J The jefferson memorial is at
K the edge of the Tidal Basin. This
L setting is beautiful in the spring.
M (No mistakes)

5
A How many times did we go
B to the park last week? I remember
* C going thursday and friday.
D (No mistakes)

6
J Nancy moved across town at
K the end of the summer. Her new
* L address is 12334 Freemont street.
M (No mistakes)

7
A Lewis and Clark explored
* B Idaho in 1805. the state's first
C settlement was a trading post.
D (No mistakes)

8
*J The people of iceland elected
K the first woman president
L in history in 1980.
M (No mistakes)

9
A Kurt watched as the parade
B passed by. When he saw his
* C sister, he yelled, "good job!"
D (No mistakes)

10
J Our dog, Bullet, loves to chase
K cars as they pass by. He barks
L until the cars are out of sight.
* M (No mistakes)

Unit 11 Test 5 Punctuation

Administration Time: 20 minutes

Say **Turn to Test 5 on page 127.**

Check to see that the students have found page 127.

Say **Look at your answer sheet. Find the part called Test 5, Punctuation. All your answers for this test should be marked on your answer sheet, not in your book.**

Check to see that the students have found the correct part of the answer sheet.

Say **This test will check how well you can find punctuation mistakes. Remember to make sure that the circles for your answer choices are completely filled in. Press your pencil firmly so that your marks come out dark. Completely erase any marks for answers that you change.**

Look at Sample A. Read the answer choices. Find the answer that has a punctuation mistake. If there is no mistake, choose the last answer. Mark the circle for your answer on the answer sheet.

Test Practice

Test 5 **Punctuation**

Directions: Fill in the space for the answer that has a punctuation mistake. Fill in the last answer space if there is no mistake.

Sample A
- A The plane landed in
- * B London We took the train
- C from the airport.
- D (No mistakes)

Sample B
- J Candace shouted to Kevin,
- K "Hurry up and close the door
- L before the cat gets out."
- * M (No mistakes)

1
- A In Oxford, England, it is
- B difficult to find a restaurant
- * C open after 900 at night.
- D (No mistakes)

2
- J James looked at Mr. Wright
- * K carefully. Are you serious?
- L James asked the man.
- M (No mistakes)

3
- * A Hes promised to go to a play
- B with me tonight, though Victor
- C rarely leaves his house.
- D (No mistakes)

4
- J "Alligators usually live
- * K in swampy water?" said James
- L as he passed through the zoo.
- M (No mistakes)

5
- A While Jessica ran downstairs,
- B her brother hid a gift. He was
- C wrapping it for her birthday.
- * D (No mistakes)

6
- J When the travelers reached
- * K Durango Colorado, they
- L decided to stay for a few days.
- M (No mistakes)

7
- A Sonja waited eagerly by
- * B the door to talk to Mrs Boswell
- C about the award program.
- D (No mistakes)

8
- J Do you have any friends
- K who live in another country?
- * L I know a girl in Mexico
- M (No mistakes)

9
- * A How many do we have left?
- B yelled Mr. Ivers. "Only two
- C more boxes, sir," said Joe.
- D (No mistakes)

10
- J As I walked, I noticed
- K that the baby ducks had
- * L arrived I love watching them.
- M (No mistakes)

127

Allow time for the students to mark their answers.

Say **Answer circle B should have been marked. A period is needed after *London* because it is the end of a sentence. If you chose another answer, erase yours and fill in answer circle B now.**

Check to see that the students have filled in the correct answer circle.

Say **Look at Sample B. Find the answer that has a punctuation mistake. If there is no mistake, choose the last answer. Mark the circle for your answer.**

Allow time for the students to mark their answers.

Say **Answer circle M should have been marked because none of the answer choices has a mistake. If you chose another answer, erase yours and fill in answer circle J now.**

Check to see that the students have filled in the correct answer circle.

Say **Now you will do more items. Look for an answer that has a punctuation mistake. If none of the answers has a mistake, choose the last answer. Work by yourself until you come to the STOP sign at the bottom of the page. When you have finished, you can check over your answers to this test. Then wait for the rest of the group to finish. Any questions?**

Answer any questions that the students have.

Say **Start working now. You will have 15 minutes.**

Allow 15 minutes.

Say **It's time to stop. You have completed Test 5. Check to see that you have completely filled in your answer circles with dark marks. Make sure that any marks for answers that you changed have been completely erased. Now you may close your books.**

Review the items with the students. Have them indicate completion of the lesson by entering their score for this activity on the progress chart at the beginning of the book. Then collect the students' books and answer sheets if this is the end of the testing session.

Test Practice

Test 5 **Punctuation**

Directions: Fill in the space for the answer that has a punctuation mistake. Fill in the last answer space if there is no mistake.

Sample **A**
A The plane landed in
* B London We took the train
C from the airport.
D (No mistakes)

Sample **B**
J Candace shouted to Kevin,
K "Hurry up and close the door
L before the cat gets out."
* M (No mistakes)

1
A In Oxford, England, it is
B difficult to find a restaurant
* C open after 900 at night.
D (No mistakes)

2
J James looked at Mr. Wright
* K carefully. Are you serious?
L James asked the man.
M (No mistakes)

3
* A Hes promised to go to a play
B with me tonight, though Victor
C rarely leaves his house.
D (No mistakes)

4
J "Alligators usually live
* K in swampy water?" said James
L as he passed through the zoo.
M (No mistakes)

5
A While Jessica ran downstairs,
B her brother hid a gift. He was
C wrapping it for her birthday.
* D (No mistakes)

6
J When the travelers reached
* K Durango Colorado, they
L decided to stay for a few days.
M (No mistakes)

7
A Sonja waited eagerly by
* B the door to talk to Mrs Boswell
C about the award program.
D (No mistakes)

8
J Do you have any friends
K who live in another country?
* L I know a girl in Mexico
M (No mistakes)

9
* A How many do we have left?
B yelled Mr. Ivers. "Only two
C more boxes, sir," said Joe.
D (No mistakes)

10
J As I walked, I noticed
K that the baby ducks had
* L arrived I love watching them.
M (No mistakes)

Unit 11 Test 6 Part 1 Usage

Administration Time: 25 minutes

Say **Turn to Test 6, Part 1 on page 128.**

Check to see that the students have found page 128.

Say **Look at your answer sheet. Find the part called Test 6, Part 1, Usage. All your answers for this test should be marked on your answer sheet, not in your book.**

Check to see that the students have found the correct part of the answer sheet.

Say **This test will check how well you can find mistakes in English usage and expression. Remember to make sure that the circles for your answer choices are completely filled in. Press your pencil firmly so that your marks come out dark. Completely erase any marks for answers that you change.**

Look at Sample A. Read the answer choices. Find the answer that has a mistake in usage. If there is no mistake, choose the last answer. Mark the circle for your answer on the answer sheet.

Test Practice

Test 6 Part 1 **Usage**

Directions: Fill in the space for the answer that has a mistake in usage. Fill in the last answer space if there is no mistake.

Sample A
*A Sally's sister growed two
B inches this year. She is taller
C than both of her brothers.
D (No mistakes)

Sample B
J Harry S. Truman became
K president after the death
L of Franklin Delano Roosevelt.
* M (No mistakes)

1
A Wilma Rudolph had polio as a
* B child. She still winned two gold
C medals in the 1960 Olympics.
D (No mistakes)

2
J Aunt Sandy and Uncle Jamal
K went to Hawaii for two weeks, but they
* L didn't get no pictures of the trip.
M (No mistakes)

3
*A John and her walked to
B the beach early Saturday
C morning. The water was cold.
D (No mistakes)

4
J Casey said that the movie was the
* K bestest she'd ever seen. It starred
L her favorite actor and had great music.
M (No mistakes)

5
A Without thinking about it, Ned
B jumped into the water and
C grabbed his mother's hat.
* D (No mistakes)

6
*J Toby asked I and Jesse to
K play the guitar at the talent
L show this Friday night.
M (No mistakes)

7
A They had to rent a different
* B video game because there favorite
C was checked out at the video store.
D (No mistakes)

8
*J Jessica hadn't done none
K of her homework Friday. She
L planned to do it on Saturday.
M (No mistakes)

9
A When we visit Uncle
B John's farm I love to watch
* C the sheeps in the pasture.
D (No mistakes)

10
J How many times had you
* K wored that bracelet before
L you lost the clasp and charm?
M (No mistakes)

GO

128

Allow time for the students to mark their answers.

Say **Answer circle A should have been marked because the word *growed* should be *grew*. If you chose another answer, erase yours and fill in answer circle A now.**

Check to see that the students have filled in the correct answer circle.

Say **Look at Sample B. Find the answer that has a punctuation mistake. If there is no mistake, choose the last answer. Mark the circle for your answer.**

Allow time for the students to mark their answers.

Say **You should have marked answer circle M because none of the answers has a mistake in English usage. If you chose another answer, erase yours and fill in answer circle M now.**

Check to see that the students have filled in the correct answer circle.

Say **Now you will do more items. Look for an answer that has a mistake in usage. If none of the answers has a mistake, choose the last answer. Work by yourself. When you come to the GO sign at the bottom of the page, turn the page and continue working. Work until you come to the STOP sign at the bottom of page 129. When you have finished, you can check over your answers to this test. Then wait for the rest of the group to finish. Do you have any questions?**

Answer any questions that the students have.

Say **Start working now. You will have 20 minutes.**

Allow 20 minutes.

Say **It's time to stop. You have completed Test 6, Part 1. Check to see that you have completely filled in your answer circles with dark marks. Make sure that any marks for answers that you changed have been completely erased. Now you may close your books.**

Review the items with the students. Have them indicate completion of the lesson by entering their score for this activity on the progress chart at the beginning of the book. Then collect the students' books and answer sheets if this is the end of the testing session.

Test 6 Part 1 **Usage**

11 A Some people love to watch themselves
B on the video screen at the mall. They
C stare and make faces as they pass by.
* D (No mistakes)

12*J The arctic fox should better be glad
K its coat is white. The color matches
L the snow and hides it from its enemies.
M (No mistakes)

13*A James Madison he was the fourth
B president of the United States
C and the oldest of twelve children.
D (No mistakes)

14 J The airplane has made the
K world a smaller place. People
* L can go anywheres they want.
M (No mistakes)

15*A There weren't nobody at
B the beach when we arrived,
C but soon it was crowded.
D (No mistakes)

16 J Only about 1,000 pandas are
* K lefted in the world, though they
L once populated much of Asia.
M (No mistakes)

17 A I'm not ready to jump off the
B high dive yet, though I've taken
C swimming lessons for two weeks.
* D (No mistakes)

18 J Mt. Rainier, located in Washington,
K is a challenge to mountain climbers.
* L That there mountain is over 14,000 feet high.
M (No mistakes)

19*A Brian watch his little brother
B every Monday night while his
C parents go to choir practice.
D (No mistakes)

20 J My grandmother lived during
* K the Depression. She selled her
L wedding ring to feed her family.
M (No mistakes)

129

Unit 11 Test 6 Part 2 **Expression**

Administration Time: 20 minutes

Say **Turn to Test 6, Part 2 on page 130.**

Check to see that the students have found page 130.

Say **Look at your answer sheet. Find the part called Test 6, Part 2, Expression. All your answers for this test should be marked on your answer sheet, not in your book.**

Check to see that the students have found the correct part of the answer sheet.

Say **This test will check how well you know English expression. Remember to make sure that the circles for your answer choices are completely filled in. Press your pencil firmly so that your marks come out dark. Completely erase any marks for answers that you change.**

Look at Sample A. Read the sentence and the answer choices. Find the answer that can take the place of the underlined part of the sentence. If the underlined part is correct, choose the last answer, No change. Mark the circle for your answer on the answer sheet.

Allow time for the students to mark their answers.

Say **Answer circle D should have been marked because the underlined part of the sentence is correct. If you chose another answer, erase yours and fill in answer circle D now.**

Check to see that the students have filled in the correct answer circle.

Say **Now you will do more items. Read the directions for each section. Mark the space for the answer you think is correct. Work by yourself. When you come to the GO sign at the bottom of the page, turn the page and continue working. Work until you come to the STOP sign at the bottom of page 131. When you have finished, you can check over your answers to this test. Then wait for the rest of the group to finish. Do you have any questions?**

Answer any questions that the students have.

Say **Start working now. You will have 15 minutes.**

Allow 15 minutes.

Test Practice

Test 6 Part 2 **Expression**

Directions: For questions 1–3, choose the best way to write the underlined part of the sentence.

Sample **A** The children enjoyed the picnic **in spite of** the rainy weather.
A although B because of C except * D (No change)

1 I only see my grandmother once a month **when** she moved away.
* A since
B while
C if
D (No change)

2 Sarita always cleans off the table **until washing** the dishes.
J while she washed
* K before washing
L when to wash
M (No change)

3 Carla **has watered** the grass five times since Saturday.
A is watered
B will water
C is watering
* D (No change)

Directions: For questions 4 and 5, choose the best way of writing the idea.

4 J Please when you go to the grocery store pick up some milk.
* K Please pick up some milk when you go to the grocery store.
L When you to the grocery store go, please pick up some milk.
M Some milk please pick up when you go to the grocery store.

5 A At our favorite restaurant, we went to dinner after we left the fair.
* B After we left the fair, we went to dinner at our favorite restaurant.
C We went to dinner after we left the fair at our favorite restaurant.
D We went after we left the fair at our favorite restaurant to dinner.

6 **Which of these would be most appropriate in a letter asking for help from a city council?**
* J Jones Elementary would like to sponsor a fundraiser to buy new computers. We ask for your help by letting us use the courthouse lawn for our rummage sale. We thank you for your time.
K Our school wants to sell some stuff on the courthouse lawn. Would it be okay with you? We need some new computers. Thanks a lot!
L The county courthouse is a really great place because it is right in the middle of town. That's why Jones Elementary wants to use it to have a rummage sale. The sale is in two weeks. See you then!
M Our teacher wanted us to write and ask if we could use the courthouse lawn to have a rummage sale. Please let us know by next week. We have a lot of work to do.

GO

130

Say **It's time to stop. You have completed Test 6, Part 2. Check to see that you have completely filled in your answer circles with dark marks. Make sure that any marks for answers that you changed have been completely erased. Now you may close your books.**

Review the items with the students. Have them indicate completion of the lesson by entering their score for this activity on the progress chart at the beginning of the book. Then collect the students' books and answer sheets if this is the end of the testing session.

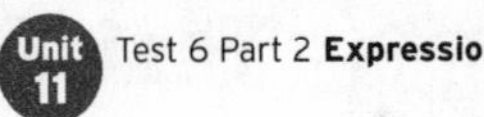

Directions: Use this paragraph to answer questions 7–12.

[1]The plans for the house must then be submitted to the county. [2]Before any building can begin, a house plan must be created. [3]After the builder has obtained the proper permits, excavating can begin. [4]He digs in the dirt where the foundation will be laid. [5]Then concrete is poured in the hole. [6]Concrete can be used to fix cracks in the sidewalk. [7]When the concrete dries it, become the foundation for the home.

7 **What is the best opening sentence for the paragraph?**
- A Houses can be built in the city or county and can be big or small.
- * B Much work is necessary before a house is actually built.
- C A house is a place where many family activities occur.
- D I learned most of what I know about building from my father.

8 **Which sentence should be left out of the paragraph?**
- J Sentence 4
- K Sentence 5
- * L Sentence 6
- M Sentence 7

9 **Where is the best place for sentence 2?**
- * A At the beginning of the paragraph
- B Between sentences 4 and 5
- C Between sentences 6 and 7
- D After sentence 3

10 **What is the best way to write the underlined part of sentence 4?**
- J He is digging
- K It is dug
- L Digging the hole
- * M A hole is dug

11 **What is the best way to write the underlined part of sentence 7?**
- A dries. It becomes
- B is drying, it becomes
- * C dries, it becomes
- D (No change)

12 **Choose the best concluding sentence to add to this paragraph.**
- J After the house is finished, the owners can move in.
- * K Once the foundation is laid, the building can begin.
- L Some houses can actually be moved on a truck.
- M Not everyone lives in a house made of wood.

131

Unit 11 Test 7 Part 1 Math Concepts

Administration Time: 20 minutes

Distribute scratch paper to the students.

Say Turn to Test 7, Part 1 on page 132.

Check to see that the students have found page 132.

Say Look at your answer sheet. Find the part called Test 7, Part 1, Math Concepts. If you need to, you may work on scratch paper, but be sure to mark all your answers for this test on your answer sheet.

Check to see that the students have found the correct part of the answer sheet.

Say This test will check how well you understand and solve mathematics problems. Remember to make sure that the circles for your answer choices are completely filled in. Press your pencil firmly so that your marks come out dark. Completely erase any marks for answers that you change.

Test Practice

Test 7 Part 1 **Math Concepts**

Directions: Read each mathematics problem. Choose the best answer.

Sample A **A mile is closest in value to**
A a meter.
* B a kilometer.
C a centimeter.
D a millimeter.

Sample B **What is another way to write *three thousand five*?**
* J 3,005
K 3,500
L 30,005
M 30,050

1 **What number is 1 less than 3,000?**
A 2,990
* B 2,999
C 2,000
D 3,001

2 **What fraction of the square shown below is shaded?**

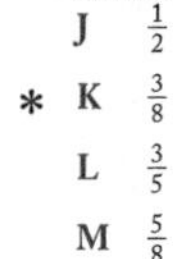

J $\frac{1}{2}$
* K $\frac{3}{8}$
L $\frac{3}{5}$
M $\frac{5}{8}$

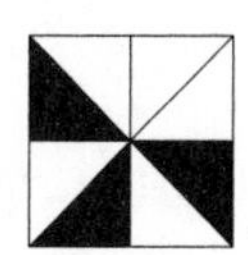

3 **How should you read 50,070?**
* A Fifty thousand seventy
B Fifty thousand seven
C Fifty thousand seven hundred
D Five hundred thousand seventy

4 **Which operation sign should replace the □ in the number sentence below?**

32 □ 2 = 4 × 4

J +
K −
L ×
* M ÷

5 **Which unit would be the best choice for measuring the distance between two lakes?**
A Tons
* B Miles
C Grams
D Centimeters

6 **Which figure has a line of symmetry drawn through it?**

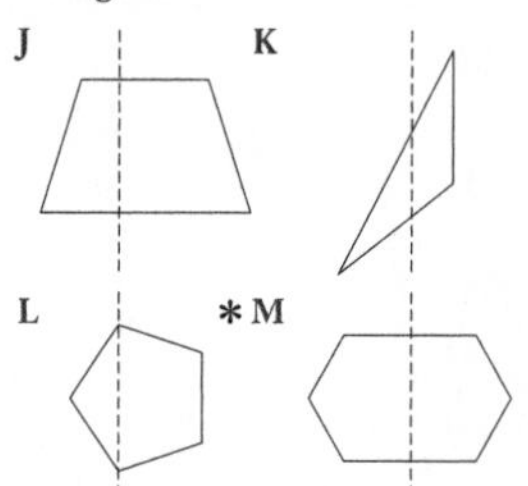

7 **Which will have a remainder when divided by 6?**
* A 32
B 48
C 54
D 78

GO

132

Look at Sample A. Read the problem and the four answer choices. Then solve the problem. On your answer sheet, find the answer circles for Sample A. Mark the circle for the answer to the problem.

Allow time for the students to mark their answers.

Say Answer circle B should have been filled in because *a kilometer* is closest in length to a mile. If you chose another answer, erase yours and fill in circle B now.

Check to see that the students have filled in the correct answer circle.

Say Now do Sample B. Solve the problem and mark the circle for the answer you find.

Allow time for the students to mark their answers.

Say Answer circle J should have been filled in. If you chose another answer, erase yours and fill in circle J now.

Check to see that the students have filled in the correct answer circle.

Say Now you will solve more mathematics problems. Work by yourself. Remember that you may use scratch paper to solve the problems. When you come to the GO sign at the bottom of the page, turn to the next page and continue working. Work until you come to the STOP sign at the bottom of page 133. When you have finished, you can check over your answers to this test. Then wait for the rest of the group to finish. Any questions?

Answer any questions that the students have.

Say Start working now. You will have 15 minutes.

Allow 15 minutes.

Say **It's time to stop. You have completed Test 7, Part 1. Check to see that you have completely filled in your answer circles with dark marks. Make sure that any marks for answers that you changed have been completely erased. Now you may close your books.**

Review the items with the students. Have them indicate completion of the lesson by entering their score for this activity on the progress chart at the beginning of the book. Then collect the students' books and answer sheets if this is the end of the testing session.

Unit 11 Test 7 Part 1 **Math Concepts**

8 What is the missing factor in the number sentence below?

$\square \times 1 \times 6 = 24$

J 0
* K 4
L 8
M 31

9 Which numeral should come next in the sequence 1, 3, 9, 27, _____?

A 29
B 30
C 34
* D 81

10 Which of these figures has the same area as the figure shown at the right?

J 
* L 
K 
M 

11 A washing machine would most likely hold

* A 30 gallons.
B 3 pints.
C 45 ounces.
D 5 quarts.

12 What should replace the □ in the number sentence below?

$79 - 6 < \square$

J 55
K 61
L 71
* M 74

13 Which piece below is part of the puzzle shown at the right?

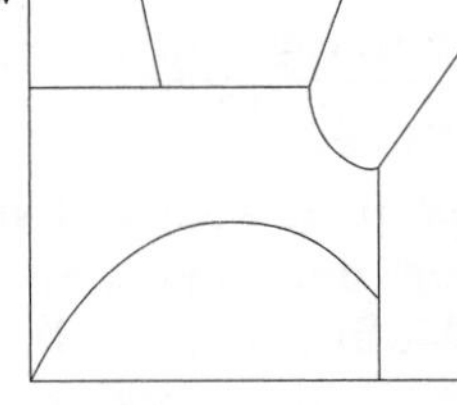

A
B

C

* D

STOP

133

Unit 11

Test 7 Part 2 Math Estimation

Administration Time: 20 minutes

Distribute scratch paper to the students.

Say **Turn to Test 7, Part 2 on page 134.**

Check to see that the students have found page 134.

Say **Look at your answer sheet. Find the part called Test 7, Part 2, Math Estimation. If you need to, you may work on scratch paper, but be sure to mark all your answers for this test on your answer sheet.**

Check to see that the students have found the correct part of the answer sheet.

Say **This test will check how well you understand and solve estimation problems. Remember to make sure that the circles for your answer choices are completely filled in. Press your pencil firmly so that your marks come out dark. Completely erase any marks for answers that you change.**

Test Practice

Test 7 Part 2 **Math Estimation**

Directions: Read each mathematics problem. Choose the answer that is the best estimation of the exact answer.

Sample A The closest estimate of 51 × 11 is between _____.
A 450 and 500
B 500 and 550
* C 550 and 600
D 600 and 650

Sample B The closest estimate of 32 × 88 is _____.
J 20 × 80
K 20 × 90
L 30 × 80
* M 30 × 90

1 Laura got inline skates for her birthday. The skates cost $49, the helmet cost $26, the wrist guards cost $13 and the knee guards cost $7. Which best shows how to get the closest estimate of the total cost of the skates and accessories?
A 50 + 30 + 20 + 10
* B 50 + 30 + 10 + 10
C 40 + 30 + 10 + 10
D 50 + 20 + 10 + 10

2 The closest estimate of 71,869 ÷ 9 is _____?
J 8
K 80
L 800
* M 8,000

3 Jason's family car can go 300 miles on 1 tank of gas. The closest estimate of the number of tanks of gas Jason's family will need to drive 1700 miles is _____.
A 5
* B 6
C 7
D 8

4 Which best shows how to get the closest estimate of $57.75 + $61.37 + $63.01?
J $50 × (2 × $60)
K $60 × (2 × $70)
L 3 × $50
* M 3 × $60

GO

134

Look at Sample A. Read the problem and the four answer choices. Then solve the problem. On your answer sheet, find the answer circles for Sample A. Mark the circle for the answer to the problem.

Allow time for the students to mark their answers.

Say **Answer circle C should have been filled in because it is the closest estimate to the solution of 51 times 11. If you chose another answer, erase yours and fill in circle C now.**

Check to see that the students have filled in the correct answer circle.

Say **Now do Sample B. Solve the problem and mark the circle for the answer you think is best.**

Allow time for the students to mark their answers.

Say **Answer circle M should have been filled in because the closest estimate to the problem is *30 times 90*. If you chose another answer, erase yours and fill in circle M now.**

Check to see that the students have filled in the correct answer circle.

Say **Now you will solve more estimation problems. Work by yourself. Remember that you may use scratch paper to solve the problems. When you come to the GO sign at the bottom of the page, turn the page and continue working. Work until you come to the STOP sign at the bottom of page 135. When you have finished, you can check over your answers to this test. Then wait for the rest of the group to finish. Any questions?**

Answer any questions that the students have.

Say **Start working now. You will have 15 minutes.**

Allow 15 minutes.

Say It's time to stop. You have completed Test 7, Part 2. Check to see that you have completely filled in your answer circles with dark marks. Make sure that any marks for answers that you changed have been completely erased. Now you may close your books.

Review the items with the students. Have them indicate completion of the lesson by entering their score for this activity on the progress chart at the beginning of the book. Then collect the students' books and answer sheets if this is the end of the testing session.

Test 7 Part 2 **Math Estimation**

5 **There are 16 black cars, 23 silver cars, and 11 red cars in a parking lot. Which best shows how to get the closest estimate of the total number of cars?**

A 10 + 20 + 10
B 30 + 30 + 20
C 20 + 30 + 10
* D 20 + 20 + 10

6 **The closest estimate of 27,436 + 18,857 is _____.**

J 500
K 5,000
* L 50,000
M 500,000

7 **One blank CD costs 95¢. The closest estimate to the cost of 8 blank CDs is _____.**

A $7
* B $8
C $9
D $10

8 **The closest estimate of $49.04 ÷ 8 is _____.**

J $4
K $5
* L $6
M $7

9 **Dante lives 74.1 miles from the coast. Marta lives 33.4 miles from the coast. About how many more miles does Dante live from the coast than Marta?**

* A 40 miles
B 50 miles
C 60 miles
D 70 miles

10 **The closest estimate of 593 × 45 is _____.**

J 400 × 40
K 500 × 50
* L 600 × 40
M 700 × 50

STOP

135

Unit 11 Test 8 Part 1 Math Problem Solving

Administration Time: 15 minutes

Distribute scratch paper to the students.

Say **Turn to Test 8, Part 1 on page 136.**

Check to see that the students have found page 136.

Say **Look at your answer sheet. Find the part called Test 8, Part 1, Math Problem Solving. If you need to, you may work on scratch paper, but be sure to mark all your answers for this test on your answer sheet.**

Check to see that the students have found the correct part of the answer sheet.

Say **This test will check how well you understand and solve word problems. Remember to make sure that the circles for your answer choices are completely filled in. Press your pencil firmly so that your marks come out dark. Completely erase any marks for answers that you change.**

Look at Sample A. Read the problem and the four answer choices. Then solve the problem. On your answer sheet, find the answer circles for Sample A. Mark the circle for the answer to the problem. If the correct answer is not given, choose answer D.

Allow time for the students to mark their answers.

Say **Answer circle C should have been filled in because the correct answer to the problem is *16*. If you chose another answer, erase yours and fill in circle C now.**

Check to see that the students have filled in the correct answer circle.

Unit 11 Test Practice

Test 8 Part 1 **Math Problem Solving**

Directions: Read each mathematics problem. Choose the best answer.

Sample A The Martin family decided to turn the television off from 6:00 P.M. to 8:00 P.M. for 5 days a week. On the other 2 days, they will shut it off from 6:00 P.M. to 9:00 P.M.

For how many hours a week did the Martins turn off the television?

A 7
B 14
* C 16
D Not given

1 **Cary, Alisha, and Colin organized a food and clothing drive at their school. To begin, they each brought 9 cans of food to school. How many cans did they bring in all?**

A 3
B 12
* C 27
D Not given

2 **During the first week of the drive they gave prizes to students who brought in 3 items of clothing and 10 cans of food. During the second week of the drive they only gave prizes to students who brought in a total of 17 items. How many more items did students have to bring the second week than the first week to get a prize?**

J 3
* K 4
L 14
M Not given

3 **Some students put up posters at school advertising their food and clothing drive. They made 3 posters for each hallway. What would you have to do to figure out the total number of posters they made?**

A Measure the length of the hallway.
B Measure the area of the posters.
C Count the amount of time it took them to make each poster.
* D Count the hallways in the school.

4 **By the end of the first week, the 3 students had 24 boxes of food and clothing to carry to the donation truck. They decided to each carry the same number of boxes. How many boxes did each child carry?**

J 12
K 21
L 27
* M Not given

STOP

136

Say **Now you will solve more mathematics problems. Remember that you may use scratch paper to solve the problems. Work until you come to the STOP sign at the bottom of the page. When you have finished, you can check over your answers to this test. Then wait for the rest of the group to finish. Any questions?**

Answer any questions that the students have.

Say **Start working now. You will have 10 minutes.**

Allow 10 minutes.

Say **It's time to stop. You have completed Test 8, Part 1. Check to see that you have completely filled in your answer circles with dark marks. Make sure that any marks for answers that you changed have been completely erased. Now you may close your books.**

Review the items with the students. Have them indicate completion of the lesson by entering their score for this activity on the progress chart at the beginning of the book. Then collect the students' books and answer sheets if this is the end of the testing session.

Test Practice

Test 8 Part 1 **Math Problem Solving**

Directions: Read each mathematics problem. Choose the best answer.

Sample **A** The Martin family decided to turn the television off from 6:00 P.M. to 8:00 P.M. for 5 days a week. On the other 2 days, they will shut it off from 6:00 P.M. to 9:00 P.M.

For how many hours a week did the Martins turn off the television?

A 7
B 14
* C 16
D Not given

1 **Cary, Alisha, and Colin organized a food and clothing drive at their school. To begin, they each brought 9 cans of food to school. How many cans did they bring in all?**

A 3
B 12
* C 27
D Not given

2 **During the first week of the drive they gave prizes to students who brought in 3 items of clothing and 10 cans of food. During the second week of the drive they only gave prizes to students who brought in a total of 17 items. How many more items did students have to bring the second week than the first week to get a prize?**

J 3
* K 4
L 14
M Not given

3 **Some students put up posters at school advertising their food and clothing drive. They made 3 posters for each hallway. What would you have to do to figure out the total number of posters they made?**

A Measure the length of the hallway.
B Measure the area of the posters.
C Count the amount of time it took them to make each poster.
* D Count the hallways in the school.

4 **By the end of the first week, the 3 students had 24 boxes of food and clothing to carry to the donation truck. They decided to each carry the same number of boxes. How many boxes did each child carry?**

J 12
K 21
L 27
* M Not given

STOP

136

Unit 11 Test 8 Part 2 **Data Interpretation**

Administration Time: 15 minutes

Distribute scratch paper to the students.

Say Turn to Test 8, Part 2 on page 137.

Check to see that the students have found page 137.

Say Look at your answer sheet. Find the part called Test 8, Part 2, Data Interpretation. If you need to, you may work on scratch paper, but be sure to mark all your answers for this test on your answer sheet.

Check to see that the students have found the correct part of the answer sheet.

Say This test will check how well you understand a graph. Remember to make sure that the circles for your answer choices are completely filled in. Press your pencil firmly so that your marks come out dark. Completely erase any marks for answers that you change. Remember that you may use scratch paper to solve the problems. Work until you come to the STOP sign at the bottom of the page. When you have finished, you can check over your answers to this test. Then wait for the rest of the group to finish. Any questions?

Answer any questions that the students have.

Say Start working now. You will have 10 minutes.

Allow 10 minutes.

Say It's time to stop. You have completed Test 8, Part 2. Check to see that you have completely filled in your answer circles with dark marks. Make sure that any marks for answers that you changed have been completely erased. Now you may close your books.

Review the items with the students. Have them indicate completion of the lesson by entering their score for this activity on the progress chart at the beginning of the book. Then collect the students' books and answer sheets if this is the end of the testing session.

Test Practice

Test 8 Part 2 **Data Interpretation**

Directions: Use the graph below to answer questions 1–4.

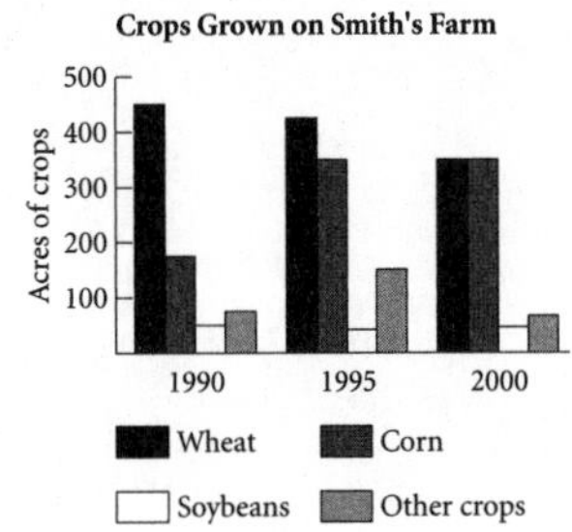

1 **In 1995, about how many more acres of wheat than corn were there on the Smith farm?**

* A 80
B 100
C 160
D 800

2 **For which crop did the number of acres increase the most between 1990 and 2000?**

J Wheat
* K Corn
L Soy beans
M Other crops

3 **Based on the information shown in the graph, which of these statements can be made about barley?**

A Barley is the smallest crop.
B Barley is planted on more acres than soybeans.
* C Corn is planted on more acres than barley.
D No barley is planted on the Smith farm.

4 **If present trends continue on the Smith farm, which crop will be planted on the most acres by 2005?**

J Wheat
* K Corn
L Soy beans
M Other crops

137

Unit 11

Test 9 Math Computation

Administration Time: 20 minutes

Distribute scratch paper to the students.

Say **Turn to Test 9 on page 138.**

Check to see that the students have found page 138.

Say **Look at your answer sheet. Find the part called Test 9, Math Computation. If you need to, you may work on scratch paper, but be sure to mark all your answers for this test on your answer sheet.**

Check to see that the students have found the correct part of the answer sheet.

Say **This test will check how well you can solve computation problems. Remember to make sure that the circles for your answer choices are completely filled in. Press your pencil firmly so that your marks come out dark. Completely erase any marks for answers that you change.**

Unit 11 **Test Practice**

Test 9 **Math Computation**

Directions: Solve each problem. Choose the answer you think is correct. If the correct answer is not given, fill in the space for the last answer, N.

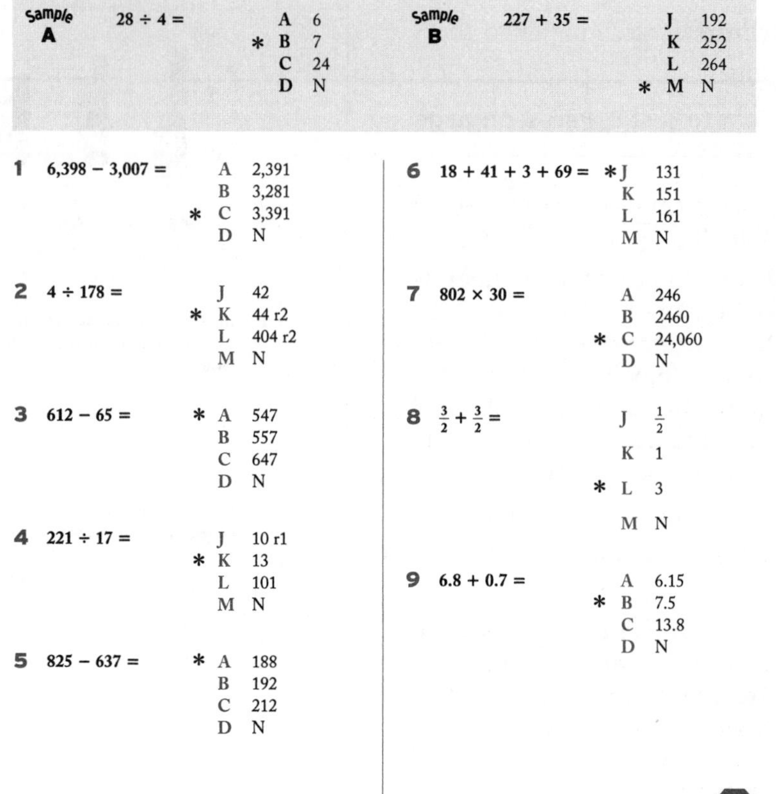

Sample A   28 ÷ 4 =   A 6   * B 7   C 24   D N

Sample B   227 + 35 =   J 192   K 252   L 264   * M N

1 6,398 − 3,007 =   A 2,391   B 3,281   * C 3,391   D N

2 4 ÷ 178 =   J 42   * K 44 r2   L 404 r2   M N

3 612 − 65 =   * A 547   B 557   C 647   D N

4 221 ÷ 17 =   J 10 r1   * K 13   L 101   M N

5 825 − 637 =   * A 188   B 192   C 212   D N

6 18 + 41 + 3 + 69 =   * J 131   K 151   L 161   M N

7 802 × 30 =   A 246   B 2460   * C 24,060   D N

8 $\frac{3}{2} + \frac{3}{2} =$ J $\frac{1}{2}$ K 1   * L 3   M N

9 6.8 + 0.7 =   A 6.15   * B 7.5   C 13.8   D N

STOP

138

Look at Sample A. Read the problem and the four answer choices. Then solve the problem. On your answer sheet, find the answer circles for Sample A. Mark the circle for the answer to the problem. If the correct answer is not given, choose answer D.

Allow time for the students to mark their answers.

Say **Answer circle B should have been filled in because the correct answer to the problem is *7*. If you chose another answer, erase yours and fill in circle B now.**

Check to see that the students have filled in the correct answer circle.

Say **Now do Sample B. Solve the problem and mark the circle for the answer you find. Mark the circle for the answer you think is best.**

Allow time for the students to mark their answers.

Say **Answer circle M should have been filled in because the solution to the problem, *262*, is not one of the choices. If you chose another answer, erase yours and fill in circle M now.**

Check to see that the students have filled in the correct answer circle.

Say **Now you will solve more computation problems. Remember that you may use scratch paper to solve the problems. Work until you come to the STOP sign at the bottom of the page. When you have finished, you can check over your answers to this test. Then wait for the rest of the group to finish. Any questions?**

Answer any questions that the students have.

Say **Start working now. You will have 15 minutes.**

Allow 15 minutes.

Say **It's time to stop. You have completed Test 9. Check to see that you have completely filled in your answer circles with dark marks. Make sure that any marks for answers that you changed have been completely erased. Now you may close your books.**

Review the items with the students. Have them indicate completion of the lesson by entering their score for this activity on the progress chart at the beginning of the book. Then collect the students' books and answer sheets if this is the end of the testing session.

Test Practice

Test 9 **Math Computation**

Directions: Solve each problem. Choose the answer you think is correct. If the correct answer is not given, fill in the space for the last answer, N.

Sample A 28 ÷ 4 =
A 6
* B 7
C 24
D N

Sample B 227 + 35 =
J 192
K 252
L 264
* M N

1 6,398 − 3,007 =
A 2,391
B 3,281
* C 3,391
D N

2 4 ÷ 178 =
J 42
* K 44 r2
L 404 r2
M N

3 612 − 65 =
* A 547
B 557
C 647
D N

4 221 ÷ 17 =
J 10 r1
* K 13
L 101
M N

5 825 − 637 =
* A 188
B 192
C 212
D N

6 18 + 41 + 3 + 69 =
* J 131
K 151
L 161
M N

7 802 × 30 =
A 246
B 2460
* C 24,060
D N

8 $\frac{3}{2} + \frac{3}{2} =$
J $\frac{1}{2}$
K 1
* L 3
M N

9 6.8 + 0.7 =
A 6.15
* B 7.5
C 13.8
D N

STOP

138

Unit 11 Test 10 Maps and Diagrams

Administration Time: 25 minutes

Say **Turn to Test 10 on page 139.**

Check to see that the students have found page 139.

Say **Look at your answer sheet. Find the part called Test 10, Maps and Diagrams. Mark all your answers for this test on your answer sheet.**

Check to see that the students have found the correct part of the answer sheet.

Say **This test will check how well you can use maps and diagrams. Remember to make sure that the circles for your answer choices are completely filled in. Press your pencil firmly so that your marks come out dark. Completely erase any marks for answers that you change.**

Look at the map and read the question for Sample A. On your answer sheet, find the answer circles for Sample A. Mark the circle for the answer to the question.

Test Practice

Test 10 **Maps and Diagrams**

Directions: Choose the best answer.

Sample A **Where are the entrances to the Art Galleries?**
A On Park View Avenue
* B On C Street
C On Market Place Avenue
D On D Street

Sample B **In what direction does Mr. Wells walk to go to the Park Place Center after checking into the Wyatt Hotel?**
J East
K West
L North
* M South

Directions: This map shows part of a city. Use the map to answer questions 1–5.

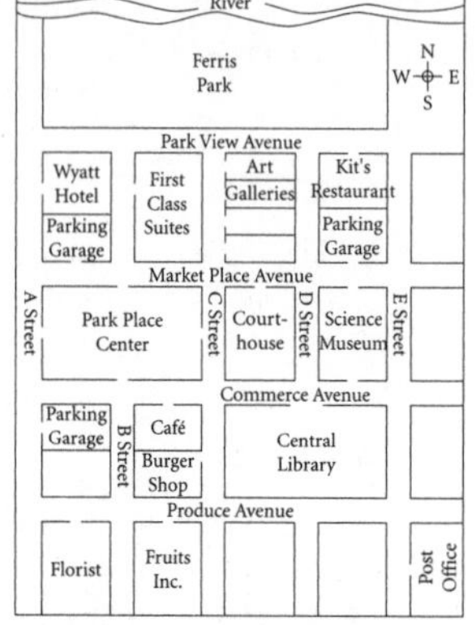

1 **Rick Wong lives on E Street, one block north of the Science Museum. To which of these does he live the closest?**
A Park Place Center
* B Kit's Restaurant
C Fruits, Inc.
D Central Library

2 **Which of these is closest to the Café?**
* J First Class Suites
K Kit's Restaurant
L The Post Office
M Wyatt Hotel

3 **A group of students left the Science Museum through the Commerce Avenue exit. They walked $1\frac{1}{2}$ blocks west and then a half block south. Where did they go?**
A To Central Library
B To the Café
* C To the Burger Shop
D To Fruits, Inc.

4 **How many blocks away from Central Library is the nearest parking garage?**
* J One block
K Two blocks
L Three blocks
M Four blocks

5 **In what direction is the Courthouse from the river?**
A East
B West
C North
* D South

GO

139

Allow time for the students to mark their answers.

Say **Answer circle B should have been filled in because the entrances to the art galleries are *on C Street*. If you chose another answer, erase yours and fill in circle B now.**

Check to see that the students have filled in the correct answer circle.

Say **Now do Sample B. On your answer sheet, find the answer circles for Sample B. Mark the circle for the answer you think is best.**

Allow time for the students to mark their answers.

Say **Answer circle M should have been filled in. If you chose another answer, erase yours and fill in circle M now.**

Check to see that the students have filled in the correct answer circle.

Say **Now you will answer more questions. Mark your answers on the answer sheet. When you come to a GO sign, turn the page and continue working. Work until you come to the STOP sign at the bottom of page 141. When you have finished, you can check over your answers to this test. Then wait for the rest of the group to finish. Any questions?**

Answer any questions that the students have.

Say **Start working now. You will have 20 minutes.**

Allow 20 minutes.

Test 10 **Maps and Diagrams**

Directions: The maps below show a farming area. The map on the top shows the geography of the farms. The map on the bottom shows what the farms produce. Use the maps to answer questions 6–11.

Map of Neighboring Farms

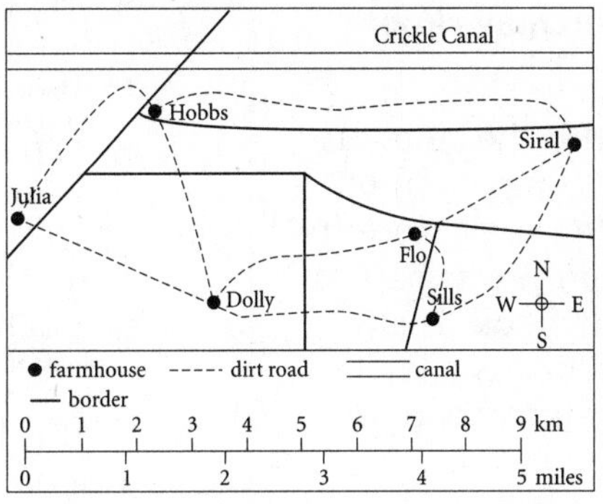

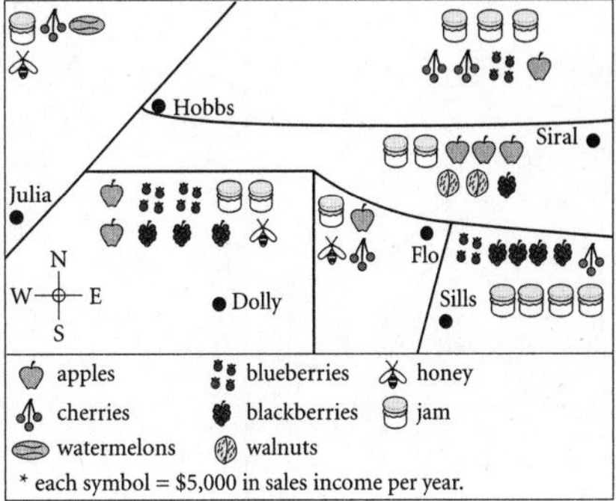

GO

140

Say **It's time to stop. You have completed Test 10. Check to see that you have completely filled in your answer circles with dark marks. Make sure that any marks for answers that you changed have been completely erased. Now you may close your books.**

Review the items with the students. Have them indicate completion of the lesson by entering their score for this activity on the progress chart at the beginning of the book. Then collect the students' books and answer sheets if this is the end of the testing session.

Test 10 **Maps and Diagrams**

6 **Which of these farms sells the most apples?**
- J Hobbs
- K Flo
- L Dolly
- * M Siral

7 **Which farm is divided nearly in half by a water source?**
- * A Julia
- B Hobbs
- C Flo
- D Siral

8 **Which farm product creates the highest dollar amount in sales each year?**
- J Cherries
- K Blueberries
- L Honey
- * M Jam

9 **Which farmhouse is southwest of the Flo farmhouse?**
- * A Dolly
- B Sills
- C Siral
- D Hobbs

10 **In which direction would you go if you were going from the Hobbs farmhouse to the Sills farmhouse?**
- J Northeast
- * K Southeast
- L Northwest
- M Southwest

11 **About how many miles is the most direct trip from the Dolly farmhouse to the Hobbs farmhouse?**
- A 1
- B 2
- * C 3
- D 4

STOP

141

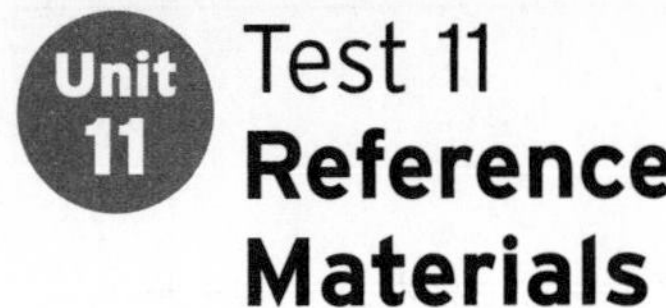

Unit 11 Test 11 Reference Materials

Administration Time: 25 minutes

Say **Turn to Test 11 on page 142.**

Check to see that the students have found page 142.

Say **Look at your answer sheet. Find the part called Test 11, Reference Materials. Mark all your answers for this test on your answer sheet.**

Check to see that the students have found the correct part of the answer sheet.

Say **This test will check how well you understand reference materials. Remember to make sure that the circles for your answer choices are completely filled in. Press your pencil firmly so that your marks come out dark. Completely erase any marks for answers that you change.**

Look at the table of contents and read the question for Sample A. On your answer sheet, find the answer circles for Sample A. Mark the circle for the answer to the question.

Unit 11 Test Practice

Test 11 **Reference Materials**

Directions: Choose the best answer.

Sample **A** **Where should you begin reading to find out about how to predict a volcanic eruption?**

A Page 7
B Page 15
* C Page 25
D Page 37

Sample **B** **Where should you begin reading to find out where a lot of volcanoes are?**

J Page 9
K Page 20
L Page 32
* M Page 35

Directions: Use this table of contents to answer questions 1–4.

Earthquakes and Volcanoes Contents

Chapter		Page
1	A Myth About Earthquakes	5
2	A Myth About Volcanoes	7
3	Shield, Cinder Cone, and Composite Cone Volcanoes	9
4	What Makes Volcanoes Explode?	15
5	The Earth Far Below a Volcano	20
6	Knowing About Eruptions Ahead of Time	25
7	How Mt. Mazama Became Crater Lake	28
8	All Cracked Up: The Earth's Outer Crust	32
9	Where Many Volcanoes Occur: Ring of Fire	35
10	How Big Was That Earthquake?	37

1 **Which chapter would probably tell how experts measure earthquakes?**

A Chapter 1
B Chapter 6
C Chapter 9
* D Chapter 10

2 **Which chapter would tell a make-believe story about volcanoes?**

* J Chapter 2
K Chapter 5
L Chapter 7
M Chapter 9

3 **What would chapter 3 tell you most about?**

A Protection from volcanoes
* B Different kinds of volcanoes
C Trees that grow near volcanoes
D How long volcanoes take to form

4 **Which chapter would tell about the many layers below the earth's surface?**

* J Chapter 5
K Chapter 6
L Chapter 8
M Chapter 9

GO

142

Allow time for the students to mark their answers.

Say **Answer circle C should have been filled in because *page 25* would tell you about predicting volcanic eruptions. If you chose another answer, erase yours and fill in circle C now.**

Check to see that the students have filled in the correct answer circle.

Say **Now do Sample B. Read the question and decide which answer is correct. Be sure to look at the table of contents. Mark the circle for the answer you think is best.**

Allow time for the students to mark their answers.

Say **Answer circle M should have been filled in because *page 35* tells where many volcanoes are located. If you chose another answer, erase yours and fill in circle M now.**

Check to see that the students have filled in the correct answer circle.

Say **Now you will answer more questions. There are different kinds of questions in this test, so be sure to read the directions for each part carefully. Mark your answers on the answer sheet. When you come to a GO sign, turn the page and continue working. Work until you come to the STOP sign at the bottom of page 144. When you have finished, you can check over your answers to this test. Then wait for the rest of the group to finish. Any questions?**

Answer any questions that the students have.

Say **Start working now. You will have 20 minutes.**

Allow 20 minutes.

Test 11 **Reference Materials**

Directions: For questions 5–8, choose the word or name that would come first if the words or names were arranged in alphabetical order.

5 A headstrong
* B headlight
C headquarters
D headline

6 J accuse
K accurate
L account
* M accost

7 A Anderson, Texas
* B Andalusia, Pennsylvania
C Androscoggin, Maine
D Andrew, Missouri

8 J Vicks, Melissa
K Vicks, Michaelia
* L Vicks, Melinda
M Vicks, Mildred

Directions: Use this encyclopedia set to answer questions 9–12.

9 Which volume would tell you whether the common wombat and the hairy-nosed wombat are native only to Australia?
A Volume 1
B Volume 2
C Volume 4
* D Volume 12

10 Which volume would tell you the most about Mario Andretti, a famous race-car driver who won the Grand Prix in 1978?
* J Volume 1
K Volume 4
L Volume 7
M Volume 9

11 Which volume would tell you the most about Julia Child, world-famous chef and author of *Mastering the Art of French Cooking*?
* A Volume 2
B Volume 3
C Volume 5
D Volume 7

12 Which volume would probably tell you about building gingerbread houses with the help of candy and icing?
J Volume 1
K Volume 2
* L Volume 4
M Volume 5

GO

Say **It's time to stop. You have completed Test 11. Check to see that you have completely filled in your answer circles with dark marks. Make sure that any marks for answers that you changed have been completely erased. Now you may close your books.**

Review the items with the students. Have them indicate completion of the lesson by entering their score for this activity on the progress chart at the beginning of the book. Then collect the students' books and answer sheets if this is the end of the testing session.

Test 11 **Reference Materials**

Directions: Use this dictionary page to answer questions 13 and 14.

accolade • atmosphere

ac•co•lade (ăc′ ə lād′) *n.* 1. any award, honor, or notice 2. the ceremony of becoming a knight

af•fa•ble (ăf′ ə bəl) *adj.* easy to talk to

a•gil•i•ty (ə jĭl′ ĭ tē) *n.* the power of moving quickly and easily

ag•i•ta•tor (aj′ ĭ tā′ tər) *n.* a person who stirs up trouble

ail•ment (āl′ mənt) *n.* a physical disorder or illness

an•noy•ance (ə noi′ əns) *n.* a person or thing that annoys: Unwanted guests are an annoyance.

ap•a•thet•ic (ăp′ ə thĕt′ ĭk) *adj.* 1. having or showing little or no emotion 2. uninterested

ap•pli•cant (ăp′ lĭ kənt) *n.* a person who applies for something, like a job

ap•ti•tude (ăp′ tĭ to͞od′) *n.* the capability or ability to do something; talent

ar•id (ăr′ ĭd) *adj.* being without moisture; extremely dry

ar•ti•fice (är′ tə fĭs) *n.* a clever trick or craftiness

at•mos•phere (ăt′ mə sfîr′) *n.* 1. the gaseous envelope surrounding Earth 2. the mood or tone of an environment

13 How should you spell the name of a person who applies for a job?

A applecant
B aplicant
* C applicant
D aplacant

14 What is the plural form of agitator?

J agitatores
K agitatories
L agitatorse
* M agitators

Directions: Use this information from a library catalog system to answer questions 15 and 16.

Thomas, Robin
570.3 The greatest inventor of all time: the
T784 biography of Leonardo da Vinci / by Robin Thomas; illustrated by Rich Geary.
–New York: Jackson-Fife, 1978.
72 p.: ill.; 26 cm.
1. Inventors. 2. Biography. 3. da Vinci.
I. Geary, Richard M.
II. Title

15 Who is Richard M. Geary?

A The publisher of the book
B The author of the book
* C The person who drew the pictures for the book
D The person who knew Leonardo da Vinci best

16 What is the title of this book?

* J The Greatest Inventor of All Time: The Biography of Leonardo da Vinci
K The Greatest Inventor of All Time
L The Biography of Leonardo da Vinci
M Inventors

STOP

144

Unit 11 Test 12 Science

Administration Time: 45 minutes

Say **Turn to Test 12 on page 145.**

Check to see that the students have found page 145.

Say **Look at your answer sheet. Find the part called Test 12, Science. Mark all your answers for this test on your answer sheet.**

Check to see that the students have found the correct part of the answer sheet.

Say **This test will check how well you understand science. Remember to make sure that the circles for your answer choices are completely filled in. Press your pencil firmly so that your marks come out dark. Completely erase any marks for answers that you change.**

Read Sample A to yourself. Think about the question and look at the answer choices. On your answer sheet, find the answer circles for Sample A. Mark the circle for your answer.

Allow time for the students to mark their answers.

Test Practice

Test 12 **Science**

Directions: Read each question and the answer choices. Choose the best answer.

Sample A **One way that animals protect themselves is by being able to escape predators. Which of these animals uses speed to escape predators?**

A Turtle
B Snail
* C Rabbit
D Clam

Sample B **When a meteor reaches the atmosphere of Earth, it will become hot and leave a fiery trail. This is the result of**

J moisture in Earth's atmosphere.
K energy radiating from the sun.
L Earth's magnetic field.
* M friction caused by the atmosphere.

1 **How does a pine tree reproduce?**

A Spores
B Cell division
* C Cones
D Root grafting

2 **What force causes objects moving on level ground to stop?**

J Gravity
* K Friction
L Tension
M Inertia

3 **Rain, snow, and sleet are forms of what?**

* A Precipitation
B Clouds
C Climate
D Cold weather

4 **Another name for rust is**

J hydrogen.
K calcium.
L carbon dioxide.
* M iron oxide.

GO

145

Say **Answer circle C should have been filled in because a *rabbit* uses speed to escape predators. If you chose another answer, erase yours and fill in circle C now.**

Check to see that the students have filled in the correct answer circle.

Say **Now do Sample B. Read the question and decide which answer is correct. Mark the circle for the answer you think is best.**

Allow time for the students to mark their answers.

Say **Answer circle M should have been filled in because *friction* causes meteors to become hot and leave a fiery trail. If you chose another answer, erase yours and fill in circle M now.**

Check to see that the students have filled in the correct answer circle.

Say **Now you will answer more questions. Mark your answers on the answer sheet. When you come to a GO sign, turn the page and continue working. Work until you come to the STOP sign at the bottom of page 154. When you have finished, you can check over your answers to this test. Then wait for the rest of the group to finish. Any questions?**

Answer any questions that the students have.

Say **Start working now. You will have 40 minutes.**

Allow 40 minutes.

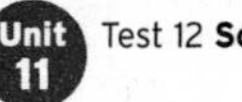

Test 12 **Science**

Directions: Use the information below to answer questions 5–8.

Angela was interested in finding out what affected the growth of plants. She decided to test one factor.

Angela put two small bean plants in glass jars using the same amount of high-quality soil. She gave them each enough water to saturate the soil. She put a lid on one of the jars and left the other one open. Both jars were placed on a kitchen window where they received the same amount of light for most of the day. After five days, the plant in the jar with the lid was drooping. Its leaves were yellow, and it had not grown the way the other bean plant had. The bean plant in the open jar seemed healthy. It stood straight and tall, its color was good, and it had sprouted new leaves.

5 What was Angela trying to find out?
* A If plants need air to grow
B How much bean plants grow in five days
C If plants enjoy growing in glass jars
D If plants need water to grow

6 What did Angela's results show?
J The bean plant in the open jar did not grow as well.
K Neither bean plant grew well in a glass jar.
* L The bean plant in the covered jar did not grow as well.
M Bean plants are hardy and can grow under most conditions.

7 What did the plant in the closed jar need to grow better?
A More water
B More oxygen
* C More carbon dioxide
D More sunlight

8 What other factor may have caused the plant to droop?
* J A disease that affected just one plant
K Using glass jars instead of flower pots
L Growing bean plants rather than peas
M Putting the jars in a sunny window

GO

Test 12 **Science**

9 What does a seed contain that provides energy for germination?

A Absorbed sunlight
B Water
C Seed coat
* D Stored food

10 Fossils suggest that a horselike animal the size of a small dog lived millions of years ago. Today's horses are much larger. What does this show about how horses have developed?

J Horses were once related to dogs.
K Horses have not changed much since the first of the species appeared.
* L Horses have grown significantly in size over time.
M Early fossils are not a good indicator of how horses have changed.

11 Heat moves through metal by

A radiation.
* B conduction.
C reproduction.
D absorption.

12 During which stage of its life is a moth most likely to damage clothes?

J Egg
* K Larva
L Pupa
M Adult

13 Which of these is a chemical change?

A Melting
B Boiling
C Condensing
* D Rusting

GO

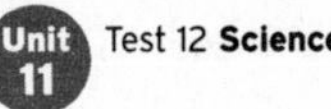

Test 12 **Science**

14 Which of these traits is inherited by a dog?

J Barking to go outside
K A preference for certain dog food
* L The color of its eyes
M Walking on a leash

15 How does the force of gravity exerted by the moon on a rocket change as the rocket approaches the moon?

A It increases because Earth's gravity is carried along by the rocket.
B There is no force of gravity on the moon.
C The force of gravity is unchanged because gravity is the same everywhere.
* D The force of gravity increases as the rocket approaches the moon.

16 A lunar eclipse occurs when

J Venus and Mercury come between the sun and the moon.
* K Earth comes between the sun and moon, and casts a shadow across the moon's surface.
L the moon passes in front of the sun and blocks the sun's light from reaching the Earth.
M the light from the sun does not reach the moon because the moon is tilted too far on its axis.

17 An animal without a skeleton is called

A an amphibian.
B a scavenger.
C a reptile.
* D an invertebrate.

18 Which statement about volcanoes is <u>not</u> true?

J Volcanoes may form under the ocean at plate edges.
K Volcanoes may be cone-shaped or almost flat.
* L Volcanoes are a result of severe tropical storms.
M Volcanoes erupt when pressure builds up inside.

GO

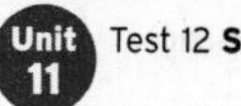

19 Which of these can be concluded about small plants that grow on the forest floor?

A They have bigger fruit than taller plants.

B They require a different climate than taller plants.

C They have fewer insect pests than taller plants.

* D They need less light than taller plants.

20 Most of what scientists know about dinosaurs comes from

* J fossils.

K books.

L pictures.

M observers.

21 When ice forms in a lake, it usually begins at the shore and moves toward the middle. What causes this?

A Streams enter lakes near the middle, so the water is moving more.

* B The shallow water near the shore cools off more quickly.

C Large stones near shore absorb heat from the water.

D Plants growing in the middle of the lake create energy from sunlight.

22 To which body part are the wings of an insect attached?

J Head

* K Thorax

L Abdomen

M Antennae

23 On cool spring days, snakes and lizards will often lie on roads. Why do they do this?

A They are hiding from predators that are afraid of roads.

B They are waiting for insects they can eat.

* C They are absorbing heat from the warm roads.

D They need the moisture the road provides.

24 Proteins are complex compounds, but they are not living things. Which of these differentiates a living thing from a protein?

J Only a living thing contains carbon.
* K Only a living thing can reproduce.
L Only a living thing is affected by gravity.
M Only a living thing gives off heat.

25 When you are in an elevator and move upward quickly, inertia pushes you against the floor of the elevator. In this situation, this force is most associated with

* A gravity.
B magnetism.
C electricity.
D friction.

26 What information does the color of a star provide?

J Its moisture content
K The galaxy in which it is located
L How many planets it has
* M Its surface temperature

27 Groups of organs that perform related functions are called

A cells.
* B systems.
C tissue.
D molecular.

28 The process through which a solid changes into a liquid is called

* J melting.
K vaporizing.
L evaporating.
M condensing.

GO

Test 12 **Science**

Directions: Use the information below to answer questions 29–32.

Melanie's teacher said that heat travels from hotter bodies to cooler bodies. Melanie decided to conduct an experiment to see if this was true.

Melanie filled two beakers with water. One beaker held water at 100°C, and one held water at 20°C, which was the temperature of the room. Each beaker was wrapped with insulation. She bent a metal rod at both ends and put one end in each beaker. She attached surface thermometers to the metal rod every two centimeters and recorded the temperature of each rod at one minute intervals. The results of the experiment are shown below.

Thermometer	1 minute	2 minutes	3 minutes	4 minutes
A	35°	42°	56°	72°
B	30°	37°	44°	51°
C	26°	34°	40°	48°
D	20°	27°	34°	41°

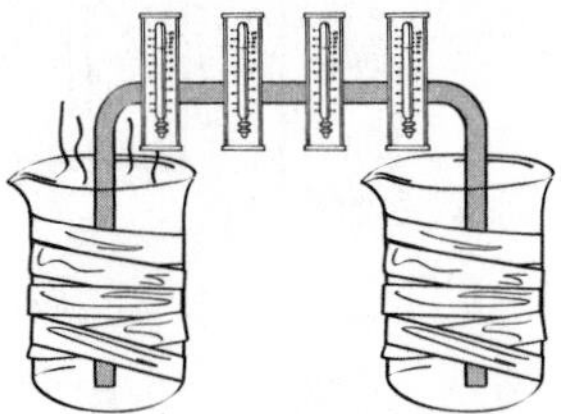

29 What was changed in order to determine the direction of the flow of heat?
- A The insulation that was wrapped around the beakers
- B The temperature of the water
- C The size of the beakers
- * D The distance of the thermometers from the beakers

30 What was most important for Melanie to do in this experiment?
- J Be sure that the temperature of the room was exactly 20° C.
- * K Record the correct temperature from each thermometer.
- L Use water that was pure.
- M Bend the rod at exactly the same place at both ends.

31 What would be the advantage of connecting a computer to the thermometers?
- A The thermometers could be moved closer to the beakers of water.
- B The amount of water for the experiment could be increased.
- * C The temperature could be measured more often and more accurately.
- D The hot water temperature could have been increased above 100° C.

32 Melanie concluded that the heat was being transferred from the hot water to the cold water through the rod because
- * J the thermometers near the hot water got warm before the ones farther away.
- K the temperature in the room stayed about 20° C.
- L the metal rod didn't melt in the hot water.
- M the insulation wrapped around the beakers kept them from becoming too cold.

Test 12 **Science**

33 **Only animals that can move quickly will migrate. This is true because**
A fast animals need a lot of food.
* B slow animals would take too long to migrate.
C fast animals are always escaping predators.
D slow animals have few enemies.

34 **During the 1930s, a great drought hit much of the American West. The area at the time was called the Dust Bowl. What happened to cause this?**
J Too many trees were planted on crop land.
K Farmers were unable to harvest crops.
L Crops were destroyed by grasshoppers.
* M Wind storms blew the dry soil away.

35 **Which of these is true of a material that is a good conductor of electricity?**
A It will attract electricity from the air.
B Appliances draw power from the material when they are connected.
C The material creates electricity when it is plugged in.
* D Electricity can flow through the material easily.

36 **Why is it unlikely that chickens will become extinct?**
* J There are so many of them.
K They can escape predators well.
L Chickens can eat almost anything.
M No animals eat chickens.

37 **Which of these weighs about a pound?**
A A gallon of ice cream
* B A pint of milk
C A cubic foot of iron
D A cubic meter of air

GO

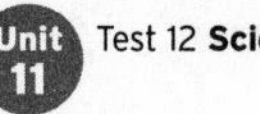 Test 12 **Science**

Directions: Use the information below to answer questions 38–40.

When Randy went to the plant store with his mother, they bought some soil called Super Soil. On the package, it said the soil absorbed more water than any other soil. Randy decided to test this.

Randy put two ounces of Super Soil in a cup. He put two ounces of soil from the family garden in another cup and two ounces of sandy soil in a third cup. He then added four ounces of water to each cup. He stirred the mixtures well, let the cups stand for a minute, then stirred the mixtures again. Randy poked a hole in each cup and let the water drain into a beaker. He weighed the water from each cup and recorded the results below.

Soil Type	Weight of Unabsorbed Water
Super Soil	0.8 ounces
Garden Soil	1.7 ounces
Sandy Soil	3.1 ounces

38 What conclusion is most reasonable, based on the results of Randy's experiment.

J Super Soil absorbs more water than any other soil.

* K Super Soil absorbs more water than garden soil or sandy soil.

L Super Soil will cause plants to grow better than garden soil or sandy soil.

M Super Soil keeps plants from drying out even in the hottest weather.

39 Why did Randy weigh the water after mixing it with soil?

A It showed that the same amount of soil was in each cup.

B It showed that no water was absorbed by the cup.

C It showed that stirring helps soil absorb water.

* D It showed which soil absorbed the most water.

40 Why was mixing the soil and water so important?

J To be sure the water was removed from the beaker each time

K To be sure none of the soil fell out of the cup

* L To be sure the soil had a chance to absorb the water

M To be sure the water would run through the hole

Say It's time to stop. You have completed Test 12. Check to see that you have completely filled in your answer circles with dark marks. Make sure that any marks for answers that you changed have been completely erased. Now you may close your books.

Review the items with the students. Have them indicate completion of the lesson by entering their score for this activity on the progress chart at the beginning of the book.

Discuss the tests with the students. Ask if they felt comfortable during the tests, or if they were nervous. Were they able to finish all the questions in each test? Which tips that they learned were most helpful? Did they have any other problems that kept them from doing their best?

Unit 11 Test 12 **Science**

41 Which of these shows that heat can be conducted through water?

* A An egg cooks in a pot of water boiling on a stove.
B A bowl of water evaporates when it is in the sun.
C People can stand on the ice on a frozen pond.
D Ice cubes float in water that is warm or cool.

42 A mushroom is a kind of

J animal.
* K fungus.
L plant.
M bacteria.

43 The center of Earth is

A a mixture of dirt, sand, and large rocks.
B about the same temperature as a desert.
C colder than the polar regions.
* D much hotter than the surface.

44 Ice is less dense than water. Proof of this is that

J water flows downhill.
* K ice floats in water.
L ice is less clear than water.
M water turns into steam.

45 When weather reporters talk about humidity, they are talking about

A the temperature of the air.
B the speed of the wind.
* C the amount of moisture in the air.
D the pressure of the air.